William C. Fletcher is professor and director of Soviet and East European studies and professor of religion at the University of Kansas. He received the A.B. *cum laude* in 1958 from U.C.L.A., the B.D. in 1964 from California Baptist Theological Seminary, and the Ph.D. in 1964 from the University of Southern California. He was president and director of the Centre de Recherches et d'Etude des Institutions Religieuses in Geneva, Switzerland, from 1965 to 1970, and before that was a research associate at the Research Institute on Communist Strategy and Propaganda in the School of International Relations at the University of Southern California. He is the author or editor of eight other books, including *Religion and Soviet Foreign Policy, 1945-1970*; *The Russian Orthodox Church Underground, 1917-1970*; *Religion and the Soviet State: A Dilemma of Power*; and *Religion and the Search for New Ideals in the USSR*; and has published numerous articles in scholarly journals, including the *Russian Review*, *Slavic Review*, *Journal of Church and State*, *Canadian Slavonic Papers*, *Worldview*, and *Communist Affairs*.

SOVIET BELIEVERS

WILLIAM C. FLETCHER

Soviet Believers

The Religious Sector of the Population

BIP87
THE REGENTS PRESS OF KANSAS
Lawrence

Library of Congress Cataloging in Publication Data
Fletcher, William C
Soviet believers.
Bibliography: p.
Includes index.
1. Russia—Religion—1917–   I. Title.
BL980.R8F53   306'.6   80-25495
ISBN 0–7006–0211–9

TO

REVENGE'S ANTIDOTE

CONTENTS

ACKNOWLEDGMENTS

Like all endeavors of scholarship, this work is indebted to many others which paved the way. Obviously, Soviet scholars are my chief benefactors, for this study is really little more than an attempt to see the realities of religion in the USSR through their eyes, their work. Many years of sociological investigation lie behind the data reviewed here, and I am indebted to the hard work and diligent effort of the sociological fraternity in the USSR. Their work is not free of errors—whose is?—and their approach at times diverges from what I might want. Nevertheless they have done a great deal of work, without which this study could not have been made.

A great many others have rendered outstanding help in clarifying obscure points for me, helping me to overcome my own denseness from time to time, and in serving as referrees. Dr. George Jerkovich, the Curator of the Slavic Collection at the University of Kansas, was wondrously ingenious and efficient in securing materials for this study. Darlene Heacock and Jackie Bryan endured more than any mortal should in preparing the manuscript. And the Graduate Research Fund of the University of Kansas merits my thanks for a grant during the early stages of this study.

And most of all, my wife suffered most as I struggled through this complex, often dull task. I suppose it cannot be helped, but it is a mark of generosity and merit on her part, and I am grateful.

1

THE
RELIGIOUS ENVIRONMENT

In this book I will examine one of the most promising recent developments in the study of religion in the USSR. During the past decade and a half, Soviet scholars have devoted much energy to the sociological study of religion, with experiments and elaborations of field-study techniques, numerous surveys of the population, many attempts to quantify the data, and the like. To date, Western scholars have not devoted intensive attention to this development in Soviet scholarship; hence, a promising source of information has as yet neither been examined in detail nor evaluated.

This is an unfortunate hiatus on the part of Western students of religion in the USSR, for religion as a field of Soviet studies has perennially been plagued by a lack of reliable source materials. Even more than most other disciplines, the study of religion must rely on the various inferential techniques of the Sovietologist. This is scarcely satisfying, because the opportunities for error and misinterpretation are manifold. There simply are no reliable sources. Almost without exception, the various types of resource materials, whether religious or antireligious, all have their individual problems—lack of objectivity, partisanship, one-sidedness, and various other forms of conscious deception and unconscious distortion abound. Hence even the possibility of actual data collection must have great interest for the study of religion. However primitive and undeveloped this infant discipline may be in the USSR, if it can increase the meager store of concrete knowledge available to the student of religion, it must be seized upon, examined, and utilized.

The sociological study of religion in the USSR is, indeed, a young discipline, and the challenges that Soviet sociologists face are great. Not only have they had to develop an entire discipline virtually from

1

nothing, with all the attendant problems of discriminating among the various techniques of study and of mastering those that are most applicable to the Soviet situation; they have also faced formidable obstacles in the religious milieu itself. The strained relations between church and state, in addition to the tensions resulting from official policy towards religion, provide a difficult context for the work of the sociologist.

From World War II onward, relations between church and state in the USSR have been defined by a tense and limited truce. The church, adhering to its policy decision of 1927, offered to the state its complete support in all political matters. Primarily in foreign affairs, but also in domestic matters, the church, or at least its leadership, has instantly and obediently served the national interests. For its part, the state has granted to the church a restricted range of concessions, thus permitting the latter to function as an institution within Soviet society.[1]

Russian Orthodoxy, which is the country's dominant religion, was able to maintain some fifteen thousand churches—enough, perhaps, to minister to the minimal needs of many of the believers.[2] In addition, a very modest system of theological schools was permitted. The church was able to maintain its national administrative offices in the patriarchate, and church publications were allowed on an exceedingly restricted basis. Perhaps most important, church members, provided they kept their religiousness within tightly circumscribed bounds, were less subject to harassment than in other times.

This pattern of church-state relations prevailed, largely unchanged, for the decade and a half after World War II. Other religions shared in the concordat more or less as Russian Orthodoxy did, with greater or narrower ranges of restrictions. With some exceptions (e.g., outbursts of official anti-Semitism between 1947 and 1953, or concurrent attacks against the underground, schismatic Orthodox), these were almost years of tranquillity for religious believers in the USSR, at least in comparison with former times. The antireligious preferences of the state were largely muted—indeed, the brief "Hundred Days Campaign" against religion in 1954 was personally terminated by Nikita Khrushchev in the first decree that he signed personally as leader of the party.[3] After the emancipation of the prisoners following Stalin's death, which returned thousands of imprisoned believers to society, the churches enjoyed a vigorous resurgence during the latter part of the fifties.[4]

Almost certainly, this revival of religion in the USSR was one of the reasons that prompted a change in state policy. Even though the church continued, indeed increased, its political services to the state in the late fifties, the regime, no longer willing to reciprocate, began to withdraw, one by one, those modest concessions which had been the hallmark of state policy toward religion during the postwar period. Instead, the prewar policy toward religion was resuscitated, as the state again embraced its commitment that religion must be eradicated from society. The antireligious campaign of the sixties and seventies emulated, and in some respects even exceeded, the bitter antireligious campaigns of the thirties.[5]

The change in policy was not immediately evident. The first harbingers of sterner times came in 1957, when some of the illegal sects (e.g., Jehovah's Witnesses and underground Orthodox groups) began to experience stern repression, including arrests and the imprisonment of members.[6] The Baptists came under attack during 1958/59, and by early 1960 the antireligious campaign had become general. The leaders of both the state and the church who had symbolized the long détente were removed from office early in 1960, and a full-scale attack against religion ensued.[7] The government now began to enforce the laws of 1929, which had never been rescinded, and a new provision was inserted into the Criminal Code, Article 227, which prescribes a penalty of up to five years in prison for religious activity that endangers the health, encourages neglect of social duties, or attracts minors to religion.[8] These legal restrictions were widely applied, and for the next four years there were hundreds of arrests and convictions of religious believers, including many clergymen and at least three bishops.[9] Particularly stern measures were applied against children: those under the age of 18 were strictly prohibited from attending church services, and there were many cases in which parents who were found guilty of teaching religion to their children were denied parental rights, and the children were forcibly removed to atheistic boarding schools.

The churches came under severe attack. Beginning in 1960, widespread campaigns of closing churches were reminiscent of the worst prewar periods. Between 1960 and 1964, half of the remaining churches were closed. The number of Russian Orthodox churches declined, during the space of these four years, from some fifteen thousand churches to seventy-five hundred;[10] other religious denominations suffered similar—sometimes worse—losses. Great numbers of believing citizens were thus denied any possibility of fulfilling their religious needs and desires. The number of churches, which had never been more than marginally sufficient, now became so small that for a great portion of the believers there was no longer any access at all to an institutionalized expression of religion.

Coupled with these measures was a seemingly infinite range of harassments against religious citizens. Investigations and interrogations of religious believers became commonplace. They suffered demotion or dismissal from their places of employment, and young people were expelled from institutions of higher education when their religious convictions were discovered.[11] A broad range of interference with worship and other religious activities was vigorously applied.[12] By the time Khrushchev was removed from office late in 1964, the antireligious campaign had made a great impact on Soviet society. The relative tranquillity of the previous decade had been replaced by extreme tension. Religious believers once again had to accept and become accustomed to the widespread hostility of a society that had been consciously mobilized against them.

As a result, movements of religious dissent began to appear. The Baptists were the first to protest against the new religious policies.[13] In 1960 the national leadership, doubtless complying with state initiatives, issued an instruction that preaching and evangelism were to be discouraged and that candidates for baptism were not to be accepted under the age of 30. This order, which was diametrically opposed to the evangelistic élan of the Russian Baptists, provided an issue around which the growing discontent that had been caused by the antireligious campaign could coalesce. By the summer of 1962 an "Initiative Committee" had been formed, and its adherents, the *Initsiativniki,* very quickly increased until they formed a nationwide movement. The movement handily survived the arrest of its leader, A. Prokof'ev, in November 1962; and the number of protests continued to increase. Essentially, the movement protested against the denominational leadership for accepting the illegal restrictions of Soviet officials and against the state for failing to abide by its own laws on religion.

This was a serious protest movement. By 1963 the state evidently considered it an important enough problem that it permitted the legalized Baptists to hold an unprecedented national convention, at which some concessions were made to the demands of the *Initsiativniki.* Immediately thereafter, a wave of arrests took place, and in response to this the movement formed a new organization, the Council of Relatives of Prisoners. The movement continued to issue and circulate open letters of protest, although up to this point the entire affair had been kept rather quiet, reports of it having appeared only in the most obscure references in the Soviet provincial press. In 1966, however, both sides escalated their challenge. The state began a widespread propaganda campaign against the *Initsiativniki,* who reciprocated by escalating their activities, holding mass baptisms in public parks, a "sing-in" on a Kiev subway train, a "sit-in" at the parliament building in Moscow, and the like. New concessions were made to the *Initsiativniki* demands at the Baptist Congress of 1966, and concurrently new laws were passed that were specifically designed against many of the activities of the *Initsiativniki.* A new wave of arrests followed,

4

this time embracing the entire leadership of the movement. Such arrests and convictions of the dissident Baptists became endemic thereafter, waxing and waning every two or three years.

Late in 1965 the Orthodox began to emulate the Baptists.[14] Two Moscow priests, N. Eshliman and G. Iakunin, made similar protests to church and state authorities, and their action quickly elicited responses from various regions of the country. While never achieving the coherence and organization of the *Initsiativniki,* the Russian Orthodox protest was potentially more dangerous to the antireligious designs of the state, both because of the vast population which still embraces Orthodoxy to one extent or another and because of the movement's ability to elicit a sympathetic response among the secular intelligentsia. As a result, stern measures followed, and key leaders were arrested in 1969. Nevertheless, the Orthodox protest continued to grow, gaining the open support of no less a figure than Alexander Solzhenitsyn in 1972.[15]

These protest movements have exercised a considerable influence on the state's religious policy since the fall of Khrushchev. The antireligious campaign, which had been rightly associated with Khrushchev's leadership, handily survived his fall; but there was one major change. From its inception the antireligious campaign had increased in intensity from month to month throughout the Khrushchev period, but immediately after his removal from office, this growth curve stabilized, and though the campaign was not radically reduced by the collective leadership, it no longer continued to accelerate. The antireligious campaign continued to be a stable element in state policy during the decade that ensued, neither increasing in intensity nor diminishing drastically. In two respects, however, modifications were introduced.

The campaign of closing churches was abruptly terminated. Since October 1964, few churches have been closed. Conversely, however, few have reopened (until very recently); so the effects of the 1960–64 campaign of closing churches remained unchanged. The institutional base of religion has been forced to operate at approximately half of its former level.

Secondly, the widespread, almost indiscriminate application of force (arrests, imprisonments, etc.) has been modified. In its place there is a selective use of force by the regime. Though arrests and imprisonment continue to take place, and in some cases, deaths have resulted, these measures are no longer applied indiscriminately. They are applied in a highly selective manner against dissenters and members of illegal denominations (e.g., Pentecostals, Jehovah's Witnesses, etc.) in order to accomplish specific results. Arrest is no longer designed primarily to intimidate the rank and file but, rather, to inhibit religious activities outside the narrowly prescribed limits of what is officially permitted.

It should be noted that the lesser measures of harassment remain in force, waxing and waning from year to year and largely depending on local administrations. Religious believers continue to experience an exceedingly broad range of discriminatory practices, including job discrimination and the denial of higher education to believing youth. Such harassment and the denial of the most elementary religious services to believers because of the small number of remaining churches ensure that the religious situation remains exceedingly tense in the USSR.

In the campaign of the sixties and seventies, as in every previous antireligious campaign, atheistic propaganda has played a major role. Concurrently with its reliance on coercion, the state invests vast resources in the techniques of persuasion. Antireligious propaganda quickly became a staple of Soviet life, and from the late fifties onward, the progress of the antireligious campaign has been reflected in the vast, seemingly ubiquitous tide of propaganda pouring forth from a great arsenal of media techniques.

The mass media play a significant role in the antireligious propaganda campaign. The Soviet state pioneered in using the mass media for persuasion and propaganda, and the resources that have been made available to antireligious propagandists are staggering.

Books and pamphlets continue to be a staple of the Soviet antireligious effort. After the lapse of nearly two decades, publishing houses began to present atheistic books and pamphlets in the late fifties. Year by year the number increased, until by 1964 the production of such materials had reached hundreds of titles and millions of copies each year. After 1964 the annual production declined somewhat, but the output of atheistic books and pamphlets is still substantial and appears to be a permanent part of the state's publishing patterns.

These books and pamphlets embraced a wide, almost limitless range of materials. Children's books, from the very crude to the highly impressive, were produced in abundance. Popular materials ranged from the most benighted levels of pulp, designed for the scarcely literate, to well conceived, artistically produced, and even (rarely) interesting treatments, designed for the mass audience. Specialized materials were produced on any number of subjects. Reference materials on discrete religions were produced in abundance, and if some of the products of atheistic scholarship were scarcely credible, others achieved respectable levels of scholarly standards. Literature and belles-lettres were produced, but in no great

6

abundance and of no outstanding quality, primarily because of the difficulty of making atheistic themes attractive to first-rate writers.

As in every other field of propaganda, the daily and periodical press constituted the major weapon relied upon by the regime. Articles on an inconceivably broad range of antireligious subjects became regular features in nearly every newspaper and magazine in the country. On the national level, newspaper stories appeared frequently, and their contents ranged from the most scurrilous attacks against religious individuals to sober editorials and well-researched background articles. In the periodical press, antireligious articles covered a broad range of subjects that were nicely tailored to the audience of the periodical, whether a highly popularized treatment in a picture magazine or an arcane, scholarly article in an academic journal was demanded. The local and provincial press followed the lead of the national newspapers and periodicals, sometimes creating their own articles of local importance, but more often reprinting a selection from the rich store of antireligious materials supplied by the national offices.

Nor were the printed media the only means of mass persuasion utilized. From the beginnings of the campaign, radio was enlisted into the antireligious arsenal. Radio broadcasts displayed a considerable variety; very often they were interview programs, but some highly imaginative experiments were included. The networks devoted considerable attention to antireligious programs, and local stations produced their own more-specific antireligious efforts.[16]

Similarly, television was enlisted in the antireligious effort, although not on so broad a scale as was radio. Early in the antireligious campaign, television was not widely available, and it has only been in the past decade that television could begin to reach a significant portion of the Soviet population. Although much of the television effort has consisted of stereotyped interview programs of limited appeal ("talking heads"), efforts have increasingly been devoted to exploring the medium's entire range of possibilities for persuading the viewer to oppose religion.[17]

One of the early emphases of the campaign was to enlist the cinema in the antireligious effort. Antireligious films had not been produced at all since before the war; now great efforts were devoted to the production of films that might be used against religion. By the early sixties, antireligious films had begun to appear in considerable number. However, the success of these films has been highly debatable, for with very few exceptions they tend to take extreme propagandistic approaches which are scarcely credible to the increasingly sophisticated Soviet audience.[18]

Finally, other public media are utilized to one degree or another.

7

Special antireligious museums have been established in several locations, and a great many of the general museums devote some of their efforts to antireligious displays. Wall newspapers are utilized against religion, as are other forms of visual media such as poster art (although not on a scale comparable to that used in the early twenties). In short, most of the means of reaching a mass audience have been explored and utilized in one way or another in the antireligious campaign.

Oral propaganda plays a great role in Soviet attempts to mold public opinion. The lecture format has always been the staple of Soviet atheistic propaganda, and it remains the single most widely promoted form used to counteract the influence of religion in society. A number of different organizations take responsibility for organizing atheistic lectures. Chief among them is the Knowledge Society, which at the beginning of the antireligious campaign had some eight hundred thousand members and has since grown to several million members.[19] This society has taken over many of the functions of the prewar League of Militant Godless, and under its auspices, thousands of lectures on atheism are delivered every year. In addition to the Knowledge Society, many other propaganda and educational organizations arrange atheistic lectures, utilizing both formal and informal settings (in factories, in schools, etc.).

One of the serious problems facing the lecture as an approach lies in finding competent lecturers. Many of the lecturers are sent out to deliver the message after receiving little or no training, and as a result the lectures are very often stereotyped, dull, and eminently ineffective. Even more difficult is the problem of attracting an audience for such lectures. As a rule, religious believers, understandably enough, have no particular desire to attend antireligious lectures, especially when an ill-trained or incompetent lecturer is likely to let his performance degenerate into insults against them.[20] Hence, many of the practitioners of Soviet atheism suspect that the lecturers talk only to atheists most of the time. Even though lectures remain the most widely utilized form of oral propaganda, there is room for much debate concerning the effectiveness of this approach.

Other approaches utilized by the antireligious establishment include the organization of clubs for atheists.[21] While ideally such clubs should combine recreation with atheistic indoctrination, very often they serve merely as an administrative unit designed to organize the various types of local antireligious agitation. Even according to their most ardent promoters, the clubs have not proved to be very successful in competing with the local church to win the affections of the local populace.

One of the more intimate forms of oral propaganda is the discussion.

8

Specially trained atheistic propagandists are instructed to hold small group discussions on atheistic themes. The discussion leader has his own agenda of points that need to be covered, but he follows a conversational method, letting the discussion proceed where it will and completing his agenda during the course of it in whatever order seems most natural. Needless to say, this is a demanding art, and many of the discussion sessions are not very successful; indeed, they can become counterproductive, when vigorous and articulate religious believers are present.

During the current antireligious campaign, the form of propaganda that has received the greatest publicity is "individual work with believers." Possibly copying the Baptists, who have had great success with personal evangelism, atheistic organizations assign their members individually to known religious believers. The plan is for the atheist to make contact with the believer, come to know him as a close friend, and then embark on a long-term attempt to persuade him to atheism. The atheistic leadership expresses great hope for the effectiveness of this form of personal propaganda.

There are many problems connected with this approach, however. First is the problem of finding qualified atheistic practitioners. While at first glance it might seem that anybody can become a friend to someone else and then exercise an influence on him, in fact this method requires a great deal of tact, inasmuch as it necessarily entails an invasion of privacy (the believer, after all, does not ask for this kind of friendship). With untrained and insensitive practitioners, such an attempt to establish personal relations can only end in the most dismal failure. Furthermore, disparate cultural levels also complicate the task: most of the atheistic workers, for example, are young, while most of the believers are elderly; hence, it becomes more difficult to establish any truly meaningful relationship on a one-to-one basis. Another problem is the risk involved in this approach: if the atheist is able to exercise a persuasive influence on the religious believer after a personal relationship has been established, the converse is also true; therefore, the practitioner of "individual work with believers" may find that he is as much subject to persuasion as is the believer.

Finally, the most debilitating problem with this approach is its cost. In terms of man-hours, this form of persuasion imposes a staggering burden, and to reach any significant proportion of the population, great armies of atheistic practitioners would have to be committed to this kind of work. Among believers, the willingness to undertake this kind of commitment of personal time and effort is common enough; it remains problematical whether atheists are willing to make a similar commitment. A lecturer can feel that with an hour of his time he has reached a large number of people with his message. But "individual work with believers" demands the investment of great amounts of time over a long period, with perhaps no tangible results whatsoever.

The educational system has naturally loomed large in the designs of the antireligious campaign.[22] Ideally, the schools should serve as the cradle of atheism, counteracting and replacing the religious nurture that may still linger on in the family. Frequent exhortations appear in the press that atheism should be introduced in every class at every level. Numerous materials and textbooks are produced for the various age groups. Nurseries and kindergartens are urged to teach atheism. Grade-school teachers are instructed about techniques for utilizing the various subjects that are taught as introductions for lessons in atheism. For the higher grades, instructional materials are presented, detailing the atheistic conclusions to be drawn from subjects as disparate as biology and philosophy or history and astronomy.

One of the chief difficulties in introducing atheism into the school system is that the majority of the teachers have never received any formal training in atheism.[23] Therefore, great efforts have been devoted to introducing atheism into higher education.[24] Courses in atheism have been introduced as requirements in many universities and teacher-training institutes, and special departments of atheism have been created at the major universities. Special "Universities of Atheism" have been set up, and numerous "universities" have been established for evening study among workers.

The massive propaganda effort has demanded that a great deal of knowledge be available for the propagandist. It has been the task of Soviet atheistic scholars to supply this background of knowledge regarding both atheism and, even more importantly, the various religions that the campaign must combat. Soviet scholarship has made considerable progress in acquiring this background and in making it available. Indeed, the chief distinction between the contemporary antireligious campaign and its prewar predecessors is in the scholarship that has accompanied the most recent campaign. This scholarship far surpasses the prewar efforts, both in the extent and range of the knowledge that has been acquired and in the quality and scholarly standards that have been sought.

Indeed, the preparation of the knowledge base was begun well before the antireligious campaign began. In his 1954 directive from the Central Committee of the Communist Party of the Soviet Union (CC CPSU), Nikita Khrushchev ordered that massive efforts be initiated to develop a sound, scholarly base of knowledge about religion:

10

The Central Committee reemphasizes that at the basis of scientific atheistic propaganda should be the popular dissemination of the most important phenomena of nature and of society in life, such questions as the structure of the universe, the origin of life and of man on earth, achievements in the fields of astronomy, biology, physiology, physics, chemistry, and the other sciences, which support the correctness of materialistic views concerning the development of nature and society.

The CC CPSU emphasizes that waging scientific atheistic propaganda requires the most attentive, careful attitude toward the selection of lecturers, authors of papers, and authors of articles and pamphlets on antireligious themes. Only cadres qualified in scientific matters should be attracted to the work—schoolteachers, faculty members of the trade schools and institutions of higher learning, doctors, agronomists, workers from the various scientific research institutions, writers and artists, and others skilled in the position of the materialistic world view, to explain the antiscientific character of religion convincingly.[25]

Immediately thereafter, the long process of developing a corps of sound, qualified scholars began, and by the end of the decade, as the antireligious campaign was gaining its stride, these efforts had begun to bear fruit. A number of highly trained, well-qualified scholars began to write, eventually providing an immense amount of research on a wide range of religious and atheistic subjects.

Led by an establishment of eminent scholars within the Academy of Sciences, the professors and, increasingly, the products of this impressive effort in higher education began to filter outward through the university system. By the end of the Khrushchev period, research was being conducted not only in Moscow and Leningrad but in a number of prestigious universities throughout the country. The range of subjects covered was vast, embracing almost every field of inquiry related to religion or atheism. The top leadership in the antireligious establishment had had lengthy experience in such work, for many of them had grown up in the League of Militant Godless.

After the fall of Khrushchev, there was a reorganization within atheistic scholarship. The older, more theoretical approaches which had been exemplified in such publications as the *Annual of the Museum of the History of Religion and Atheism* and *Problems of the History of Religion and Atheism* were replaced by more practical, immediately usable approaches. In effect, pure research on religion was replaced by applied research in various disciplines exemplified by the new semiannual *Problems of Scientific Atheism*. During Khrushchev's last year in power, the atheistic

11

effort had been brought under the central direction of the Institute of Scientific Atheism in the Academy of Social Sciences of the Central Committee of the Communist Party,[26] and now that reorganization quickly filtered out into the various research facilities for atheism throughout the country. The result was that from the middle sixties onward, a considerable output of high-level research has appeared, which concentrates on disciplines and approaches that can be immediately applied by field workers in the antireligious campaign. This has generated an impressive increase in the fund of information that is available to antireligious propagandists, for great effort is now being expended to provide a more-detailed picture of the needs and problems connected with atheism and religion in the USSR.

2

SOCIOLOGICAL METHODS

In the proliferation of new academic approaches that accompanied the contemporary antireligious campaign, few innovations have enjoyed the glamour associated with the sociology of religion. Other disciplines appeared in the burgeoning academic area of scientific atheism—psychology of religion, biblical studies, contemporary theology, and the like—but as the campaign progressed, it became clear that the sociological study of religion would receive great emphasis.[1]

This precipitate rise in popularity was conditioned by the evolution and the needs of the antireligious campaign. It was also due, however, to the belated entry of sociology itself into the panoply of Soviet academia. One of the more stultifying attributes of Stalinist Neo-Scholasticism was its almost paranoid suspicion of Western intellectual developments. Discomfort with regard to sociology was aggravated by the fact that it was heavily emphasized in America, and after World War II the United States became the symbol and citadel of all that was hateful to Stalinist Russia. While Stalin lived, then, sociology was derided but otherwise ignored by Soviet scholars.

After the death of Stalin in 1953, new winds began to blow in Soviet scholarship, fitfully at first but with increasing assurance. An awareness began to grow that sociology did promise results that would be useful to many of the concerns of Soviet society. Soviet scholars began the challenging process of embracing and assimilating this new discipline. By 1967 the concrete study of social processes could be called "the most characteristic trait of the contemporary stage in social science."[2] In the process, sociology of religion came into its own as a major emphasis in scientific atheism.

Finding a sociological theory of religion presented no problem whatsoever to Soviet atheistic scholars, for a complete, ready-made theory was already at hand. Indeed, little more than a change in name was required, for the received philosophy could just as easily be called a sociological theory. Marxism, after all, is not primarily dialectical materialism, although this metaphysical construct is prominent in its system; nor is it really historical materialism, for its deep and vital concern with history is motivated by the desire to apprehend social processes; more than anything else, Marxism is the study of society. As such, it has, by definition, eminently sound credentials for being admitted to the sociological fraternity.

In his analysis of social phenomena, Marx did not neglect religion; and his theories, elaborated upon by Lenin, presented a basic approach to understanding religion as a product of society. These theories have been sufficiently complex and satisfying to inspire a small army of Soviet scholars, some of whom are highly qualified and very intelligent indeed, to devote their lives to exploring and elaborating upon the received doctrine. Nevertheless, it can be summarized fairly succinctly.

According to Marxism, religion, like every other social phenomenon, is ultimately dependent on the economic base. Economic relationships—or more exactly, the ownership of the means of production—determine all other relationships. Literature, the arts, philosophy, and even politics form a superstructure that is dependent upon and reflects the economic base. Religion is a part of this superstructure. In the capitalist stage of economic development, religion reflects man's exploitation of man, upon which capitalist society is built: "*Religious* distress is at the same time the *expression* of real distress and the *protest* against real distress. Religion is the sigh of the oppressed creature, the heart of a heartless world, just as it is the spirit of a spiritless situation. It is the *opium* of the people."[3] More specifically, religion is a tool of the dominant class and helps it to stay in power. According to Lenin, "Those who live by the labor of others are taught by religion to practice charity while on earth, thus offering them a very cheap way of justifying their entire existence as exploiters and selling them, at an attractive price, tickets to heavenly bliss. Religion is the opium of the people. Religion is a sort of spiritual booze, in which the slaves of capital drown their human image."[4] Naturally, when the economic base has been changed, when the Revolution has returned the means of production to the workers themselves, and when exploitation of man by man has been eradicated at its economic base, religion will disappear. Religion is an unscientific, even superstitious, approach to reality; when

14

the economic conditions that give rise to religion have been removed, religion will vanish.

Unfortunately for the theory, religion has not disappeared. According to the Soviet understanding, the Revolution of 1917 marked the end of capitalist exploitation in what was then proclaimed to be the Union of Soviet Socialist Republics. The ruling and oppressed classes were abolished, all power reverted to the workers, and the classless society came into being. Capitalism, that hoary nemesis of modern man, was finally and decisively overcome. With the end of exploitation, exploitation's handmaid, religion, should also have disappeared. But it did not.

The persistence of religion for more than half a century after its economic roots have been eliminated is somewhat of a theoretical anomaly. The strict theory, rigorously applied, demands that religion not exist in the post-Revolutionary society. Soviet theoreticians have, perforce, developed a number of elaborations upon Marxist-Leninist doctrine to account for this uncomfortable persistence.[5]

Most obvious is the explanation that the Revolution, while decisive, was not a simplistic, single act, all of whose benefits would suddenly, indeed magically, appear overnight. The Revolution was not complete on the morning after that hallowed October day, and to some degree it is not yet complete. This argument must be used with great delicacy, for if allowed to proliferate too far, it might cast doubt upon some of the most sacrosanct pillars of the Soviet system; but it can be used in moderation. After all, Lenin himself used a variant of this argument in justifying the inauguration of the New Economic Policy (NEP) in the twenties. If, then, the Revolution is not yet absolutely complete, the continued existence of one relatively minor aspect of the former superstructure—namely, religion—is not terribly embarrassing.

A variant of this theory of the incomplete revolution is the suggestion that mistakes have been made that may provide causation for the persistence of religion:

> In socialist society, where the social roots of religion are disrupted, the epistomological roots that exist in unity with them are also dying out. In the developing Communist society the liquidation of the social roots of religion without doubt drags along in its train, in the last analysis, the disappearance of its epistemological roots also. Of course, the possibility remains for specific mistakes in the process of understanding, but still they will not develop into a system of a perverse world view—religion.[6]

Again, this argument must be used with discretion, because the contemporary climate is not entirely auspicious for implying that the Communist Party can be mistaken. Nevertheless, once Khrushchev, in his de-Stalinization campaign, had endorsed the possibility that individual Communist leaders could make mistakes, inadequacies and human error could be used to account for certain aspects, at least, of the viability of religion. Many cases of religiousness among individuals are ascribed to the inadequate provision for their needs by society and its leaders.

A second major rationale explaining the continuing existence of religion in the USSR is the venerable theory of "capitalist encirclement." Since the end of the Stalin era the term itself has not been much used. Nevertheless, expressions of its content continue to appear from time to time:

> First of all, while imperialism exists, the possibility that it may provoke new wars is not excluded. Of course, in contemporary circumstances the world's system of socialism is the decisive power in the anti-imperialistic struggle, and the developing countries have come forward as an important factor in the development of international relations. However, the threat of war exists. This finds expression in the psychology of part of the Soviet people and stimulates the development of eschatological and apocalyptic movements among the believers.[7]

This theory can be used with impunity. While it is true that on inspection this argument is not always terribly persuasive—what contact, after all, does the religious peasant woman in her hut deep in the endless taiga, or forest, have with the encircling capitalists?—it is also true that the seemingly ubiquitous Western religious broadcasting targeted at the Russian people, the occasional instances of religious literature smuggled in from the West, and the various indirect contacts do provide indubitable, absolutely solid evidence in support of this theory: "To some extent, religious ideology in our country is supported by bourgeois propaganda which flows to us through various channels (tourism, foreign students, showing of foreign films, foreign industrial and art expositions, radio transcriptions, dispatch of religious literature, etc.). Several foreign clerical organizations try by every means to revive religious views among Soviet people."[8] Another author complains: "In recent years alone many hundreds of religious books and pamphlets have been sent by mail [from abroad] to the addresses of institutions and private citizens of Penzensk region."[9]

The most widely used rationale for explaining the incongruity of the persistence of religion in Soviet society is the theory of "survivals of capitalism." To be sure, the economic base has been removed once and

16

for all. The superstructure, though, ephemeral as it may be in the ultimate philosophical sense, has a momentum of its own. Thus, prolonged effort and continued patience will be needed before religion will disappear completely from Soviet society. At first glance this theory seems tenuous—perhaps even risible—in view of the fact that the fourth generation since the Revolution is now present in Soviet society, and many of its members are religious; but closer inspection of the phenomenon would indicate that this theory of survivals of capitalism is not at all untenable. The intimate degree to which each generation is dependent upon its predecessors makes it very credible indeed that some phenomena may persist long after the causes for them have vanished. One of the chief advantages of this theory, of course, is that it can be used indefinitely—weakened by time, perhaps, but not refuted.

Thus, Soviet sociologists of religion have no difficulty in finding an acceptable theoretical basis for their work. Marxism, because it is essentially a sociological theory, is fully usable by the sociologist. The difficulty arises in distinguishing sociology from other disiplinary approaches to Soviet theory, particularly the philosopher's.

Soviet sociologists can define their discipline easily enough: "Sociological study of religion consists of the analysis of its relationships with other phenomena of the social life of people—with economics, politics, morality, living conditions, culture, etc., and also the converse influence of religion on these phenomena."[10] So far so good. But "the methodology of sociological study of religion is dialectical and historical materialism," and therefore it becomes difficult to distinguish sociology from Marxist philosophy.[11] After all, the methodologies are the same, and one Soviet sociologist, Nemchinov, simply states flatly that "historical materialism is Marxist sociology."[12]

Some scholars find the difference not so much in theory as in the approach, inasmuch as the sociologist strives for the concrete more than the theoretical.[13] For others, such as Cherniak, the distinction is more subtle:

> The various points of view found in Soviet philosophical literature on this problem may be grouped around two basic opinions. The one, which equates historical materialism and sociology, considers these concepts as synonyms. The other asserts that historical materialism and sociology are different sciences, and therefore their separate, independent existence is proper. These divergences are based upon a number of factors. Among them, disagreement concerning the particular subjects of these sciences has substantial significance.

The common factor between historical materialism and sociology, in the aspect which interests us, is that both the one and the other science study sociological laws, i.e., laws which relate to the field of the interrelationship of various spheres of the life of society, and also that the one and the other science use concrete sociological methods. The difference, in particular, is that historical materialism, as a philosophy of history, accepts these methods primarily for the study of general sociological laws of social development; whereas, sociology, basing itself on this theory, accepts the stated methods for studying the interrelationships of general, special, and specific sociological laws applicable to the given formation.[14]

Obviously, then, the distinction is great enough to interest and concern Soviet sociologists, many of whom devote intricate, complex, and tightly reasoned disquisitions to this difference.[15] To the non-Marxist, however, these differences may not appear to be so striking; and the understanding of the Marxist position on religion which he brings from other disciplines will serve very adequately indeed in attuning him to Soviet sociological theory. In any event, this study will concentrate, not on the theory, but on another aspect. This aspect receives far more attention among Soviet scholars than does the dubious distinction between sociological, philosophical, dialectical-material, or other nuances of Marxist theory. The branch of sociology that this study will examine is called "concrete sociological research."

By "concrete sociological research" Soviet scholars mean, essentially, the collection of data, or field studies. This emphasis on concrete data is really what marks the new departure in the contemporary Soviet study of religion. While it would not seem that gathering actual information from the individual citizens themselves would represent a particularly bold or startling innovation, inasmuch as such data would appear to be needed for verification and development of almost any social theory, under Soviet conditions it does represent a significant advance. Since the Soviet Union always emphasizes planning and the complex development of social theory, it has been somewhat weak in testing and demonstrating its theories and plans. In fact, at various phases and in various segments of the bureaucracy, modification of facts to fit the theory, rather than the other way around, has not been unknown. Therefore, the serious attempt to obtain objective, reliable data through concrete sociological research on religion is highly significant.

It should not be inferred that the need for concrete data was entirely ignored in earlier years—indeed, some Soviet scholars become rather indignant at such suggestions.[16] During the twenties, concrete sociological research was conducted in Moscow, Leningrad, Saratov, and Perm;[17] and after the 1921 Plenum of the Communist Party's Central Committee, such studies of religious sects took place in at least six regions throughout the country, including the Ukraine, where forty-seven districts were examined.[18] By and large, however, this early research was localized and sporadic.[19] "Individual attempts at conducting concrete social research in the field of atheism and religion were undertaken earlier, even at the end of the twenties and beginning of the thirties, but this research was insufficiently effective, insufficiently reliable for working out strictly scientific recommendations. Not infrequently it contained mistakes of a subjective order."[20] Nor did subjective mistakes—the conscious or unconscious biasing of the data—constitute the only problems: sheer inexperience and overenthusiasm could vitiate the efforts as well. For example, one questionnaire that was developed by adepts of the League of Militant Godless consisted of 14 sections and no fewer than 165 questions.[21] The famous nationwide census of 1937 represents perhaps the most ambitious single effort at gathering data on religion ever attempted in the USSR. In the original version of that census there was the question "Are you a believer or not?" The census was aborted, and its results were suppressed, but indirect indications suggest that as much as 56% of the population answered the question affirmatively (which would not only be astonishing to the enthusiasts of atheism but would also represent a grave setback for their hopes).[22]

By and large, however, concrete sociological research on religion remained inconsequential until the late fifties, when the impetus supplied by the 1954 decree of Khrushchev's Central Committee began to bear fruit, and a number of serious and intelligent field studies began to appear.[23] By the later stages of the Khrushchev antireligious campaign, sociology of religion had become an integral part of the atheistic establishment in Soviet academia. During that period (1954–64) it was not yet the leading emphasis in Soviet atheism, or even one of the leading ones. More venerable disciplines, such as philosophical refutations of religion, theoretical studies of the origins of religion, and the history of comparative religions, which had been established in the times of E. Iaroslavskii and the League of Militant Godless, still commanded the greater resources.

After Khrushchev was removed from power late in 1964 and the atheistic establishment was reorganized, sociology of religion was "renewed and has acquired significant scope."[24] Sociological research was endorsed by A. N. Kosygin at the Twenty-third Congress of the Communist Party in 1966,[25] and the scope of the research began to expand rapidly.[26] In 1971, "at the extended session of the group, Concrete Sociological Research on Problems of Atheism and Religion, the plan of work for 1971–75 was considered. Basic directions were noted: the working out of methodo- logical and methodical problems of sociological study of religion and atheism; the organization and conduct of experimental research; joint work with other problem groups, laboratories and scientific institutions, and also Party committees; the study of the experience of concrete sociological work in socialist countries; the working out of problematical questions of criticism of bourgeois sociology of religion; and the preparation of highly qualified specialists."[27] Efforts devoted to sociology of religion have ex- panded at an impressive rate. By the end of the sixties, the production of books, pamphlets, and articles on sociology had reached 750 titles per year,[28] and the sociology of religion reflected this increase.[29]

Fairly detailed and complex approaches have been worked out over the years. The leading scholars in these field studies have acquired two decades of experience,[30] and in the course of these years devoted to field studies, a great deal has been learned about the organization, conduct, and methodology of the concrete sociological study of religion.

The keys to the successful acquisition of data, of course, are what kind of research team gathers the information and what the qualifications of its members are. In the better efforts, the researchers are given spe- cialized training after they have been recruited,[31] and when properly done, this training provides a thorough and careful preparation.[32]

The typical approach is the use of small research teams:

In 1962, in the Orenburg region, an expedition consisting of eight people was working under the leadership of Docent Iu. F. Bor- unkov. In the summer of 1963, two expeditions were sent out: one consisting of ten people in the Krasnodar district (the leader was Docent Iu. F. Borunkov) and another consisting of seven people in the Karaganda region (the leader was Candidate of Philosophical Sciences I. D. Gorokhov). In July and August 1965, in the Orlov region, an expedition was working, consisting of ten people under the leadership of Senior Scientific Associate I. N. Iablokov. In 1966 the Department [of the History and Theory of Atheism, Moscow State University] organized sociological research in the Lenin region of Moscow. In addition to the complex ex- pedition, there was a practice made of sending groups consisting of two to four researchers with a goal of studying particular prob- lems. In the last three years such groups have been sent out to Central Asia, the western Ukraine and Belorussia, to the Baltic area, to the Mari ASSR, and other places.[33]

The work of these expeditions can be fairly brief or can be extended over a period of several weeks.[34] More complex expeditions have included larger numbers in the research team; for example, in one case a group of 80 atheists studied two rural villages.[35] These expeditions are usually led by experienced senior scholars.[36]

Some of the most ambitious surveys have involved very large numbers of researchers. As early as in the middle sixties, 1,196 people were involved in one project.[37] Perhaps the most ambitious organizer of data-gathering is M. K. Tepliakov of Voronezh. He dispatched as many as 3,500 researchers into the field,[38] and he eventually involved more than 7,000 people in the process of acquiring data.[39] It should be noted, however, that in this vast project the ratio of respondents to researchers was ·fewer than 9 to 1, and therefore a large proportion of the 7,000 researchers may not have been very intimately involved in the research.

The subjects of these research projects range from a relatively small group of people to very large numbers. In a small village, for example, Safronov's survey of only 177 people covered one-quarter of the population of the village.[40] One and one-half months were devoted to Krasnikov's study of 500 families in another project ("O nekotorykh voprosakh," p. 7). Tepliakov's study of the religious attitudes of students included 880 subjects (*Problemy*, p. 71), while Eryshev and Kosukha surveyed 1,247 young men and women.[41] Perhaps more typical are projects that embrace somewhat larger numbers. Thus, for example, Duluman and his colleagues selected 1,443 believers and former believers (*Sovremennyi veruiushchii*, p. 5), while Tepliakov surveyed 1,577 collective farmers in one study ("Pobeda," p. 137) and 1,933 students in another ("Pobeda," p. 137). On two occasions, Kniasev studied 3,000 workers,[42] while Kolbanovskii's studies of collective farmers have surveyed as many as 3,661 individuals.[43] Earlier studies reached larger numbers (more than 6,000 believers in one case [Duluman, *Sovremennyi veruiushchii*, p. 5], 9,000 people in another [Krasnikov, "O nekotorykh voprosakh," p. 4]), while more-recent studies have attempted even more comprehensive surveys. In the Mari Republic, Guzev surveyed 11,000 people, including 4,000 selected as a 1% sample of the entire adult population.[44] One of Tepliakov's surveys covered 21,557 respondents ("Pobeda," p. 134), and Selivanov's covered 30,674, including 9,015 who represented a 1% sample of the entire population of the region (*Partiinoe rukovodstvo*, p. 7). More than 32,000 young people were surveyed by Galitskaia ("K voprosu," p. 391), while in the middle sixties, Tepliakov studied 37,519 inhabitants of the Voronezh region ("Pobeda," p. 134). Again in Voronezh, Tepliakov surveyed 46,820 citizens,[45] while the most ambitious project reported on to date covered 59,288 citizens (Tepliakov, *Problemy*, p. 132).

There has been considerable desire to survey the entire population of the region under study, as is evident above. In the city of Iaroslavl, for example, approximately 1% of the families have been surveyed by Vasilevskaia,[46] while Cherniak's study included more than 70% of the total number of workers in Alma-Ata.[47] On a smaller scale, Solov'ev's survey of 832 people was all that was necessary to accomplish a 10% random selection of a small city in the Mari ASSR.[48]

With regard to geography, some of the pioneering efforts of the late fifties and early sixties were concentrated in south-central European Russia, in the regions of Tambov, Lipetsk, and Voronezh.[49] Repeated studies were conducted in these areas; and in the Voronezh area, at least, continuing intensive research has been conducted on a rather large scale (Mering, "Konkretno o samom vazhnom," p. 40). By the middle sixties, research had extended throughout the Russian republic and in the national republics as well—Lithuania, the Ukraine, Moldavia, Belorussia, Mordvinia, the Chuvash Republic, Central Asia, and so forth (Galitskaia, "K voprosu," p. 391). From 1970 to 1972 there was an ambitious attempt to make a profile of the entire multinational population of the Chechen-Ingush ASSR, in the hope that the data derived might be applicable to all of the northern Caucasus republics.[50] In the mid seventies, researchers in the Leningrad area attempted to select a nominal 100 respondents in each of a series of classifications, winding up with more than 4,000; this survey was coordinated with similar research in other regions: the Odessa area (1,300 respondents), the Arkhangelsk area (1,000), Kareliia (1,017), and Khabarovsk (1,000) (Kobetskii, *Sotsiologicheskoe izuchenie*, pp. 66–67).

A broad variety of populations has been studied in the research. Urban citizens of a large number of cities have been surveyed,[51] while other studies have attempted to reach out into the rural population (Iablokov, *Metodologicheskie problemy*, pp. 100–101; Koshevnikov, "Ateisticheskoe vospitanie," p. 2). In general, Soviet sociologists have studied most of the major population strata in the country.

A considerable range of methods of gathering data in these field studies is employed:

> Some Western sociologists tend to identify concrete sociological research with the taking of popular polls. In our opinion this is an erroneous point of view. Public polls can provide reliable results only if they are scrupulously prepared and conducted in conjunction with other methods of sociological research. Questionnaires are valid instruments of sociological science only if they can be compared with a mass of subjective answers to definite objective data and if they expose the natural link between objec-

tive and dependent subjective processes of comprehension. In our opinion, all information gathered from polls should be checked and supplemented with data gathered by other methods.[52]

Particularly when dealing with more furtive groups—the vow of silence is not unknown in Russian religious practice—direct questions simply cannot be used, and instead, other forms of research must be pressed into service (Klibanov, *Religioznoe sektantstvo*, p. 46).

Direct observation is an obvious possibility. While its range is limited, certain information can be acquired through simple observation.[53] Particularly with regard to religious gatherings, a great deal of data (age, gender, etc.) can be obtained.[54] This approach, for all its limitations, has the signal advantage that if the observations are made discreetly, the risk that the researcher himself will influence the data is minimized.

Less directly, a documentary research can be utilized by the field expedition. Working through the archives of the local press can yield considerable amounts of data on religion, even though, given the nature of the journalistic profession in the Soviet countryside, such data may not always be especially valid (e.g., Tepliakov, *Problemy*, p. 146). Particularly where the cooperation of local authorities and institutions is secured, a fairly rich harvest of knowledge may be gathered in materials produced by religious people: "Among research materials are compositions of a theological character, documents of religious polemics, religious belles-lettres, poems, songs, and tracts. As a rule, these are handwritten and typed compositions, less frequently compositions printed on duplicating apparatuses, and even more rarely printed by typographic means" (Klibanov, "Nauchno-organizatsionnyi i metodicheskii opyt," p. 22).

Soviet scholars are usually scrupulous in acknowledging help received from local authorities, with one curious exception. For no immediately apparent reason, the state's Council for Religious Affairs is never mentioned among the bodies that facilitate the gathering of field data.[55] This is so even though the council is specifically charged with issuing registration to churches and with keeping records concerning them. Thus it would be the logical first point for a field expedition from another state agency to contact. And when a scholar such as A. I. Klibanov (*Religioznoe*, p. 76), the leading Soviet authority on the Baptists, states, "According to our data, at the present time on the territory of the Ukrainian SSR no less than ⅓ of all the Evangelical Christians–Baptists congregations which exist in our country are distributed," and when he attributes this sweeping knowledge to correspondence from Ukrainian researchers that has been sent personally to him, one may perhaps be forgiven for hypothesizing that the good offices of the Council for Religious Affairs may have provided some help. Indeed, on numerous occasions when exceedingly precise data on the number of registered churches are given, the possibility must remain that official data have been used (e.g., Tepliakov, *Problemy,* p. 169).

Similarly, field expeditions in search of documentary research materials have on occasion been given access to otherwise absolutely secret files of materials—interrogation reports, confessions, court transcripts, material evidence, and the like—from the archives of the Secret Police.[56]

An additional approach consists of the detailed observation and analysis of sermons and liturgical activities:

> This method was selected in particular for the study of attendance and liturgical practice and its influence on parishioners of three Orthodox churches of the Lenin district of Moscow. The investigators attended all divine services during the course of the entire period of the investigation. The program of investigation was devoted to determining the number of parishioners (specifically, men, women, children, adolescents, youth, people of middle age, and people over fifty), the forms of liturgical activity (worshiping icons, bowing, participating in general singing, lighting candles, etc.), the activity of various groups of parishioners in liturgical activities, elements of divine service (collective prayers, reading the Bible, giving the sacraments, preaching, etc.), the composition and form of religious propaganda, and the results of the influence of the divine service on its participants (changes in conduct, expressive movement, etc.). [Iablokov, *Metodologicheskie problemy,* p. 105]

Iarygin analyzed 800 Baptist sermons,[57] Tepliakov (*Problemy,* p. 41) studied 308 sermons in Orthodox churches and 205 Baptist sermons in Voronezh, while in Soviet Central Asia, Nikonov analyzed 103 Baptist sermons in detail ("O nekotorykh tendentsiiakh," passim). This form of research has the additional benefit of being cost-free in some cases, for at various times and places it was a very common practice of local party and governmental agencies to station observers in the churches in an effort to exercise maximum supervision and control during the antireligious campaign. Thus, these observations could be acquired and utilized by sociologists without additional expenditure of effort on the part of the sociological research team.

The most costly form of research, in terms of man hours, is the conduct of discussions with individual respondents: "Discussions took place as a rule under noncoercive conditions, in an atmosphere of good will, and they often were prolonged to 4 or 5 hours. Usually the conversation or interview was conducted by two researchers; one of them, with the agreement of the believer, took notes. There were only isolated cases of refusing to take part in the discussion."[58] Provided sufficient time can be found for conducting these discussions, this technique surpasses all others in its ability to penetrate deeply into questions and to clarify shadings and nuances in the answers.

Generally, the discussions were carefully planned in advance; according to Iablokov (*Metodologicheskie problemy*, p. 106): "Unstandardized as well as standardized interviews were used. In the first stage of the research in the course of the work of the Orenburg, Karaganda, and Krasnodar expeditions, recourse was made to the nonstandardized, open interview. Although the researcher was also armed with a grid of basic questions, he was able to raise them in any order, in order to change the formula, and even to raise unforeseen questions which were dictated by the situation. The reworking of them was difficult." For the researcher this is a tantalizing approach because of its richness; however, even relatively modest attempts, such as Ignatenko's project ("Opyt," p. 251), which used this method with some 110 people, or 1% of the total number studied, represent a formidable achievement in terms of research time devoted to the subject. The expenditure would seem to be worthwhile, however, for these interviews yield some of the most enlightening insights into the contemporary Russian believer that are to be found anywhere in Soviet scholarship.[59]

The primary tool of Soviet sociology of religion, however, remains the questionnaire. Once the other forms of study have been practiced, the essence of the research effort is usually the prepared set of questions (Pantskhava, "Vvedenie," p. 7). Soviet researchers consider this to be the key to success in the concrete sociological study of religion:

Inasmuch as the given research dealt with a question that was so delicate and sensitive for an identifiable part of the population as the relationship to religion, during the time of preparation for it not a few doubts were expressed about the possibility of receiving frank answers from believers concerning their religious convictions and feelings. The researchers themselves also had doubts of this sort. However, after completion of the work the team came to a unanimous conclusion that frank conversation with believers on religion is fully possible. Much depends on the preparation of the questionnaires, their political and vital maturity, tact, amiability, good will, and comradely attitude toward those studied. No little significance for the acquisition of objective data on the internal world of believers is borne by the composition of the questionnaire itself and even the order of the questions posed.[60]

The researchers can select from among a considerable range of types of questions. Iablokov's questionnaire "included open, closed, and semi-closed questions. Open questions did not foresee variant answers in advance. Questions of such a type are good in that they permit free expression and do not bind the subject to one opinion or another. But far from always do they permit a clarification of the opinion on precisely those aspects of the phenomena that interest the researcher. Closed questions foresee various answers. If these variants are meaningful and representative, if they are correctly worked out, then such questions serve as an effective means of studying precisely those problems that the researcher faces" (*Metodologicheskie problemy*, p. 107). Generally, of course, closed questions (alternate answers or multiple choice) are preferred because of the ease with which they can subsequently be processed (Cherniak, *Formirovanie*, p. 76).

Quite rightly, Cherniak recognized that the questions are the ultimate determinant of the value of the project, for not even the most elaborate analysis will be fruitful if the questions are poorly chosen:

> As is well known, in a survey used as an instrument for receiving detailed information, the problems of the program of research are transformed into concrete questions. One and the same program problem appears in the survey in a number of variants. If, for example, it is necessary to explain the relationship of the believer to religious holidays and rituals, this problem appears in the survey in a number of concrete, more or less direct, oblique, and control questions scattered in various parts of the survey. For example, "What holidays do you observe: Soviet or religious or both?"; "Let us suppose that in your family they wish to observe a religious holiday or ritual. How would you react?"; "Did you baptize your children?" Naturally, during reworking and analysis, the answers to these questions are brought together and considered as a group. [*Formirovanie*, p. 76]

There is nothing very arcane in the descriptions that Soviet scholars have written regarding the construction of their questionnaires. Indeed, questionnaires that have been designed for use among students sound very similar to ordinary diagnostic testing procedures in Western academic circles.[61]

Typically, a questionnaire will be designed to provide data on an array of parameters. One representative survey dealt with the following:

1. Sex.
2. Age.
3. Education.
4. Family situation.
5. Social situation.
6. Professional circumstances.
7. Material circumstances.
8. Participation in social life.
9. How does he spend his free time?
10. What brought him to religion?
11. How often does he visit church or a house of prayer?
12. Does he pray to god?*
13. When does he receive greater satisfaction from prayer; when he prays alone or when he prays in church?
14. What impression does the believer have of god?
15. What convinces the believer of the existence of god?
16. Does he believe in prophetic dreams, fortunetelling, sorcery?
17. Does he believe in life beyond the grave?
18. Can an unbeliever be moral?
19. Does he know the Moral Codex of the Builder of Communism?
20. In what is the meaning of a man's life?
21. In what is man's happiness?
22. For what does man work?
23. How does he understand the commandment about "love of enemies"? [Pantskhava, "Vvedenie," pp. 8–9]

In Alekseev's questionnaire ("Metodika," p. 142) only one-eighth of the space was devoted to religion; the bulk of the questionnaire was devoted to external demographic and other data which could be used to clarify the responses to the specifically religious parameters that were included. Tepliakov's survey (*Problemy*, p. 118) covered seventeen indices, while another concentrated on the following fifteen "working questions";

1. What circumstances of life brought you to faith?
2. What does religion give you?
3. In your opinion, how did stars, the sun, the earth, and man originate?
4. How can one, in your opinion, prove the existence of god?
5. What phenomenon, in your opinion, best illustrates religion?
6. Do you read the Bible, and what passages do you read most often?

---

* When quoting from Soviet sources, I will reluctantly comply with the Soviet insistence on "orthographic atheism," whereby the dignity of capitalization is denied to the Divinity.

7. Do you believe in miracles?
8. What do you consider good, evil, sin?
9. How do you understand the goal and meaning of life, fortune?
10. What is for you an example of virtue?
11. Does religion help in labor, in family life?
12. Which is more important, the interests of personal salvation or the interests of the common good?
13. How do you understand the command, "Love your enemies"?
14. Can an unbeliever be a person of high morals?
15. Do you know the Moral Codex of the Builder of Communism? What do you accept in it and what do you not accept?[62]

A questionnaire that was prepared for school children in Kazakhstan was much more direct, and in many respects it showed an intelligent comprehension of parameters that can be informative when school children are subjects,[63] even though, to some extent, the questions may seem more applicable to primary-school pupils rather than the secondary-school students who were the subjects of the questionnaire research.

The form for Russian schools included the following question: "Explain the words: 'cosmonaut,' 'god,' 'heaven,' 'hell.' What is the Bible and have you seen it? Which holidays do you like most of all and why? Do you pray? Do you believe in god? Who tells you about god?" The form for the Kazakh school . . . included such questions as: "Explain the word, 'cosmonaut,' 'god,' 'heaven,' 'hell.' What is the koran? Have you seen it? What are the *Uraza* and *Ait* and do you observe them in your home? Do you believe in god? Who tells you about god?"[64]

The following is an example of a multiple-choice question:

Which of the following assertions about a person's fate expresses your opinion?
1. A person's fate depends entirely on himself.
2. It depends on him in part.
3. A person's fate does not depend on him at all.
4. It is ordained by god.
5. I do not know.
6. I have another opinion (specify). [Cherniak, *Formirovanie*, p. 115]

Utilizing these techniques, an almost infinite array of approaches may be employed, depending primarily on the ingenuity and intellectual habits of the organizer of the research. The historian A. I. Klibanov, for example, has derived some very interesting conclusions by making comparisons over time. He is careful to compare contemporary data with earlier data that was acquired in the same locale, and in one unusual innovation he utilized data that had been gathered during the twenties and thirties, or ten to twenty years after the Revolution, as comparisons with data gathered in the late fifties and early sixties in western areas acquired during World War II (i.e., a comparable period of time after the introduction of Soviet rule; Klibanov, *Religioznoe sektantstvo*, pp. 76, 79–81). Other scholars have derived similar comparative data by repeating a field expedition after a lapse of some years. From 1970 to 1972, for example, A. I. Dem'ianov attempted to repeat the pioneering research on the underground Orthodox (the True Orthodox Christians) that had been carried out in 1959/60.[65]

Other insights may be derived by making a careful selection of the population to be studied (e.g., comparing figures from heavy industry with light industry, in view of the fact that more women will be employed at the enterprises of light industry; Cherniak, *Formirovanie*, passim). Indeed, Soviet scholars are coming to realize that the permutations that are possible while conducting concrete sociological research on religion are unlimited, and it is by no means unusual for Soviet scholars to examine the approaches of their counterparts in other countries, both in Eastern Europe and elsewhere, including the U.S., in order to enrich their methodologies.[66]

3

WEAKNESSES

Soviet sociology of religion is still in its infancy; so a number of problems have not yet been satisfactorily resolved. Some of these problems are endemic to the approach and probably can never be completely eliminated; others, however, arise from the particular environment in which these studies are conducted and could, in time, be corrected. Whichever the type, these problems represent a weakness in contemporary sociological research on religion in the USSR, and they must be kept in mind when one is reviewing the data. To a degree, these weaknesses may reduce the reliability of some of the data, and the conclusions drawn from these studies must be tempered by the awareness that the studies are not always absolutely accurate and comprehensive.

The first problems, a large group, arise during the planning and application of the field research. Other problems interfere with the analysis and interpretation of the data after the process of acquisition has taken place. Finally, some problems are encountered from the way in which the data is presented for use by other scholars and observers. These groups of weaknesses will be discussed in sequence.

One of the less immediately apparent of the problems that arise in the course of planning the research is the selection of a representative population to serve as subjects of the survey. Much of the time, Soviet scholars are scrupulous in selecting geographies and populations that are representative, and thus the findings of the research among these respondents can have some applicability on a more general scale. However, in some cases, often by chance but doubtless sometimes by design, more unusual sites are selected. Thus, for example, a fairly elaborate research project on religion and religious behavior was conducted by Gaidurova in two rural towns. But there was no church in either of the towns; the nearest church was some fifteen miles away.[1] Similarly, in another project, Kolbanovskii studied three collective farms. There had been an Orthodox church in one of them until 1960, but now the nearest church is outside its boundary. The second had had an Orthodox church until it was closed in 1930, but now the nearest church is eleven miles away. The third collective farm had not had any churches even in pre-Revolutionary times; the nearest church is some thirty-seven miles away.[2] To their credit, both of these scholars made no secret of the anomaly that the populations to be studied did not have access to churches. In such cases, care must be taken to ensure that any conclusions drawn from such data be applied only to noninstitutional religious environments. Many of the parameters—particularly concerning such factors as church attendance, participation in religious rituals, and the like—may be quite different in other areas which enjoy the services of functioning churches. Data from such studies as these cannot always be applied to a larger, more generalized framework without some correction, and some of the specific points may not be applicable at all beyond the immediate location in which the data were gathered.

In another example, Duluman selected 675 religious believers for study, along with 768 former believers who had renounced religion (*Sovremennyi veruiushchii*, p. 5 and passim). Surely this selection was made without malice aforethought, because under Soviet conditions, such former believers will tend to be identifiable and cooperative, while it is sometimes difficult to search out and secure the cooperation of believers. But this introduces a problem. In this example, the majority of the respondents did not find lasting satisfaction in religion. In their answers, the experiences that led up to the break with religion, and the unavoidable selective coloration that has been added by memory during subsequent experiences, must surely have an influence. The result, then, is not a profile of the actual situation of contemporary believers but a skewed picture dominated by people who were dissatisfied with religion. Obviously, a poor selection of subjects for the research undermines the accuracy of the results.

Not all the weaknesses, unfortunately, seem to be as innocent or inadvertent as the above. Although vast advances have been made since the Stalin era, there is still the occasional tendency in Soviet scholarship to present only a part of the data. It is the perennial temptation of the propagandist—and the bane of Soviet scholarship—to present only data that are favorable to the desired conclusion and to ignore or suppress the rest (e.g., Cherniak, "Nuzhen nauchnyi podkhod," p. 26 and passim).

Even when the researcher exercises the most scrupulous care and objectivity, he may find that conditions conspire against him. For example,

Alekseev, in a study of schoolchildren, discovered that "almost all cases of religiousness among school children were predicted by their teachers prior to the survey" ("Metodika," p. 149).[3] While this may be indicative of an unusual (and wholly admirable) rapport between teacher and student, it may also raise the question of whether indeed the students were able to answer freely and without having the teacher influence their answers. It should not be supposed that such pressures cannot happen: "One must bear in mind one more danger to the acquisition of objective data by the questionnaire method: the administrators and teachers of particular schools, from falsely understood considerations of prestige, have tried to exert pressure on the pupils and have conducted belated educational work directly before the survey" (Alekseev, "Metodika," p. 145).

Conversely, the research may run afoul of outright hostility on the part of Soviet officialdom: "Certain organizers of atheistic work in businesses, in institutions, and in schools relate negatively to concrete sociological research, fearing that its results will disclose inadequacies in the establishment of atheistic education and thereby cause damage to the 'honor of the regiment,' will 'air dirty linen.' In one of the highest teaching institutions, when ambiguous results were acquired by an anonymous questionnaire on problems of religiousness, they even instituted an official interrogation of students, rudely destroying by that very action the most elementary principles of concrete sociological research."[4] The researcher thus finds that even his studies are not immune from bureaucracy. Similarly, there have been cases in which researchers have discovered that the clergy had learned of the impending survey and had instructed their congregations to give answers that would be conducive to a false picture that the clergy wished to present (Saprykin, "Ateisticheskaia rabota," p. 226).

A more general problem is the complexity of religion as a subject for sociological research. Galitskaia has asked whether methods that have been devised for studying statistical laws governing the behavior of large groups are applicable at all when one is studying so subjective a matter as religion ("K voprosu," p. 395). And indeed, often the subject can become absolutely unmanageable: "Of 2,762 who broke with religion, 117 'recollect' only one circumstance that influenced their departure from religion, 805 named two motives, 808—3, 610—4, and 422—5 or more motives. Consequently, departure from religion is the result of many interconnected and intersupplementing causes" (Tepliakov, "Pobeda," p. 140). When a sociological study begins to produce results that are as complicated as this and as subject to random influences, one is tempted to conclude, with C. de Grunwald, that "a Gallup poll is not very effective in the areas where the innermost life of the human soul is concerned."[5]

Many problems arise from mistakes made while constructing the array of questions. Some of these problems are caused by the Soviet system itself. According to Paul Hollander:

> Sociology and the social sciences in general represent a most sensitive area of inquiry in a society whose leaders adhere to firm ideological preconceptions and insist that a body of social thought conceived more than a century ago—namely, Marxism—remains largely applicable and relevant to the present. The continued penetration of Soviet sociology by philosophy, and the acknowledged Soviet desire to saddle sociological investigation with the task of providing empirical support for the official system of values, make for uneasiness among those who see sociology as a means of expanding knowledge about society, regardless of the preferences of those who rule it. The lack of institutional autonomy for Soviet sociologists is yet another reason for misgivings, because it is seen as impinging upon the questions they can ask, the methods they can use, and the conclusions they can reach.[6]

Surely there is little direct evidence that the Soviet scholars who design and lead these expeditions of concrete sociological research on religion find themselves under official constraint, whether from the political or the academic authorities. Yet Hollander's point has some merit, in that these researchers do subscribe to Marxism-Leninism and do support the official social system. Thus, each will have to struggle against this sort of prejudicial approach with greater or lesser success.

Perhaps in part because of these unavoidable commitments on the part of the researcher, many of the questions are poorly phrased for the believer. For example: "When do you receive greater satisfaction from prayer, when you pray alone or when you pray in the temple (house of prayer)?"[7] Note that because this question is ambiguous (what, after all, does an individual believer consider to be satisfaction?), the answer may very well depend on the atmosphere and mood that the believer senses at the time of the question. (In this case, 61.54% preferred collective prayer; 10.77%, individual prayers; and 27.69% rated them equal [Iablokov, "Obshchenie," p. 55].) Especially when trying to ascertain the primary reasons that the believer gives for being religious, the distinctions suggested by the researcher (e.g., "intellectual," "moral," "traditional," etc.) will often be confusing; and which motivation receives emphasis will depend to some extent on the believer's mood or whim at the moment (Duluman, *Sovremennyi veruiushchii*, pp. 71-81). This is such a complex subject that only rarely, if ever, will an individual not only understand his own motivations completely but also have the clarity needed in order to make such distinctions. The problem is aggravated by the inherent liability that the questions must be at the simplest, least educated level if they are to be valid for all the respondents (Baltonov, *Sotsiologicheskie problemy,* p. 127). This necessarily limits the ability of the method to penetrate the more complex matters.

Similarly, often when a researcher is using open-type questions (ones that do not have standardized answers), his results will depend in part on how articulate or taciturn the individual believer is, and as yet this has not been measured as a corrective to the researcher's conclusions. For example, in an attempt to determine the relative importance of reason versus feeling among believers, it seems likely that the researcher might ascribe reason to the articulate believer and feeling to one who is inarticulate or taciturn.[8]

One of the most difficult problems in designing a field project is to ensure against letting the researcher unconsciously skew the data: "It is especially important to take into account the danger of subjectivism. What is stated in the questionnaire is not fact but only expression—not always clear, occasionally incompetent and sometimes even insincere. Furthermore, the determination of expressions (for example, in an interview), and especially their interpretation, in greater or lesser degree are 'colored' by the researchers themselves. All of this 'contaminates' the materials gathered. Prevention and 'filtration of contaminants' is by no means a simple task."[9] Sometimes it is simply impossible to filter out such contaminants. For example, if a question on work motivation is phrased "Why do you work?" it will probably elicit more secularized responses than if it is phrased "Is work a religious duty?"[10]

Some errors, of course, are simply caused by inadequate understanding of religion on the part of the atheistic designer of the questionnaire or by the failure to think about all the ramifications of his questions. Thus the questionnaire that Cherniak gave to factory workers in Kazakhstan almost never takes into account the fact that the dominant religion in Kazakhstan is Islam; instead, it explores parameters that, however important they may be for the Christian, are of much less importance for the Muslim (e.g., "Do you go to the church/prayer house/*mechet*?"; Cherniak, *Formirovanie,* passim). Indeed, one suspects that such unconscious Russian presuppositions are rather more debilitating to Soviet sociology when the minority nationalities are being studied than is the prior commitment to Marxism.

Occasionally, Soviet researchers demonstrate an unfortunate insensitivity to the results of their research. For example, "Research conducted among 2,057 convinced believers belonging to Orthodoxy and the Christian sects showed that only 29% of them know the Christian mythology, and only 11% believe in 'the triune god'" (Tepliakov, "Pobeda," pp. 154–55; cf. Selivanov, *Partiinoe rukovodstvo,* p. 71). Surely, in view of the almost absolute, unanimous loyalty of Christians (especially of the Orthodox) throughout history to the doctrine of the Trinity, this researcher should have suspected that something may have been wrong with the question or with the questionnaire procedure if it produced such startling and inexplicable results. In a similar case, 129 of 538 respondents were unable to answer a question at all; in this case, there is a distinct possibility that the question was poorly conceived and that the results should not have been included (Iablokov, "Obshchenie," pp. 63–64).

Conversely, the reach may at times exceed the grasp. One sociologist claims that in research conducted among Siberian Baptists from 1969 to 1976, it was discovered that 92.5% thought that the Holy Spirit is the source of the Bible, while the remaining 7.5% accepted the theory of "progressive revelation," that the Bible comes from two sources, the divine and the human as well.[11] Surely such a result must cause some doubt, other than whether this minor matter was indeed pursued for seven years. In view of the generations-long blockade of religious literature and the complete lack of religious education for Baptists (except for the small correspondence course for pastors that was begun in 1968), it seems most unlikely that 100% of the Baptists surveyed would be able to state a clear position on so fine a distinction as this. And if they were able to, it would be an extraordinary atheist who could be sure that he really understood all of the answers.

A much more subtle problem is the need to construct a question so that it will preclude an intentionally ambiguous or even seemingly false answer. For example, when Kozachishin asked, "Do you consider yourself a religious person?" he received only 4 yes answers out of 127 responses.[12] But even a believer could answer this question negatively without overmuch rationalization, simply by telling himself that despite his belief, in fact he is naturally less inclined to heroic feats of religiousness than he feels he should be. Similarly, the question "Do you consider it essential to teach religion to children?" produced the astonishing results of only 11 affirmative answers from 58 believing respondents and 54 others who were in doubt about whether they believed in God (Safronov, "Chto," p. 71). These strange results were almost surely caused by the failure of the question to specify "your own children"; one of the sorest points in the antireligious campaign has been the teaching of religion to other people's children. While it is usually but not always permissible to teach religion to one's own children, to teach religion to other people's children or even to advocate Sunday School, and the like, have been consistently and severely punished. Hence only a brave or foolhardy person would answer this question, as phrased, in the affirmative, for such an answer might seem to be advocacy of what has been treated as a crime for the past two decades.

The readiness of believers to seize upon any possible ambiguities in order to avoid committing themselves—and thereby risking the possibility of incurring penalties—presents extraordinary difficulties to Soviet researchers.

> The task of maximizing the scientific value of the conversations runs into difficulties of another sort, of which two are the most substantial. Let us take the following questionnaire dialogue:
>
> Researcher: Tell me please, do you believe in god?
>
> Believer: Well, how to tell you. I don't know myself whether there is a god or not.
>
> Researcher: Do you attend church?
>
> Believer: When do we have time to go to church?
>
> Researcher: And why do you keep icons?
>
> Believer: The parents hung them way back when. Rather than leave the corner empty, let them sparkle there.
>
> "Waverer" [between belief and unbelief] decides the researcher. It is evident that the person is wavering, but the important thing consists of explaining whether he wavers in his own faith or is shy about speaking to an outsider about his most secret feelings.[13]

A third hypothesis might suggest that the believer is actually trying to avoid giving any direct, unequivocal answers.

Even when a workable questionnaire has been devised, great problems remain in the recruitment of field researchers to conduct the survey. Sociological research is by no means a simple task, as Iablokov points out (*Metodologicheskie,* p. 106):

> During an interview with believers, the researcher comes up against a number of difficulties. They are connected with the fact that the questions deal with the inner world, the intimate aspect of the personality of the person being questioned. In order that the conversation take place and give satisfactory material, believers should experience confidence in the researcher. In the course of the conversation the Marxist researcher cannot, of course, "play games" with religion or pose as a representative of

the religious group to which the subject belongs. Furthermore, open approval or disapproval of the statement of the believer is also inappropriate, in our view. If the researcher tries to teach or persuade the believer, then the influence of subjective factors on the information is strengthened, and its quality is severely reduced.

The researcher must assiduously avoid polemics or arguments, and certainly must not get drawn into proselyting for atheism (Alekseev, "Metodika," p. 143). At times this is a counsel of perfection. In one case, a research team was talking to a young lady who was very proud of the village church, even though the village club house was run down: "When we tried to make fun of her pride, remonstrating with her for the fact that, look, the old people build a church but the youth are satisfied with such a club . . ." (Gaidurova, "Zavisimost'," p. 23. The following is a more pronounced example of an argumentative approach (Stel'makov, "O sootnoshenii," pp. 45–46):

We shall give a characteristic excerpt from a conversation with the Baptist Iu. (city of Saran', Karaganda, works as a doctor). The topic of the conversation was whether the world is indeed created with goals and intelligence corresponding to a merciful and good creator.

Question: And the tuberculosis bacilla—this is from a good creator? And the death of children—this is from his wisdom? And war—this is from the love of the creator towards people?

Answer: The devil is responsible for this.

Question: And why does the infinitely wise creator of the world permit this "devil" to create so much sorrow for what god has created?

Answer: God gave freedom—to pursue good or to choose evil. And people themselves are guilty in their misfortunes.

Question: And a little child who is ill with tuberculosis is also himself guilty?

Answer: The wisdom of god is incomprehensible to an unbeliever.

Not only is there the danger that an unskilled or aggressive researcher may distort the data; there is a perennial problem of errors creeping into the results of the field research. Krasnikov notes ("O nekotorykh tendentsiiakh," p. 10): "The researchers kept records (filled out questionnaires) extremely concisely (and this caused their inaccuracies)." Great demands are made on the field worker's memory: "The researcher should remember exactly the questions which are to be raised" (Iablokov, *Metodologicheskie problemy,* p. 106). "In order to guarantee the frankness of the relationship with a believer the answers were written down after the conversation" (Pantskhava, "Vvedenie," p. 7). Or in the case of observations of church attendance, Iablokov says: "The difficulty consisted of the fact that in order to achieve minimal influence on the conduct of believers, the researcher had to write down the results, not during the course of divine service (not in the church), but after it (outside the church building). Certain mistakes which might arise in the course of this technique caused a small degree of distortion in the research conducted" (*Metodologicheskie problemy,* p. 105). This is certainly a real problem, for unless an individual has taken care to train his memory, the introduction of error during the period between the observation and the taking of notes is difficult to avoid.

One of the problems, of course, is that the people recruited for field work simply are not highly trained experts. "Sociological research is basically conducted by people who do not have special preparation" (Baltanov, *Sotsiologicheskie problemy,* p. 67). The subject has become fashionable, and some inadequately qualified individuals are likely to be attracted to the field work, as Evdokimov notes ("Konkretnye sotsial'nye issledovaniia," p. 24). In the most elaborate research project to date, the collecting of data involved more than 7,000 people, including directors of Party propaganda organizations, secretaries of Party committees, secondary-school administrators, surgeons, and three writers. It seems highly unlikely that this large mass of research workers received more than rather modest training, particularly in view of the small average number of individuals (9) that each research worker contacted (Tepliakov, *Problemy,* p. 32). A similar project embraced 1,196 workers drawn from various professions, and again their training may have been insufficient (Tepliakov, "Pobeda," p. 134). Even where the director of the project, Nikonov, took the time to give specialized training to his field researchers, when such researchers were drawn from so remote a source as the Technical Institute of Fish Production and Husbandry, surely their level of expertise was somewhat less than professional ("O nekotorykh tendentsiiakh," p. 174). Given the necessity to work with amateur or nearly amateur field researchers (this handicap is by no means confined to the USSR), Soviet sociologists face real problems in minimizing and correcting for errors that are introduced by the researchers.

A final problem in the staffing of research teams is an endemic problem for atheistic work in the USSR. This is the problem of the age discrepancy between the predominately young atheists and the predominately elderly believers.[14] Young people very often have not had enough general experience to be able to find an effective approach to the older subjects of the research (Duluman, *Sovremennyi veruiushchii*, p. 170). Soviet scholars have noted and discussed, but have yet to find an answer to, this "psychological barrier" which arises when research is conducted by young researchers who have been atheists all their lives and therefore may not have any deep understanding or appreciation of the believer's approach to life and its problems (Tepliakov, *Problemy*, p. 34).

In addition to these problems of approach and personnel, other problems arise among the subjects of the research, the religious people themselves. In designing and evaluating the research, the researchers must continually deal with the question of the reliability of the data supplied by the believers themselves. "For example, answers to questions of a questionnaire may be sincere or insincere, correct or mistaken, etc." (Baltonov, *Sotsiologicheskie problemy*, pp. 135–36). In many instances there are also indications—and it is sometimes obvious—that the respondent is refusing to provide candid information.

Part of the problem lies simply in the official aura that surrounds the investigators, "for the very association of the sociologist with the government raises the crucial problem of eliciting candid responses and trustworthy information from the Soviet citizen" (Hollander, "Dilemmas," p. 323). Cherniak points out that Soviet researchers are very much aware of this problem: "The fact that, when studying attitudes toward religion, the researcher is dealing with very intimate aspects of individal consciousness (people, as a rule, are embarrassed to recognize their religiousness, and have a complete right not to talk about it) presents the study of questions of the relationship to religion with a very delicate and complex task, much more difficult than study of problems connected with other forms of social consciousness" (*Formirovanie*, p. 61). Baltanov shows that a great deal depends on the approach and that "the questions should not insult their religious feelings," lest believers either refuse to respond or give a distorted answer (*Sotsiologicheskie problemy*, p. 58).

Cooperation with the researcher is voluntary for the subject, and coercion is not employed, according to Alekseev ("Metodika," p. 141); however, as will become apparent below, indirect pressures are sometimes present, which may tend to distort the data.

According to Ugrinovich, respondents are prone to call themselves believers when in fact they are not: "As research in the socialist countries shows, people in conversations or interviews personally consider themselves believers. Nevertheless their consciousness and especially their behavior bear an almost completely secularized character. In this way a contradiction arises between the subjective consideration of one's self as a believer and the real condition of consciousness and conduct of a given person."[15] This may indeed be true; it repeats a venerable observation of Lenin's widow, N. Krupskaia, during the era of the 1937 census (*Izvestiia*, 27 April 1937). However, in the Soviet Union today, there is every incentive for the opposite to take place, for religious believers to seek to mask their true positions. Often a great deal of tact is required in order to penetrate the initial barrier of reticence (Mitrokhin, "O metodologii," pp. 318–19).

The problem of general reticence, Iablokov points out, is compounded by conscious insincerity on the part of some respondents (*Metodologicheskie problemy*, p. 109). Gaidurova says ("Zavisimost'," p. 15):

> Even when gathering primary data in the field, as in no other sociological research, one must overcome this special "resistance" of the subject matter: here, after all, we are dealing with believers —the least developed part of the population of our country (sometimes not united in institutions), not infrequently living a very private form of life. To attract them to participate in research (as not infrequently happens in the study of other objects) is almost impossible. With many of the believers (among the illiterate), even to elicit their trust is an overwhelming task. And furthermore, subjectively the believer is interested in preserving the faith and not in studying the causes of religiousness.

In order to filter out such conscious and unconscious distortion, Duluman and his associates advocate that the responses be verified by comparing them with the behavior of the respondent himself (*Sovremennyi veruiushchii*, p. 71).[16] Unfortunately, such verification may make it seem to the believer that his answers have led to further unwanted involvement in the research project, and thus the process of following up the interview may engender hostility and suspicion which make the acquisition of reliable data even more difficult. After all, if an honest answer leads to further annoyance from these atheists, why should one be candid at all? Not infrequently, Soviet researchers are confronted with outright hostility from the religious believers, some of whom absolutely refuse to talk with atheists, as Duluman notes (in ibid., p. 171): "They do not allow atheists who try to conduct individual work with them into the house. In the majority of the cases they interrupt the 'blasphemer' with the words, 'None of your business! You don't believe in god, then shut up! What do you have to do with god? God himself knows what he is doing. If believers suffer misfortune, then it is the will of god!' 'I don't even want to listen! And don't talk to me, anti-Christ dwells in you!' 'You don't know anything, and you are not going to prove that god doesn't exist! God is!' " Other believers move from the defensive to an offensive position, seeking to draw nonbelievers into untenable positions through trap questions and the like. Religious people of this sort take care to be exceedingly well informed about atheism and the activities of the atheistic organizations (Duluman, ibid., p. 169).

On occasion, the researchers themselves will inadvertently exacerbate the latent hostility which awaits them among the subjects of their research. For example, Alekseev ("Metodika," p. 141) says that "the most convenient time period for conducting the questionnaire with the collective farmers (if it is conducted in the summer) is the morning hours prior to going out to work, the lunch break, which in rural localities lasts 2–2½ hours, and evening time after the work is done." Thus, because the researchers interrupt the free time of the respondents (after all, it is the State, not the believer, that is primarily interested in such research), any annoyance that the religious believer feels will be amplified, and the resulting hostility will increase. If, on the other hand, the cooperation of the local authorities could have been secured and the interviews could have been conducted during working hours, they might have elicited an opposite reaction from the respondents, increasing their willingness to cooperate.

Complicating the picture still further is the possibility of fear of reprisal on the part of the respondent. "The practice of the questionnaire survey showed that the sincerely believing person never uses guile in reference to his active relationship to religion. Believers in our country are prepared for this by Soviet legislation, which guarantees every citizen genuine freedom of conscience. Difficulties in acquiring objective data, apparently, may arise where there have been cases of violation of Soviet legislation in the field of religion on the part of boundlessly zealous partisans of the liquidation of religion by administrative means" (Alekseev, "Metodika," p. 142). The problem, of course, is that such outbursts of enthusiasm have taken place with some frequency during the past two decades, and those areas of the country that have not experienced illegalities with regard to Soviet religious legislation are very few indeed. Baltanov (*Sotsiologicheskie problemy*, p. 129) recognizes the problem quite frankly: "Interviewing believers is an exceedingly delicate and complex affair, for religion in our society is a foreign world view, an object of scientific criticism and social censure. Under these conditions, believers approach the various attempts to penetrate into their inner world cautiously, and in a number of cases they conceal their true attitude to religion, fearing undesired consequences (difficulties for themselves and their family members caused by the administration, closure of the church or temple, etc.)." Religious believers may give all sorts of evasive answers to avoid being identified as religious: for example, in responding to a question concerning one's mental image of God by saying, "I have not seen him," "I do not have any mental image," "I do not know," "God—that's all" (Tepliakov, *Problemy*, pp. 140–41).

This fear of reprisal creates some extraordinary results from research. For example, in Ignatenko's survey ("Opyt," p. 252) 69.6% of the Baptists asserted that they do not exercise a religious influence on their children. This is an astonishing percentage, and it is so at odds with normative Baptist attitudes toward Christian education that it quite possibly reflects fear of Soviet reprisal against those who advocate religious education. Similarly, the discovery that students hold religious convictions frequently results in their being expelled from higher education. Therefore, when students are asked to classify themselves, it is not surprising that very few indeed admit to being religious believers.[17] Lebedev, apparently without noticing anything unusual, faithfully notes that 91% of the students who are atheists and 88% of the nonbelievers do not believe in God ("Studencheskaia molodezh'," p. 202). Ugrinovich finds that a general reluctance to admit to being believers can very well include "a conscious desire to lead the researchers astray" ("Izuchenie," p. 143).

So that fear of reprisal will not distort the answers, Pismanik notes that it is absolutely essential that the anonymity of the respondent be scrupulously preserved: "How to guarantee a relationship of good will, the conscious 'collaboration' of the subjects in the survey? The most primary condition: the subject should be absolutely convinced of the strict observance of anonymity, inasmuch as many of the data, especially those imparted by them in conversation with the researcher, may have a confidential character" ("Metodika," p. 215). The problem is that despite assertions to the contrary, religious people may not be completely sure that confidentiality will be honored (Hollander, "Dilemmas," p. 326 n.29), especially in cases in which the interviewer is personally present during the entire time the respondent is filling out the questionnaire (Kobetskii, *Sotsiologicheskoe izuchenie*, p. 67). Consciously or unconsciously, violations of anonymity are permitted to occur. This can happen unintentionally, in a perfectly innocent attempt to achieve maximum clarity: "When we receive the completed questionnaire from the student, we immediately verify that it has been filled out correctly, and we make specific all unclear or incomplete places" (Alekseev, "Metodika," p. 145). If a student were apprehensive, there would be every possibility that he might interpret even such questions for clarification as violations of his confidence. Even without such overt suggestions that the procedure may not finally prove to be completely anonymous, in a general atmosphere of tension, such suspicions arise rather frequently. Bland assumptions that the suspicions are no particular problem do not really change the situation: "The mistrust of the believers was overcome by the fact that the questionnaire was given to all the inhabitants of the villages mentioned, both believers and unbelievers" (Iablakov, *Metodologicheskie problemy*, p. 107). However, in a society in which the secret police traditionally have maintained a covert, ubiquitous presence, it is not certain that such simple expedients will necessarily allay all doubts.

In some cases, Soviet religious policy renders sociological field study difficult or impossible. Thus Klibanov notes, "We have not succeeded in gathering data that would allow one to establish a generalized characteristic of the social and demographic structure and dynamics of development of the Pentecostal and Jehovah's Witnesses sects" (*Religioznoe sektantstvo*, p. 95). This is necessarily the case, inasmuch as both denominations have been declared illegal by the state, and anyone who affiliates with them risks imprisonment.

Even without such extremes, however, the promise of anonymity is sometimes subordinated to the desire to conduct antireligious work that is designed to eradicate religion. Even though Pismanik points out most forcefully that "these measures can disrupt the relationship with the believers and thereby distort the data acquired" (Metodika," p. 215) and though Baltanov notes that the respondent must be assured that the interest is exclusively scientific and no negative consequences will ensue (*Sotsiologicheskoe problemy*, pp. 129–30), Saprykin indicates that the temptation to utilize the data in constructing a local campaign against religion may be too strong to resist. "To every questionnaire form the atheists attached a note of their personal impressions concerning the believer with whom they conducted the conversation. This material was studied and analyzed. In accordance with it, concrete measures were worked out for working with the given congregation of Baptists" ("Ateisticheskaia rabota," p. 226). In another case, the results of a sociological survey were utilized in local Party meetings; and countermeasures, including the assignment of individual atheists to attach themselves to particular believers for protracted attempts at persuasion, were worked out on the basis of the results of the survey.[18] Such uses of research that is premised on the preservation of anonymity can only confirm any doubts in the believers' minds that candid answers are not in their best interest, and hence there remains the possibility that the data will contain distortions motivated by fear or apprehension.

The basic problem is that in the last analysis, Soviet sociological research on religion is not detached or dispassionate. The goal of sociological research is to change society (Baltanov, *Sotsiologicheskie problemy*,

p. 11 and passim). Whatever inclinations an individual scholar may have towards seeking truth for its own sake, the primary, overwhelming motivation of the research is to utilize sociological data in order to facilitate and enhance the state's commitment to overcome the influence of religion in society. "Religious survivals can be quickly overcome only on condition of knowledge of those real forms in which religion exists today, knowledge of the condition and tendencies of change of religious consciousness. Acquisition and broadening of this knowledge is facilitated by the concrete sociological research which has been developing in our country in recent times" (Pantskhava, "Vvedenie," p. 4). The primary motivation for such research, and therefore its ultimate justification to the authorities, is its practical application in the interests of atheism: "It offers the possibility of utilizing the information acquired to the end of working out practical recommendations with regard to the organization of atheistic education in local sites."[19] This research is one of the means utilized by the state in combating religion, and thus distortion due to the respondent's fear of reprisal can be a real problem.

Once the acquisition process has been completed, numerous problems arise in processing and analyzing the data. Some of these problems are minor, but others are serious enough to place severe limitations on the success that Soviet sociologists of religion can achieve.

Perhaps the least important is a tendency (fortunately not terribly widespread) towards simplistic approaches to the data. For example, confidence in the accuracy of responses simply because "it is usually considered a serious sin for one who is truly a believer to deny his faith" (Cherniak, *Formirovanie*, p. 60), would not seem to be universally applicable in view of the factors discussed above. From his findings, Tepliakov concluded that the incidence of people who have broken with religion increases as the age of the respondent increases ("Pobeda," p. 139). This relationship would seem only to be natural—the longer people live, the more chance there is that they will have experienced change.

Simplistic interpretations due to ideological presuppositions frequently occur. Some of these are technical and relatively minor: for example, Mitrokhin asserts that believers are prevaricating when they mention miracles, voices from heaven, and so forth ("O metodologii," pp. 319-20); they very well may be, but without empirical evidence, the canons of pure scholarship would prefer that such data be presented without comment. Similar, but more worrisome, are the more sweeping conclusions that are drawn from ideological presuppositions. For example, Cherniak's statement "Today the absolute majority of the workers, without doubt, accept for themselves the scientific materialist explanation of the world, and are in

this manner opponents of religion" ("Nuzhen nauchnyi podkhod," p. 26)—
which assumes an absolute and total incompatibility between religion and
science—would scarcely seem self-evident to observers who do not share
these ideological presuppositions.

Other lapses into simplicity can be relatively harmless, consisting of
an unnecessary pedantry. After noting that 2% of the inhabitants in one
village belonged to a certain religious sect, as compared with 65% in
another village, Tul'tseva discovered that the sect's ideas "have a broader
dissemination" in the second village, which would scarcely seem to be
surprising.[20]

Given this tendency toward simplistic conclusions, one cannot always
be confident that Soviet scholarship is fully alert to possible subtleties in
the data. "There was a case as follows. Explaining the reasons for his
religiousness, one 'believer' unexpectedly stated, How should I not believe
in god? For an entire year I have been going and asking for an apartment;
I live with my wife and two kids in one room, no facilities whatsoever, a
communal apartment. Look, let them give me an apartment—and I will
renounce religion" (Duluman, *Sovremennyi veruiushchii*, p. 50). The
Soviet scholars conclude that this is a shallow, hypocritical case, and indeed
it may be that this offer of reverse simony represents no more than that.
But it is not impossible that a much more profound philosophical point
might be at issue in this response. The believer might be referring to
Marxism's inadequacies in providing even the relatively simple material
necessities of life that it promises, thereby concluding that the ideology
itself is mistaken ("If your materialism is so great, why can't I get an
apartment?").

A related problem is the uncritical use of sources. Particularly when
they find support for an ideological presupposition, some Soviet sociologists
will on occasion fail to exercise discrimination with regard to the nature
and applicability of the sources. Tepliakov's presentation of the claims of
local journalists as facts is but one illustration of this unfortunate tendency
(*Problemy*, p. 146). One scholar who writes about women continually
quotes assertions by Lenin's widow, Krupskaia, forty years in the past,
without commenting on the applicability of such statements to contemporary circumstances.[21]

On occasion, Soviet researchers draw conclusions that are more sweeping than the data warrant. Evdokimov rightly criticizes a 1929 study: "Of
11,000 questionnaires distributed, only 3,000 (less than 30%) were returned;
among the completed questionnaires of workers, 88.8% were unbelievers
and 11.2% believers; this result was incorrectly extended to all workers,
which distorted the actual picture of religiousness during those years"

46

("Konkretnye sotsial'nye issledovaniia," p. 25). But in a number of cases, contemporary Soviet researchers do not report on such matters as the rates of return, spoiled interviews, and the like; therefore, it is not completely certain that such errors as this are entirely phenomena of the remote past. Krasnikov's recent questionnaire, which contained three simple questions on atheistic activity, was distributed to propagandists who were attending seminars in three cities. It had a return rate of only 19% ("O nekotorykh voprosakh," p. 7).

One of the greatest problems in analyzing the data is the poorly developed state of mathematical analysis. In some cases, a primitive understanding of the role of mathematics in sociological study results in a fairly misleading approach. It is not unusual for an article to present impressive statistics on a large number of parameters with regard to religion, but then to jump to conclusions about the inevitable and necessary decline of religion, conclusions that are neither required nor necessarily suggested by the data (e.g., Mamaeva, "O nekotorykh . . . faktorakh," pp. 77–92). More often, there will be the appearance but not the substance of mathematical analysis—for example, complex graphs and intricate formulae, which, on closer inspection, turn out to be simple, repetitious arithmetic manipulations (e.g., Tepliakov, *Problemy,* pp. 118–25 and passim).

The tremendous savings in time and effort that mathematical techniques can yield is poorly understood. Galitskaia complains that "an exact picture of the religiousness [of youth] has not been acquired. The research has not been conducted on a scale of the entire country, republic, or even one region. Despite its great scope, it has not been able to embrace such a number of youth that the conclusions acquired might be extended to all the youth of our country. This is a task for further research" ("K voprosu," p. 392). Apparently she is unaware of statistical-sampling techniques. Random selection is used fairly often (Solov'ev, "O vliianii," p. 187), and in one case, at least, Cherniak used a "two-step, combined, random 10% mechanical selection" ("Nuzhen nauchnyi podkhod," p. 25). More sophisticated sampling techniques are seldom utilized, however.

A large part of the problem is simply the lack of equipment. On occasion, machine-grading of questionnaire answers was used (Cherniak, *Formirovanie,* p. 76), and indeed, the trend towards using closed questions (multiple choice, etc.) is largely explained by the desire to utilize machine-grading (Alekseev "Metodika," pp. 143–44). However, counting by hand is by no means unknown. Alekseev (in ibid., p. 144) commented in 1967: "Inasmuch as processing the questions at mechanized counting facilities is an expensive operation, it follows that one must also have in view the possibility of processing them manually. Small mass questionnaires of 2–3,000 pages with a quantity of questions of about 40 can be processed by hand by a 10-man team, with intelligent and planned organization of labor, in the course of 10 days. A small questionnaire of 10–15 questions with a mass of 2–3,000 pages may be processed by the same team in 3 days." The insuperable problem is the lack of computers in Soviet civilian institutions. Very often, Soviet scholars display a desire to use mathematical techniques, and indeed, they will attempt some functions (e.g., comparison of paired questions) without the aid of a computer (Cherniak, *Formirovanie*, pp. 337–42). In 1966, Osipov told Westerners ("Some Principles," pp. 302–3):

> We believe that the use of mathematical and statistical methods (the law of averages, the law of multitudes, theory of gains, etc.) will be fruitful in concrete social research, for they provide an accurate and objective description of quantitative aspects of social processes and events. Laboratories for mathematical methods in economics, created at the Section of Economics of the Academy of Science of the USSR and at the Siberian Section of the Academy, are beginning to use mathematics more and more as a means of analysis of concrete economic processes. A large role is reserved for mathematics in modeling social processes and events as well. Economic science has already started work on social modeling, deemed a matter of utmost importance with a promising future. Sociology is following the same course. By feeding data into an electronic computer, it is possible to obtain comparisons between social events and concrete social conditions in the laboratories. These studies help us to find ways of influencing social events through public opinion and support.

Unfortunately, to date, this early optimism has been frustrated by the scarcity of computers in the civilian sector, and use of them in analyzing the results of sociological surveys of religion is relatively infrequent. When a computer is used, it is generally a Minsk-22,[22] which is a fairly complex, second-generation computer—that is, it utilizes transistorized, solid-state circuitry but not microcircuits (integrated circuits, etc.)—similar to the Elliot 803 or perhaps the IBM 1130.[23]

Because of relative inexperience in the use of cybernetic techniques, the mathematical manipulations of the data continue to be exceedingly primitive. Cherniak calculated the coefficents of association according to the formula $Q = \dfrac{ad - cb}{ad + cb}$.[24] According to Korolev ("Rol'," p. 153 n.1):

The coefficient of relationship is calculated by the formula

$$Q = \frac{ad - cb}{ad + cb},$$ where a, b, c, and d are the frequency of alternative

indices: participation or nonparticipation in particular types of social activity of religious and nonreligious population.

The formula for the coefficient of conjugation:

$$\phi = \frac{ad - cb}{(a + b)(c + d)(b + d)(a + c)}.$$

The numerical expressions that are obtained as a result of calculation with the aid of these formulae of coefficients are different, because the coefficient ϕ not only gives a more precise evaluation of the closeness of relationship but also reflects measures of interrelationship of indices that are somewhat different from Q. Therefore, in considering the interaction of several types of social activity with the religiousness of the personality, the author made the calculation by the formulae of both coefficients.

In addition, coefficients of correlation are used (again, these are derived through arithmetic formulae; Cherniak, *Formirovanie,* pp. 238–40). On one occasion at least, the Latin Square method was utilized (see table 3.1).

One severe problem that faces Soviet researchers is that official nationwide data on religion are not available (Cherniak, *Formirovanie,* pp. 60–61). Published nationwide figures, with very rare exceptions, are absolutely unreliable and bear no relationship whatsoever to facts.[25] Gaidurova cites official policy in explaining this lack of data ("Zavisimost'," p. 15; cf. *Izvestiia,* 30 August 1966): "It is well known that in socialist society, religion is the private matter of the citizen. In conformity with laws enforced among us concerning freedom of conscience, governmental organs do not conduct a statistical count of believers. Their religious adherence is not registered in documents. Because of this, we do not have national data on the condition of religiousness." This is only partly true. The Council for Religious Affairs (mentioned above) issues and supervises the registration of churches, and local organs of government (or, presumably, local offices of the council) are by law required to keep records concerning the legalized churches.[26] So, some data at least are extant; that these data have not overtly been made available to Soviet sociologists remains something of an anomaly. Furthermore, the secret police have such a tradition of internal surveillance, and there have been so many reports of the secret police having kept track of local churches and believers that a considerable

49

TABLE 3.1
AN EXAMPLE OF LATIN-SQUARE METHODOLOGY

Question 1:
Choice of answers:
A   Religion and science are incompatible.
B   Religion and science are separate.
C   Religion and science are complementary.
Question 2:
Choice of answers:
D   Religion is harmful.
E   Religion is neither harmful nor useful.
F   Religion is useful.
Question 3:
Choice of answers:
G   One should help to free believers from religion.
H   Indifferent to religiousness of believers.
I   One should leave believers alone.

Answer clusters, using rating scale from 1=atheistic to 6=contradictory to 7=indifferent to 10=religious

	A			B			C		
	D	E	F	D	E	F	D	E	F
G	1	2	6	2	3	6	6	6	6
H	2	3	6	3	7	8	6	8	9
I	4	5	6	6	8	9	6	9	10

Absolute Numbers of Respondents

	A			B			C		
	D	E	F	D	E	F	D	E	F
G	1,066	172	11	64	42	1	10	5	1
H	77	61	0	7	55	3	1	1	1
I	115	100	4	12	55	9	9	3	4

Answer Clusters by Percentage on the Rating Scale of 1 to 10

		1	2	3	4	5	7	8	9	10	No Answer or Ambiguous
Boys	807	48.0	15.5	5.9	5.4	4.8	2.8	2.7	0.1	0.0	14.8
Girls	1,436	54.5	13.1	5.5	4.9	4.2	2.2	2.5	0.02	0.02	13.06
Totals	2,275	51.2	14.3	5.7	5.1	4.5	2.5	2.6	0.06	0.03	14.04

SOURCE: *Gertsenovskie chteniia* 1 (1970): 18–20.
NOTE: Unfortunately, this promising attempt is absolutely vitiated by errors. Among the more immediately apparent are the following. First, the number of responses entered into the Latin Squares total only 1,889, rather than the 2,275 (or some other total) demanded by the tabulation of answer clusters (adding figures suggested by the No answer/ambiguous column does not resolve this anomaly). In that tabulation, 807 boys plus 1,436 girls yield a total of 2,243, not 2,275. In column 1, 48% of 807 boys and 54.5%

fund of data on the nationwide scale may be presumed to exist (or could be generated very quickly). At least since 1937, however, the statement that religion is excluded from the list of questions of the national census is certainly true enough (Duluman, *Sovremennyi veruiushchii*, p. 30).

A much more serious problem is a pervasive lack of coordination in this field, doubtless due to the fact that sociological research on religion is a relatively new arrival in Soviet academia. The result is an as yet insuperable lack of compatibility in data that has been gathered by different research teams. Alekseev notes that "lack of coordination in the methodology of the research, in the definition of criteria of religiousness, and other questions makes it difficult to compare the results acquired by the various research teams" ("Metodika," p. 148). Baltanov says that "it is difficult to render the great mass of factual material that has been gathered by Soviet sociologists studying problems of religion and atheism into a common denominator due to the lack of a single methodological, methodical, and technical approach" (*Sotsiologicheskie problemy*, p. 153).

One of the more difficult problems with Soviet sociological scholarship on religion is the presentation of misleading data. Perhaps because many of the practitioners of this discipline were trained primarily as propagandists rather than as detached scholars, disingenuousness is not always a rare phenomenon. In a number of cases, statements such as the following will appear: "In 1964 the number of religious baptisms diminished by more than 35% from the 1963 figure."[27] When the author neglects to give any concrete figures, however, such a comparison really is not very instructive. In another case, studying the reading habits of 675 believers, Duluman's group discovered that 355 read no religious literature and that 267 were poorly acquainted with the fundamentals of the faith (*Sovremennyi veruiushchii*, p. 107). They make no mention, however, of the fact that religious literature, including the Bible, is exceedingly difficult to obtain in the Soviet Union due to state restrictions against the publication and distribution of it. Not even Klibanov, who normally eschews

---

of 1,436 girls totals approximately 1,170, rather than the 1,066 of the Latin Square space ADG. The "total" line in the tabulation is derived by adding the percentage of boys and that of the girls and then dividing by 2, rather than weighting the percentage of girls by 1.8 times that of the boys. The "total" line adds up to 100.03%, due to errors in computing certain of the entries according to the mistaken formula of boys plus girls divided by 2; thus the total in column 1 should be 51.25; that of column 4, 5.15; that of column 10, 0.01; and that of the last column, 13.93 (with these corrections, the line totals 100%). Finally, even without these mistakes and such others as may be less conspicuous, if one in seven answers was ambiguous or blank, such a high rate of spoilage may indicate that the procedure itself was sufficiently crude as to cast all of its findings, whatever they may actually be, in doubt.

such devices, is completely immune from occasional disingenuousness (*Religioznoe sektantstvo,* p. 89):

> Thus, in contrast to 1959–1961, when the Alma-Ata [Baptist] congregations were replenished primarily by youth, in 1962–1963 people aged 30 and older constituted 82–83% of the newly baptized. What lies at the basis of this change? How fundamental is it from the point of view of objective processes developing in religious sectarianism? One thinks that the large scale of this change requires a very cautious evaluation. Under the given circumstances, a role might be played by various factors which have escaped the attention of the researchers, in particular, tactical considerations of the leadership itself of the Alma-Ata congregations of the Evangelical Christians-Baptists.

In actual fact, the cause of this change is nothing like as mysterious as Klibanov pretends. In 1960, the national Baptist leadership, doubtless under pressure from the state, issued its "Letter of Instructions," which prohibited baptisms for people under the age of 30. As has been noted, this letter, which became a cause célèbre, resulted in a serious, enduring nationwide schism among the Russian Baptists. Klibanov has been perhaps the leading scholar to chronicle the rise and development of the schismatic movement; indeed, in this same work he discusses the "Letter of Instructions" (*Religioznoe sektantstvo,* p. 105). Why he felt constrained to treat the matter so delicately, failing even to mention this obvious cause for the shift in the data, remains unexplained.

In some cases, unfortunate lapses from scholarly norms do occur. In one jointly authored work published in 1960, which is otherwise a fairly sophisticated, solid sociological study, a statement by an English tourist about his observations in 1954 was cited in support of the contention that the overwhelming majority of the believers are old people (Duluman, *Sovremennyi veruiushchii,* p. 33). The authors fail to explain what importance such dubious testimony has in an otherwise scholarly analysis. Similarly, Pivovarov, in a solidly researched work, states in passing that 99% of the Russian Orthodox baptisms take place before the age of one.[28] Inasmuch as actual studies of baptismal practices among the Orthodox unanimously deny this (see below, pp. 186–94), it seems obvious that in this case the author has merely stated an unfounded assumption in the course of his presentation of otherwise well-researched data.

Mere carelessness represents a further problem in contemporary Soviet sociological scholarship on religion. In some cases, one senses a willingness to accept conclusions without submitting them to thorough analysis. For example, in one study, Tul'tseva stated that only some 2% of a formerly Sabbatarian village were religious; yet 94% of the children were circumcised, a fact that might impeach this datum ("Evoliutsiia," p. 214). Mistakes in arithmetic can happen,[29] and simple misprints occasionally appear: "Thus of 614 propagandists and lecturers . . . 264 people, i.e., 4.9% [*sic;* should read 43%] had no special atheistic preparation" (Tepliakov, *Problemy,* p. 68). One author will quote a statement, ascribing it to a believer named M.; another author will use the same statement, verbatim, but ascribe it to believer P.[30] Fortunately, whatever its faults, the exceedingly cumbersome apparatus of Soviet academic publishing, where editors and subordinate editors abound, is fairly successful in ensuring that this sort of error will slip through only occasionally.

Sometimes, however, this apparatus itself causes errors to be introduced. One of Solov'ev's tables, dealing with the age at which former believers broke with religion, indicates that 9 such former believers were in the age group 18 to 20 at the time of the research; 66.6% of these 9 believers were 13 years old or younger when they broke with religion; 33.3% were aged 14 to 17; and 0.1% of these 9 people were aged 18 and over ("*O vliianii,*" p. 193). Quite obviously, some copy editor was assigned to check the figures in each table; he discovered here that 66.6 plus 33.3 equals 99.9, so he simply added 0.1 to the third column to make the figures come out even. A much more serious error of this sort occurs in an article by S. V. Koltuniuk.[31] He reprints a table (without attribution) that was originally presented by E. Duluman and his associates (*Sovremennyi veruiushchii,* p. 164); but serious errors have been introduced into the table (see table 3.2; Koltuniuk's changes are italicized in parentheses below the original datum as presented by Duluman et al.). From Koltuniuk's narrative it would appear that he had access to the original figures and that in the course of writing and editing the manuscript, the changes were introduced. Koltuniuk used the incorrect figures at times in the narrative; but the peculiar pattern whereby internal consistency was maintained in the table so that each line or category would add up to the correct total would suggest that again a copy editor, attempting to compensate for errors, had made matters worse.

Much of the time, however, the errors remain inexplicable. "By age, believers present the following picture: of 538 people, 66, or 12.26%, fall among youth up to 30 years of age; 180 people, or 33.46%, are people of middle age, from 31 to 50 years old; and 230 people, or 42.75%, are elderly, over 50 years of age."[32] But this leaves 62 people, or 11.52%, unaccounted for. Tepliakov on occasion commits similar errors (*Problemy,* p. 132): "In the selection of representative research, of 59,288 surveyed

TABLE 3.2

An Example of Numerical Discrepancies in Data

Relationship to atheistic propaganda	Number	Degree of religiousness			Denomination			Do you conduct propaganda of religion?		
		Convinced believer	Habitual believer	Wavering believer	Ortho-dox	Bap-tist	Other	Yes	No	Not es-tablished
Positive and acquainted with the arguments of atheists	116	20	28	68	99	7	10	6	102	8
Indifferent but acquainted with the arguments of atheists	155	61	27	67	119 (129)	21	15 (5)	15	130	10
Negative but acquainted with the arguments of atheists	57	47	4	6	31	20	6	14	39	4
Negative and not acquainted with the arguments of atheists	148	111	7	30	98	34	16	29	101	18
Indifferent and not acquainted with the arguments of atheists	153	70	20	63	117	21	15	17	125	11
Not established	46 (66)	19	5 (25)	22	31 (51)	4	11	3	34	9 (29)
Totals	675 (695)	328	91 (111)	256	495 (525)	107	73 (63)	84	531	60 (80)

citizens, 49,978 (77.6% [*sic*; actually 84.3%]), both through their own testimony and through objective data, were nonreligious as of 1968. Of the total number of nonreligious, 35,575 (77.3% [71.2%]) answered negatively to the question of whether they ever were believers, while 10,403 (22.6% [20.8%]) stated that they had been believers but had broken with religion during the early years of Soviet rule." Klibanov is also careless on occasion: "In actual fact, the age group from 20 to 40 constitutes 19.6% among the Baptists and 16.2% in Orthodoxy; believers from 40 to 60 among the Baptists 9.6%, and in Orthodoxy 15.1%; people older than 50 [*sic*; should read 60] years among the Baptists 70.8% and among the Orthodox 65.8%." Unfortunately, his figures for Orthodoxy total only 97.1%.[33]

Perhaps the worst problem is the outright misuse of data. Furov, for example, appeals to the sociological datum that only 2 to 3% of the young people in Leningrad are believers, in his justification of the exceedingly small number of churches that are allowed to operate in the city as compared with the pre-Revolutionary situation.[34] Nowhere, however, does he mention that because of the many disadvantages and possible sanctions against them (including expulsion from higher education), young people have by far the lowest incidence of overt religiousness, vastly below that of the general population. Such an extreme selection of data has little, if any, real bearing on the need for churches for the religious sector of the population.

In summary, in its present development, Soviet sociology of religion has a large number of problems and weaknesses. Some of these problems would seem to be inherent in the approach and will probably never be completely resolved. Many of the problems, however, can be solved rather easily if enough efforts are devoted to the research and if the degree of prejudgment continues to diminish.

It does not seem certain, however, that radical increases in the efforts devoted to this form of study of religion will take place in the near future. Religious studies have traditionally been low-priority items in the USSR. Because the society is avowedly secular and materialistic, the other disciplines and professions receive far more emphasis. This is one reason that professional atheism in the USSR has often included practitioners who are, by and large, second- or third-rank scholars; the more able often gravitate to other professions. The other reason is perhaps due to the essentially negative character of the subject. Atheism, logically and philosophically, has nothing positive to contribute; its portfolio consists solely of refuting theism. The first-rate minds who stay with the study of atheism rather than moving on to other, more positively interesting subjects are relatively few, and among the ranks of professional atheists, some enthusiasts may be found who in many important respects are much closer to the believer than to the true secularist, who cares not one whit about religion.

The result is a degree of neglect of the subject outside of those rather small circles for whom religion and atheism are prime concerns. For example, in the first five volumes of the annual scholarly publication *Problems of Philosophy and Sociology,* begun in 1969, there is nothing on the sociology of religion, even though the publication's statement of purpose includes the assertion that "a significant place in the collection is devoted to works on Marxist sociology, social psychology, and the theory of scientific communism."[35] Some of the surveys of the field of sociology in the USSR completely ignore sociological study of religion.[36] Of 1,646 papers entered in a national Lenin Centennial competition, only 25 were in the field of atheism, according to Sheptulin ("Zadachi," p. 15). Soviet sociologists of religion, then, must contend with a degree of neglect among their colleagues in other areas of sociology; and it is a continuing problem to attract the increased resources that are needed in order to improve the fledgling discipline and to overcome its weaknesses.

Thus, it does not seem probable that the resolution of problems such as those that have been described will occur immediately. Therefore, the achievements of the sociology of religion in the USSR will continue to experience some limitations. It should not be inferred, however, that these problems and weaknesses are necessarily ruinous. Some few of the weaknesses that have been described above may, perhaps, apply to all of the studies; utilization of the data must then be tempered to some extent on this account. Most of the weaknesses occur only occasionally, however; and once these potential problems have been taken into account, the data can be used with some modest degree of assurance. Almost never do all of these problems impinge together on a single study; naturally, when this happens, or when there is evidence of an unusually heavy concentration of their influence, prudence would dictate that that particular study be excluded, lest the overall findings be unduly distorted.

For all its weaknesses, however, and despite a number of unresolved problems, the contemporary sociology of religion has generated information on a considerable number of parameters. Provided it is approached with due caution and with whatever insights may be available from experience with other approaches to the subject (and, perhaps, with a modicum of good taste), this research provides a highly instructive avenue to an increased understanding of religion in the USSR.

4

THE
NUMBER OF BELIEVERS

The most fundamental information that is needed by Soviet sociologists who are seeking to analyze religion is how many religious people there are in the country. This datum is, of course, a logical prerequisite to most of the problems that the sociologist may subsequently seek to elucidate. Indeed, at first glance this might seem to be the simplest problem that will face the sociologist, a merely dichotomous question that should be relatively easy to answer. Unfortunately, the matter is not nearly so simple to resolve.

The first dilemma is the question of definition. Soviet researchers are by no means agreed on how to define a religious person. There are two basic approaches that can be used.

The first is ideational, suggesting philosophical or theological criteria that must ultimately deal with the question of the belief system. "On the basis of the analysis of objective and subjective factors of the preservation of religion, the authors of the monograph make an attempt to define the criteria regarding the religiousness of a person. The most substantial indices, according to their opinion, by which one may expose the specifics of a person's relation to the object of faith is the degree of its consciousness and the degree of its intensity."[1] More simply, the researcher can seek to determine whether the individual believes in God, taking this single criterion as enough for adjudging him to be religious or not. "The basic idea of any religion is the idea of god" (Kobetskii, *Sotsiologicheskoe izuchenie*, p. 36); "the central idea of every sort of religion [is] the existence of god" (Selivanov, *Partiinoe rukovodstvo*, p. 70). In this regard, the researcher can appeal to the classics of Marxism: " 'The concept of "god",' as F. Engels remarked, 'is the substance of religions.' "[2] More specifically,

57

the criterion for religiousness can be defined as "the concept of god as a higher supernatural power who created the Universe and Man and rules over them" (Alekseev, "Metodika," p. 133). Especially when the concept is so narrowly delimited in advance, this reduction of religiousness to the single factor of belief in God severely limits the scope of the concept of religion, and in many societies, such a narrow definition would scarcely embrace more than a fraction of the religous people.

The second basic approach for attaining a workable definition of religiousness is the behavioral approach. In view of the fact that religion plays no observable role whatsoever in the lives of some of those who nevertheless call themselves believers (Ugrinovich, *Vvedenie,* pp. 109–10), some Soviet researchers, such as Ugrinovich ("Religiia," p. 157), place more emphasis on behavioral characteristics:

> Whom can one ascribe to the deeply religious people, and according to what indices? Those who at the time of the survey state that they do not doubt the validity of all the basic positions of the Christian faith? Or those who observe all the Christian festivals and rites, regularly attend church, and actively take part in the activities of religious organizations? It is apparent that here the word "or" is not appropriate. It is essential to analyze both the condition of the religious consciousness of the believers and also the manifestations of their religious conduct, and furthermore, not only to analyze but to establish the connection between them.

Iablokov subdivides this behavioral approach into matters of belief, ethics, church activity, liturgical participation, and proselyting *(Metodologicheskie problemy,* pp. 111–12). Obviously, this approach, particularly when it includes ideational factors, furnishes a much broader, more reliable grasp on whether the individual is religious or not. The disadvantage is that insistence upon reliable behavioral data vastly increases the complexity of the identification task for the researcher, compared with the more simple criterion of asking a person whether he believes in God.

In practice, the problem of identifying whether or not the respondent is a believer is often simplified to a point that introduces some question concerning the validity of the identification. Typically a questionnaire will include the direct question "Do you believe in God?"; it may also add a few similar questions (e.g., belief in heaven) as controls on this determinative question (Gaidurova, "Zavisimost'," p. 17 n.5).

> The preliminary study of the ordinary consciousness of the collective farmers showed that from the point of view of attitude

toward religion, the collective farmers may be divided into three basic groups: believers, waverers, and unbelievers. As the criterion for assigning an individual to one of these groups or another, we took the attitude of the collective farmers to the fundamental concept which concentrates the understanding of the religious world in itself—the understanding concerning god. The question was given to those surveyed: "Do you believe in god?" Those who answered "Yes, I believe" we included in the category of believers; those who answered "No, I do not believe," in the category of unbelievers; and those who answered "I do not know," in the category of waverers. Furthermore, we asked the collective farmers to explain precisely what convinces them of the existence or nonexistence of god. [Kolbanovskii, *Kollektiv,* pp. 227–28]

Not all researchers exercise even this minimal care in amplifying the answers. Alekseev confidently asserts, "All possible nuances and variants of answers come down to three basics: Yes, I believe; No, I do not believe; I find it difficult to answer that question" ("Metodika," p. 134). He than assigns the respondents to the category of believer, unbeliever, or waverer, respectively, and goes on to the analysis of further parameters on the assumption that the problem of classification has been solved. In cases such as this, it would seem prudent to retain some reservations concerning the accuracy of the classification of the respondents, and use of the results of the survey should be tempered accordingly.

The problem is further complicated by observable differences within each category. Among believers, for example, at least two subcategories can be distinguished by separating out the "convinced" believer from the remaining believers (Iablokov, *Metodologicheskie problemy,* p. 120). The differences within the category can be distinguished still further:

In our literature it has been shown that in the USSR, believers may be divided into three basic groups according to the degree of religiousness: those whose consciousness is in a significant degree under the influence of religion; those among whom religion does not occupy a large place in life, although it is part of the world view; and those who in essence do not believe in God but observe religious rites only through tradition and inertia.

The first group is comparatively small, while the overwhelming majority of believers in the USSR belong to the second and third groups.[3]

More simply, Tepliakov ("Sostoianie," p. 31) refers to the degree of belief, ranging from deep belief, through moderate, to slight. And Duluman reports that, for example, several researchers divide believers into four types: (1) deeply convinced believers, fanatics (a small group); (2) believers by conviction, but not fanatics (a small group); (3) believers through tradition, but not convinced (more numerous); and (4) wavering (the most numerous group). . . .

Other authors think that one can establish the presence of the following groups of believers: believers in whose lives religion occupies a very large place; believers among whom religion undoubtedly enjoys some recognition, but in fact is put back in the consciousness to a secondary rank and does not play a substantial role in life; believers who only formally and with certain doubts count themselves such; and finally, those who hypocritically consider themselves to be believers. [*Sovremennyi veruiushchii*, pp. 50–51]

Alternatively, Iablokov (*Metodologicheskie problemy*, p. 111) suggests four categories, corresponding to the combinations of faith that is strong versus that which is weak and that which is conscious versus that which is blind. Other quadripartite schemes are possible:

The sociologist V. G. Pivovarov made a monographic study of the Orthodox parish in the Ardatovsk district, Gorky region. The researcher divided the parish into four groups of believers: (1) clergy, (2) consistent parishioners, (3) inconsistent parishioners, and (4) peripheral parishioners. The peripheral parishioners occupy a small place in the makeup of the parish. The researcher determined their number at 2–5%. Then the consistent parishioners constitute 55–60% of all the believers, and the inconsistent, 30–35%. Pivovarov characterizes these two groups in the following manner: " (1) Consistent parishioners believe deeply. They have attended church for a long time, constitute the fundamental part of the religious corps of activitists and those close to the clergy, and externally take part in all the activities that complement the liturgy. The religious impressions of this group are comparatively systematized. They have a definite level of knowledge of religious dogma, cultus, and structure of the church. (2) The inconsistent parishioners are believers who are not convinced of the possibility that god exists or who relate indifferently to religion and the church. They attend church services on the major holidays or in case of illness or memorial services for relatives. Their religious impressions are amorphous." [Klibanov, *Religioznoe sektantstvo*, pp. 121–22]

Obviously, nonbelievers can similarly be differentiated according to the degree of nonbelief. A spectrum can be found, ranging from those who are against religion in every respect, to those who are inconsistently against it, to those who most of the time are indifferent, to the completely indifferent.[4]

The hazy, uncertain territory between religious belief and unbelief causes great complications. "Unfortunately, in our literature one makes only occasional references to the presence among the workers in our country of those who relate indifferently to religion, and these people are usually classified either as waverers, or as those who have no point of view on this account. It is clear that explanations of this sort are completely inadequate and even simply invalid" (Cherniak, *Formirovanie*, p. 129). The concept of "waverers" between belief and unbelief looms large in Soviet sociological research on religion, and indeed, nearly every Soviet scholar relies on the concept to one degree or another.

One theoretician, Sukhov, has devised an interesting analogy to contemporary Soviet theories of international relations, in which he compares the waverer to Third World countries that are neither capitalistic nor socialistic:

> When religious morality, social doctrine, and other appurtenances of spiritual and social life, which formerly were connected with religion, are washed away, these links are lost. A man who continues to consider himself essentially religious gradually loses his religious impressions. In theological sociology, the concept of the "third man" has appeared. This is the man who is on the way from religion to atheism. One must not consider him a wavering [believer]. In many respects he has firmly renounced religion, but in some things he still maintains special connections with it. He accepts his belonging to a religious congregation, but in his practical life not infrequently he is only formally a believer. This peculiar world phenomenon at the present time attracts considerable interest, and it is typical to use such formulae as "unbelieving believer," or "believing unbeliever" when referring to it. [*Religiia*, p. 141]

Thus the problem of the intermediate area between the obviously convinced believer and the equally obviously convinced atheist introduces considerable ambiguity into Soviet research on religion. While some scholars reserve this area for people whom most would consider to be nonreligious, the majority seem to ascribe to it people who quite obviously remain religious in the sense that religious considerations continue to exercise a role, even if a relatively modest one, in their lives.

Indeed, even the classification of some respondents as waverers, rather than believers, can be open to some doubt: "Not infrequently, waverers sincerely consider themselves to be religious people, they do not hide this. In a number of cases they state their adherence to religious faith more guardedly; however, their religious consciousness and profession are not distinguished by fullness and consistency, even to the point that some waverers express deep doubts about the truth even of some of the most convincing proofs of their religiousness, aside from the assertion: 'I believe, like everybody'" (Selivanov, *Partiinoe rukovodstvo*, p. 96). Given the tension surrounding many of these interviews, the atheistic researcher may be placing rather more reliance than he should on his own judgment when he makes firm distinctions concerning ambiguous cases such as these. For example, Kobetskii discovered that 39.5% of the waverers prayed at home, but only 7.7% did so daily (*Sotsiologicheskoe izuchenie*, pp. 41–42). Such a finding might well impeach his classification of these people as waverers, rather than believers.

The cognate classification "unbelievers" (but not atheists), also raises some perplexities.

> These people completely, definitely relate themselves to the number of unbelievers. In complementary questions, in which they are required to specify their relationship to religion, they almost uniformly classify themselves in the following manner: "Although I do not consider myself a believer, nevertheless I see definite sense in religion," "I am indifferent to this question," "I have difficulty answering," etc.
>   . . . People entered in this group most often of all at the advice or insistence of believers may episodically fulfill religious rites (baptism, wedding, funeral, etc.), sometimes may even attend church. Their world view is inconsistent; often precisely from representatives of this category one may meet judgments of the type, "We were baptized and we baptize, there will be no harm in that," "We are Russians—that means Orthodox, although we do not believe in god." [Kobetskii, *Sotsiologicheskoe izuchenie,* pp. 59–60]

Hence, one cannot be entirely certain that such a classification pattern may not cause some people to be excluded from the ranks of believers who more properly might be considered religious to some degree or other.

Even when there are no such overt suggestions of religiousness, the classification of unbeliever entails other dilemmas. One antireligious author, Kobetskii, suggests yet another classification: "Adherents of a future faith—they have been disenchanted with the forms of religion known to them, but have not yet proceeded to full unbelief, they consider that there should be some sort of belief; their thesis: the known religions are the belief of the past, atheism is the belief of the present (for themselves they consider it unacceptable), the belief of the future has not yet been discovered, but it, allegedly, will be discovered" (*Sotsiologicheskoe izuchenie*, p. 48). Thus, Soviet researchers have discovered agnosticism, and it has always been a problem whether an agnostic should be classified as religious or unreligious.

There is also a real danger in the unbeliever classification, for the researcher cannot be certain that those who are assigned to this classification, over the long term, will remain outside the camp of the believers. "In their judgment on problems of the world view they often do not display implacability toward the religious ideology, and sometimes their views agree with religious norms. Some have icons in the family, they observe religious holidays at home, and they fulfill religious rites of one sort or another. In this group the reappearance of religion is quite possible" (Selivanov, *Partiinoe rukovodstvo*, p. 102).

In short, the uncertain territory between belief and unbelief raises many problems, and time may demonstrate that the contemporary figures for the number of believers might well need revision upward to some degree.

Nevertheless, the tripartite divisional scheme (believer—waverer—nonbeliever) continues to be standard for most Soviet researchers, according to Ugrinovich (*Vvedenie*, pp. 116–18). Those who work within this tripartite approach, however, often find it somewhat too crude an instrument and tend to add subdivisions. Thus, Alekseev suggests the schematic arrangement shown in the accompanying chart ("Metodika," p. 135). Other scholars, attempting to break away from the comparatively simple tripartite division, suggest more elaborate schemes. Thus Tepliakov's spectrum has five categories, corresponding to atheists, convinced nonbelievers, nonreligious, wavering, and convinced believers (*Problemy*, pp. 118–21); or by shifting the spectrum somewhat toward the religious, atheists, nonreligious,

I		II	III	
Believers		Waverers	Nonbelievers	
Active	Passive		Passive	Active
Consistent				
Inconsistent				

waverers between religion and atheism, convinced believers, and fanatics ("Pobeda," pp. 132–34).

Finally, fairly elaborate categorical schemes can be suggested. Iablokov (*Metodologicheskie problemy*, p. 111) suggests seven categories, dividing each of the three standard categories into two subdivisions and positing a seventh category—the indifferent—between second-degree waverers and first-degree atheists. He carries matters even further by suggesting three distinct divisions within the single category of believers.

> 1. Believers whose definitive approach to life is the religious orientation. Believing in god, at the same time they are convinced in other dogmas that are essential for religion. Their moral consciousness is under the influence of religion. Believers of this type play an active role in the religious group, regularly take part in liturgical activities and try to disseminate religious views.
>
> 2. Believers for whom the religious orientation is important but not determinative. Believing in god, they simply are not convinced of certain other dogmas that are essential for religion. Their moral consciousness experiences the influence of religion only partially. Believers of this type do not play an active role in religious groups, and they reduce liturgical activity to a secondary place in their system of conduct. They do not take an active part in the dissemination of religious views.
>
> 3. Believers for whom the religious orientation is subordinate. Maintaining a belief in god, they have lost certain other essential elements of religious belief. Their moral consciousness, in practice, is free from the influence of religion. They take part in liturgical activities irregularly and do not consciously participate in the dissemination of religious views. [*Metodologicheskie problemy*, pp. 111–12]

Other scholars assign waverers to the third division of the believers category. "Thus, [there are] three types of believers: the convinced, the habitual, and the wavering (we exclude from the classification 'hypocrites,' for whom there is hardly a basis for considering them believers)" (Duluman, *Sovremennyi veruiushchii*, p. 30).

Thus, the problem of classification has by no means been resolved to the satisfaction or agreement of all Soviet researchers. A large number of distributive schemata are utilized (Cherniak, *Formirovanie*, pp. 331–32). The result is that standardization is nonexistent, the potential for comparing data derived by different research projects is severely reduced, and in many cases, comparison becomes quite impossible.

The process of actually determining the number of religious believers in the USSR is complicated; at no time have figures been derived or even suggested which are broadly acceptable. Duluman's group reports that in 1930 the incidence of religiousness varied from 28.1% to 71.8% (*Sovremennyi veruiushchii*, p. 30). A Moscow study in 1931 discovered that only 11.2% of the workers were religious, although 57.7% still adhered to church weddings, and 70.4% had their children baptized.[5] During the middle thirties a little less than half the population was thought to be religious,[6] while Tepliakov (*Problemy*, p. 123) inferred from the census of 1937 that somewhat more than half were still religious. Not even the relative waxing and waning of religiousness has been identified with any great degree of confidence. Ugrinovich (*Vvedenie*, p. 134) has suggested that, at least in one region, religiousness declined during the 1930s, grew somewhat in the forties, and was relatively stabilized in the fifties. It is difficult to consider these findings typical, however, in view of the general resurgence of religion in the late fifties (Tepliakov, *Problemy*, p. 156; cf. Struve, *Christians*, pp. 291–92).

With regard to the contemporary period, widely varying results have been presented.

In view of the prediction of Marxist-Leninist theory, the lower the incidence of religiousness, the better the ideological requirements will be met; and indeed, Soviet researchers very often present exceedingly low figures for the incidence of religiousness. These figures run well under 10% at times. However, on inspection it becomes evident that most of the time a selection process has been used that will yield the low figures.

Thus, for example, if specific age groups are selected, low figures very often result. Sytenko discovered that "among people aged 30–45, 4.8% are believers and 5.8% are waverers; among youth under 30, 2.8% are believers and 3.2% are waverers" ("O nravstvennom oblike," p. 126 n.1).

Secondly, exceedingly low figures can result if selected occupational groups are surveyed. Thus, one research project, which used a seven-part scheme of classification, reported the figures shown in table 4.1. When the white-collar workers were subdivided even further into scientists and technologists, even lower figures resulted (Ugrinovich, *Vvedenie*, p. 182). Typically, studies that single out white-collar workers will show that 1% or less of them are believers (Tepliakov, "Sotsial'nye issledovaniia," p. 109), with even lower figures for the technical intelligentsia (Tepliakov, *Problemy*, p. 129). Even in rural surveys if skilled workers are selected, an incidence of believers lower than 10% can be derived.[7]

An alternative procedure that yields low figures is geographic selectivity. Figures showing the incidence of religiousness to be below 10% are not unusual in cities. "Of 15,942 urban inhabitants studied, only 7.9%

TABLE 4.1

POSITIONS ON RELIGION ACCORDING TO SOCIAL GROUP

Social Group	Position on Religion or Atheism						
	B1	B2	K1	K2	I	A1	A2
Workers	1%	5%	2%	7%	36%	37%	12%
White-collar workers, exclusive of management	1	3	2	4	26	30	34
Management	....	1	1	2	21	41	34
Students	....	....	....	....	15	50	35
Retired people	6	33	6	12	19	14	10
Housewives	6	37	6	15	16	16	4

SOURCE: Ugrinovich, *Vvedenie*, p. 181.
NOTE: B1=believers who disseminate religion; B2=believers; K1 and K2=waverers, more or less religious; I=indifferent; A1=atheists; A2=atheists who disseminate atheism.

belonged to the convinced believers, including fanatics; 7.2% expressed doubt in the existence of supernatural powers . . ." (Tepliakov, "Pobeda," p. 134). Refining the selection even further, certain areas within a city or region will yield very low figures.[8]

Other parameters can also result in low figures. For example, Cherniak's studies of a heavy-machinery factory and a construction combine yielded figures of 4.80% and 7.49%. It should be noted that according to the same survey, in a light-industry enterprise that employed a large number of women, the percentage of religiousness was 12.83 (Cherniak, *Formirovanie*, pp. 120–21). Alternatively, by varying the criteria for religiousness, different answers can be obtained. In Korolev's survey, for example, when people were asked whether religion was harmful or helpful, only 3.2% felt that it was helpful ("Rol'," p. 154). In a study of Jews in Birobidzhan, the researchers found that only 8 of 300 (2.67%) were religious.[9]

A more common means of deriving low figures on the incidence of religiousness is to utilize subcategories. To some degree, distinguishing between believers and waverers, when other researchers might include both in the general category of religious, will accomplish this function. When finer distinctions are drawn, even lower figures can be derived. Thus, for example, Ugrinovich found the incidence of "convinced believers who disseminate religious views" to be 1.3%; convinced believers, 7.6%; "waverers of the first order," 2.3%; "waverers of the second order," 6.8%; and the indifferent, 30.0% (*Vvedenie*, p. 179).

Even relatively straightforward studies of the general population, which do not resort to various means of limiting the purview to parameters where the incidence of religiousness will be low, derive some figures below 10%. In a large-scale study in the Voronezh region, for example, Tepliakov discovered that only 9.8% of the population were convinced believers, although an additional 12.6% were waverers (*Problemy*, pp. 118–21).

Such low figures are atypical, however. Levels of religiousness above 10% are found more often. In studies conducted in 1965 in one region and repeated in 1970, a fairly constant 12–13% level of religiousness was found.[10] In another large-scale study, "of 46,820 adult citizens of the Voronezh region surveyed from 73 rural population points and six cities, 35,052 (74.8%) were nonreligious, 6,110 (13.1%) were waverers, and 5,658 (12.1%) were believers" (Tepliakov, "Sotsial'nye issledovaniia," p. 108).[11] Another study in the same region indicated that 12.6% of the population were convinced believers, and 12.5% were waverers (Tepliakov, "Pobeda," p. 137). Similarly, a study of 21,557 citizens indicated that 15% were convinced believers, and 17.1% were waverers (ibid., p. 134).

Levels of religiousness in the range of 15% to 25% are reported quite frequently by Soviet sociologists of religion. "Selective research on religiousness in the Ukraine, Belorussia, Kazakhstan, and in Voronezh, Orlov, and a series of other regions of the RSFSR, testifies that among urban inhabitants, in several cases the number of believers reaches 15%, and in several rural districts, 30%."[12] In a survey of 59,288 citizens in 1968, Tepliakov discovered that 49,978 were nonreligious; presumably the remainder, or 15.7%, were religious (*Problemy*, p. 132). In a study of 1,577 unskilled collective farmers, he found that 15.5% of them were believers and 28.6% were waverers ("Pobeda," p. 137). Another village had 89 believers in 109 families, constituting 17.4% of the total number of family members.[13] "According to the data of V. M. Martynov, religiousness in the village of Gor'kaia Balka and in a series of neighboring villages (Stavropol region) wavers between the limits of 18–25%."[14] In the Voronezh region, according to Pivovarov's study, 13% of the nonagricultural workers were religious, while 20% of manual laborers employed in agriculture were religious.[15] Researchers in the Penza region discovered that 19.5% of the population were believers and 8.9% were waverers.[16] Sytenko's earlier study in the same region disclosed that 600 of 2,944 workers, or 20.4%, were religious or borderline believers ("O nravstvennom oblike," p. 126). Among 4,710 city dwellers, there were 989 believers (21%).[17] According to Tepliakov, "the data of concrete social research testify to the fact that in the Voronezh region, people who are free from religious influences constitute three-fourths of the population," which would imply that 25% are religious to some degree ("Pobeda," p. 138).

Even higher levels of religiousness have been reported (Nikitin,

"Dialektika," p. 55 n.42; cf. Selivanov, *Partiinoe rukovodstvo*, p. 40). In the Penza region, "in all, 30,674 people were surveyed, of whom 28.4% displayed one or another degree of religiousness, and 15.5% in the city of Penza."[18] The results shown in table 4.2 were obtained in three collective farms, none of which, incidentally, had a church on its territory. In a fairly large-scale study in 1968, it was discovered that 69.7% of the population of one region were nonreligious; hence, presumably 30.3% were religious (Tepliakov, *Problemy*, p. 123 n.4). In Belorussia, 16% of the urban inhabitants and 39.6% of the rural population considered themselves to be believers; whereas in a Russian region, from 23.5% to 33.2% of the rural inhabitants considered themselves to be believers (Duluman, *Sovremennyi veruiushchii*, p. 32). According to Safronov's survey of one-fourth of the total population of a Belorussian village, 58 of 177 people (or 33%) considered themselves to be believers ("Chto," p. 69). An even higher level of religiousness was discovered on three collective farms, as shown in table 4.3. Kolbanovskii's study of 3,661 rural inhabitants showed that 56.5% of the women and 15.7% of the men, or an aggregate of 41.5%, considered themselves to be believers; and an additional 21.2% were classified as waverers (*Kollektiv*, p. 232). Particularly when the population

TABLE 4.2
RESULTS OF A SURVEY OF THREE COLLECTIVE FARMS

Name of Farm	Believers		Waverers		Unbelievers	
	Men	Women	Men	Women	Men	Women
K. Marx	17.0%	59.5%	22.3%	23.5%	60.7%	17.0%
I. S. Turgenev	14.5	50.7	7.8	26.9	77.7	22.4
Way to Communism	10.9	47.0	8.3	13.4	80.8	39.6

SOURCE: Kolbanovski, *Kollektiv*, p. 237.

TABLE 4.3
RESULTS OF A SURVEY OF THREE COLLECTIVE FARMS

Collective Farm	Believers	Waverers	Unbelievers
A	43.5%	23.1%	33.4%
B	38.1	20.3	41.6
C	33.2	11.5	55.3

SOURCE: Alekseev, "Metodika," p. 149.
NOTE: Incidentally, on p. 146 he indicates that in collective farm A, 84% of the schoolchildren are religious believers; this may be a typographical error, for at farms B and C, the figures are 56% and 46%, respectively, and this high figure for farm A evokes no special comment.

group studied becomes more selective, a wider range of results may be expected. Thus, for example, in a Sabbatarian village, 65.5% (400 of 611 inhabitants) were still Sabbatarian, according to Tul'tseva ("Evoliutsiia," p. 219). As will become evident in the following chapters, when specific population groups are studied, even higher figures may be expected (e.g., Tepliakov, "Pobeda," p. 137), with the incidence of religious believers ranging above 95% for some groups (ibid., p. 132 n.2).

As has been noted, the data are disparate. When the population at large is referred to, levels of religiousness below 10% and above 35% are found relatively infrequently in contemporary Soviet sociological studies (Kalashnikov, "Religiia," pp. 22–23; Baltanov, *Sotsiologicheskie problemy*, p. 180; Kobetskii, *Sotsiologicheskoe izuchenie*, p. 24). However, figures of up to one-third of the population being religious are by no means uncommon (cf. Kozhevnikov, "Ateisticheskoe vospitanie," p. 2). Duluman's research extrapolates a figure of 15 to 20% for the entire adult population (*Sovremennyi veruiushchii*, p. 31), but it would not appear that there is an adequate data base for this generalization. Furthermore, inasmuch as Soviet scholars are not always precise as to whether or not the category of waverer is included in their figures, it becomes difficult to judge the persuasiveness of a given estimate (Klibanov, "Veruiushchii," p. 73). Particularly when a researcher distinguishes between those who are indifferent to religion and those who are waverers between religious belief and unbelief (cf. Tepliakov, *Problemy*, p. 15), without disclosing exactly how such a fine distinction can be made in every case, the usefulness of his results is necessarily diminished.

Even were there enough reliability and comparability present to allow generalizations to be made, deriving an estimate of the incidence of religiousness for the entire USSR would still be a formidable task. Minority nationalities complicate the religious spectrum immensely. Half of the population of the USSR is of non-Russian stock, and in many of the national republics, patterns and traditions of religion are vastly different from those that prevail in the Russian areas. A few examples may suggest the degree of complexity.

In some areas of the Russian republic the prevailing religion is a pattern of tribal practices and beliefs that have been modified by some decades of Orthodox missionary endeavor prior to the Revolution. Naturally, the patterns of religious belief in such areas will not necessarily replicate those in traditionally Russian areas. In the Mari Republic, for example, 11,000 inhabitants, including a 1% sample of the entire population, were surveyed by Gusev: "The research conducted in the republic demonstrated that 62.4% of the adult population are free from the influence of religion, 19.8% consider themselves to be believers, and 17.8% are waverers between belief and unbelief" ("Konkretnost'," p. 24). However, Solov'ev's survey of 832 people found that only 288, or 35%, had never been under the influence of religion ("O vliianii," p. 189). In western regions of the country, which were acquired by the USSR as a legacy of World War II and hence have been subject to antireligious efforts for a quarter-century less than other areas, the incident of religion in the population is very high. In the western Ukraine, religious people constitute 50 to 60% of the population (Koltuniuk, "K probleme," p. 145). Similar patterns obtain in the Baltic states, although here the national religion (Roman Catholicism in Lithuania; primarily Lutheranism in Latvia and Estonia) prevails.[19] With regard to Muslim areas, although Ashirov's study found that only 25.7% of the inhabitants considered themselves to be religious believers,[20] this study was probably atypical, for by all accounts religion retains a much stronger influence among the Muslims than is the norm elsewhere in the USSR.[21] In rural Dagestan, Filimonov found that 46% of the population were believers ("Sotsiologicheskie issledovaniia," p. 74).

In summary, whatever the figure that might be derived for an average incidence of religiousness in the Russian parts of the USSR, whether it would support a fairly conservative estimate in the range of 15 to 20% or whether it would confirm other findings ranging upwards to 33% or more of the population, if this figure were to be applied to the entire population of the USSR, it would almost certainly have to be revised upward to some considerable degree because of the relatively high incidence among the national minorities.

An even less satisfactory picture emerges from Soviet sociological research with regard to specific denominations. Much of the work that has been done, of course, concerns Orthodoxy, which remains the dominant religion in the USSR. Kolbanovskii, an otherwise careful scholar, for example, estimates that 99% of the religious population in one fairly broad, representative region profess Orthodoxy (*Kollektiv*, p. 232). But it is difficult to accept this figure, for this would indicate a comparative advantage for Orthodoxy greater than it has ever before enjoyed during recent times, whether pre-Revolutionary or during the Soviet period.

The Baptists have received by far the most attention among Soviet sociological studies devoted to denominations other than Orthodoxy. This is only in part explainable by the fact that the Union of Evangelical Christians-Baptists (or, more simply, Baptists) is the only non-Orthodox Christian denomination that is legally permitted to operate on a nationwide scale. In larger measure, the research attention that the Baptists have received is related to the antireligious campaign, which has expended an extraordinary amount of energy on the Baptists, far more than their numerical size would appear to warrant.

Particularly in the south of Russia, the Baptists are a strong force. Some 75% of the non-Orthodox religious people in the Ukraine are Baptists (Klibanov, *Religioznoe sektantstvo*, p. 77). One-third of the Baptists in the Ukraine are to be found in the western regions acquired during World War II (ibid., p. 79). Outside the Ukraine, Baptists of Ukrainian nationality are prominent in the local churches. In the Voronezh church, for example, 43% of the members are of Ukrainian nationality, while the incidence of Ukrainians in the general population of Voronezh approximates 7.4% (ibid., p. 77). In other areas the Baptists, while they may outnumber rival non-Orthodox groups, are not so predominant. In Belorussia, for example, there are one-eighth as many Baptists as in the Ukraine, even though the Belorussian population is one-fifth as large (ibid., p. 82).

There is no agreement concerning what percentage of the total Soviet population is Baptist. In one region, Baptists were discovered to account for 0.5 % of the population, and in another, 0.25 (Duluman, *Sovremennyi veruiushchii*, p. 32).[22] The problem is complicated, however, by the widespread phenomenon of Baptist believers who find that it is expedient to refrain from publicly joining the official church. Thus, official figures, however they are derived, are not likely to represent an accurate picture of the actual size of the Baptist minority in Soviet society. Klibanov estimates that these nonmembers have ranged from 5.15% to 4.3% of the total number of members (*Religioznoe sektantstvo*, p. 84). His figures are probably two orders of magnitude too low.[23]

Studies of the Baptists over the past fifteen years show a considerable decline in their number. For example, in the Voronezh region, according to Tepliakov,

> 1957 was the year of the maximum number of members of the Evangelical Christians-Baptists (ECB). In 7 registered congregations there were 1,471 people, and in 44 congregations and 79 unregistered groups, 2,138.
>
> In the period under observation it was noted that receiving new members came to a halt. A significant part of the ECB departed from religion under the influence of atheistic propaganda. By 1970 there were 8 registered congregations, 20 nonregistered congregations, and 103 nonregistered small groups. The aggregate number of ECB in 1970 consisted of 2,378 people, instead of 3,609 in 1957. The increase in the number of groups of the ECB is

explained by the fact that some congregations, when they had lost part of their members, broke up into groups of 3 to 10 people.[24] [*Problemy,* p. 156]

Data such as these have an intrinsic credibility, in that they reflect the effects of the intensive efforts of the antireligious campaign against the Baptists. The magnitude of the decline, however, may be atypical. Klibanov notes that in one area, where there were 2,500 Baptists in 7 registered and 69 unregistered congregations in 1957, "from 1958 to 1964 the growth of the Baptists stopped and went backwards, although at a slow rate. By 1964, in the registered and unregistered congregations of the region, there were 2,270 Baptists, and there were only 53 congregations" (*Religioznoe sektantstvo,* p. 72). For the Ukraine as a whole, he notes a 14% decline in the number of Baptists during the most severe years of the antireligious campaign, 1963–65 (ibid., p. 26). Similar declines during the period of antireligious effort are observable elsewhere (e.g., Ugrinovich, *Vvedenie,* pp. 134–35; Tepliakov, *Problemy,* p. 116).

Rather less attention has been devoted to other religious denominations. Some research has been devoted to the Seventh Day Adventists, Pentecostals, and Jehovah's Witnesses, but apparently the efforts in these directions have not been exhaustive (Klibanov, *Religioznoe sektantstvo,* pp. 95, 98–99). Old Believers (who derive from the great schism in Orthodoxy in the seventeenth century) have received some attention. As will become apparent below, they appear to be relatively impervious to the downward trend that Soviet researchers have found in other religions.

However widely the views are disseminated that Old Believers are declining significantly faster than other religious denominations, in our view this is completely unfounded. To support this conclusion we cite several facts. According to our count, in 10 years (1956–1966) the number of Old Believer congregations in Latvia declined by 3.8%, while all other religious denominations in the Republic have diminished by 16.4%. But maybe the process of departure of believers from religion takes place more rapidly among Old Believers? The analysis conducted shows that one must give a negative answer to this question also. For example, from 1962 to 1966 among Catholics the number baptized has declined by 6.5%; among Old Believers, by 16.1%; among Orthodox, by 17.4%; and among Lutherans, by 39.2%.[25]

Klibanov has studied such indigenous Russian sects such as Molokans, Dukhobors, and Sabbatarians (*Religioznoe sektantstvo,* pp. 90, 93, 68–70), but due to the relatively small numbers of adherents, these groups are not receiving major attention. So long as they exist, however, Soviet sociology must maintain an awareness of such religious believers.[26]

The need for increased research is rather more apparent with regard to Islam and Buddhism. The former embraces more than 35 million Soviet citizens, in its cultural aspects at least (and it remains problematical whether religion is separable from culture in Islam), and while there have been sociological studies of various aspects of these populations, studies specifically devoted to religion are conspicuous by their scarcity. With regard to Buddhism, the situation is completely obscure. Great changes have taken place due to the virtual elimination of institutional Buddhism in the 1930s, and so much syncretism with indigenous folk beliefs has taken place in the forty years since then that exhaustive study would be needed before Soviet sociologists would be able to say anything at all about the contemporary situation of Buddhism in the USSR.[27]

On the whole, then, the task of determining who is and who is not religious in the USSR is far from complete. Soviet sociologists have not yet developed completely satisfactory criteria to answer this question, nor have they achieved general agreement, even among themselves, concerning what criteria should be used. The introduction of a considerable variety of classification schemes confuses the picture further. A great deal of data on this subject has been collected; but much work remains to be done before Soviet sociology will be able to differentiate clearly between the religious and the nonreligious citizen.

5

AGE AND GENDER

One of the parameters of intense interest to Soviet sociologists of religion is the relationship between religiousness and age. The primary reason for this interest stems from the atheistic presuppositions of the ideology. If religion is doomed to disappear, then—so the reasoning goes— concrete data concerning the age of believers will provide a useful predictive tool for projecting the rate and timetable of this disappearance. As will become apparent below, such a confident assumption that there is a correlation between the advanced age of believers and the demise of religion must ignore a number of factors, not the least of which has been the persistence of this pattern for more than half a century. Some researchers, taking a more limited approach, find that knowledge of the age patterns among believers is potentially useful for the structuring of antireligious propaganda.[1]

One approach that Soviet scholars have taken is to attempt to determine the percentage of religious believers in various age groups in the general population. Thus, Sytenko's survey of 2,944 workers disclosed that believers and waverers constituted 7% among youth under 30, 10.6% among those aged 30 to 45 and 31.5% among those over 45 ("O nravstvennom oblike," p. 126 n.1.) A study by Tepliakov revealed a similar upward progression from 6.5% for those aged 18 to 25 to 65.4% for those over 65, with the average incidence of religiousness for all age groups being 25.1% ("Pobeda," p. 138). The findings of his large-scale survey of nearly 60,000 citizens in the Voronezh region from 1965 to 1967 may be found in table 5.1 Results in the Penza region showed a similar degree of religiousness, with religious people accounting for 8.1% of those aged 21 to 30, 20.3% of those aged 41 to 50, 56.9% of those aged 61 to 70, and 72.2%

75

of those 71 to 80 years old (Tepliakov, *Problemy*, p. 126 n.5; "VII . . . kongress," p. 328; Selivanov, *Partiinoe rukovodstvo*, p. 89).[2] In a number of Tatar villages, however, believers accounted for 21% of the 18 to 30 year olds, 49% of those aged 31 to 45, 64% of those aged 46 to 60, and 86% of the people over 60.[3]

While such high percentages are atypical in Soviet research, the direct relationship between advancing age and an increasing percentage of religiousness in the population is a unanimous finding of Soviet religious sociology.

Soviet researchers devote a great deal of their attention to the younger generation. This, of course, is the sector of society that will determine the future, and hence the ideology would suggest that this is where the greatest antireligious efforts should be focused.

Generally speaking, the researchers find gratifying results. Thus, in Tepliakov's study of 1,933 pupils and students, there were no religious believers at all, and only 37 (1.9%) were waverers ("Pobeda," p. 135). In a Georgian village founded by Dukhobors, there were no believers under the age of 25.[4] In a study of students matriculating at institutions of higher education, Kozachishin found that only some 5%, although they denied religion, nevertheless found some positive aspect in it ("Konkretno-sotsiologicheskie issledovanii," p. 216). Cherniak discovered that a greater number of young people approve of religion than might be expected (*Formirovanie*, pp. 125–26). According to one study, 31 of 175 science students (17.7%) doubted the proposition that there is no God.[5] Other

TABLE 5.1
RESULTS OF A SURVEY IN THE VORONEZH REGION

Year of birth	Number surveyed	Convinced atheist	Convinced unbeliever	Non-religious	Wavering believer	Convinced believer
1895–99	6,682	3.7%	22.3%	16.3%	26.0%	31.7%
1900–1905	4,426	5.4	24.9	22.6	26.2	20.9
1906–10	4,262	5.8	30.3	22.5	22.2	19.2
1911–14	4,503	7.3	32.6	26.0	18.6	15.5
1915–19	3,581	11.6	38.5	27.5	13.1	9.3
1920–25	4,052	14.3	41.3	30.5	8.0	5.9
1926–30	4,677	12.7	44.0	29.5	9.5	4.3
1931–35	5,244	13.8	44.5	29.5	7.2	5.0
1936–40	9,833	13.6	42.3	33.8	8.3	2.5
1941–45	6,381	18.3	43.8	32.8	3.5	1.6
1946–50	5,638	19.1	45.5	32.2	2.6	0.6

SOURCE: Tepliakov, *Problemy*, p. 126.
NOTE: The data for 1936 to 1940 total 100.5%.

projects found that 25 to 30% of the young people studied were indifferent to questions of religion and atheism (*Gertsenovskie chteniia* 3 [1972]: 24). Ershov commented with regard to indifference toward religion: "The optimists say that this is a growing phenomenon, that life is completely changing. But look at what is shown by research on the religiousness of the population of Kareliia which was conducted by the Laboratory of Sociological Research of the Kareliia Pedagogical Institute in 1965. It seemed that among people under 30, 26% relate to religion 'indifferently.' The optimists' conclusion was not borne out. The group of 'indifferent' to be found in the schools is not diminishing in practice."[6]

This is a worrisome phenomenon for Soviet analysts, for those who are indifferent today may not remain indifferent tomorrow. With regard to Latvia, for example, Freiberg notes that "research conducted in several districts among youth who have finished school and have begun an independent life showed that only 60 to 70% of the young men and women are consistently guided by atheistic convictions in their lives; the remainder express inconsistency of world view, indifference in relation to religion and atheism. In various circumstances of life, such young people may waver and in certain cases even depart from atheistic positions."[7]

Among young people in general, many researchers find that fewer than 5% are religious. Thus, Alekseev found that only 0.5% of the children in grades 5 to 11 were religious ("Metodika," p. 149). According to a study of religiousness among working youth, from 2% to 4% were religious, with as many as 4.4% among youth working in small industrial enterprises (Galitskaia, "K voprosu," p. 394). Among students, Lebedev found that religious believers and waverers constituted 2.2% of the student body ("Studencheskaia molodezh'," p. 201), or, as a rule, not in excess of 3% (*Gertsenovskie chteniia* 3 [1972]: 24). "As the research has shown, believing youth aged 14 to 25 constitute 2.5 to 3% of the total number of all youth researched. (Note 1: it should be emphasized that 2.5 to 3% represents the average figure. In some cities and regions, because of specific historical and economic circumstances, there is a higher percentage of believing youth [in the Western regions of the Ukraine, Belorussia, Moldavia and elsewhere], while in other cities and regions [Moscow, Leningrad, Perm', and others] it is lower)" (Galitskaia, "K voprosu," p. 392). Approaching the matter obliquely, Vimsaare found that 3.5% during the academic year 1971/72 and 1.6% during the following year answered that religion was useful when they were asked, "In your opinion, is religion harmful; bears neither help nor harm or is it useful?" ("Ob ispol'zovanii," p. 225). One wonders whether the rather awkward construction of the question might have influenced the answers.

Not all studies have yielded such low figures for religiousness among youth. Tepliakov's study of 461 beginning students in higher education disclosed that 5% were religious to some degree (*Problemy*, p. 71). In the Moscow Engineering and Physics Institute, Lebedev classified 5.2% of the students as waverers ("Studencheskaia molodezh'," p. 201). Two researchers found that 5.5% of young people aged 16 to 30 were religious (Kolbanovskii, *Kollektiv*, p. 232; Alekseev, "Metodika," p. 149). "E. K. Arnaut notes that among young workers of the city of Bel'tsy, 8.8% are believers; while among young collective farmers, 14.8% of the total number of youth surveyed are believers. According to the data of Iu. S. Gurov, among young laborers in rural localities, 10.2% are religious; while in urban areas, 3.9% of the total number surveyed [are religious]" (*Gertsenovskie chteniia* 1 [1970]: 16).[8] Galitskaia's studies of rural youth have found that 10% and even 12.7% are religious ("K voprosu," p. 394). And in a survey of 932 eighth and tenth graders, 12.8% of the former and 15.8% of the latter felt that religion could be helpful (*Gertsenovskie chteniia* 3 [1972]: 21).

Finally, isolated cases of studies of young people have yielded fairly astonishing results. Thus, 20% of 141 college students did not give a negative evaluation of religion (Kozachishin, "Konkretno-sotsiologicheskie issledovanii," p. 216). In 1972, studies disclosed that 23% of those questioned among Lithuanian young people (16 to 25 years old) supported religious traditions,[9] and 24.77% of another group of students had read the Scriptures (Ulybin, "Iz opyta," p. 103). According to a Ukrainian study, conducted by Eryshev, "during a concrete sociological research program 'attitude of Soviet youth toward religion,' which was conducted in the Odessa region, 1,247 young men and women under 30 were questioned. These included workers . . . and senior students from Odessa's School No. 44. Over 70% of those polled reject faith in god and all supernatural forces, and look upon religion as a harmful phenomenon in our life" ("Instilling," p. 136). The corollary is that nearly 30% do not. Finally, Filiminov, in a study of 5,226 young people between the ages of 14 and 30 in the Northern Caucasus republics, found that 19.3% were believers and 14.5% were waverers, a total of more than one-third of those studied ("Sotsiologicheskie issledovaniia," p. 75).

Approaching the matter from an alternate position, aggregate data from research conducted throughout the country indicate that "in Orthodox churches the percentage of youth varies from 2 to 6%, and in the congregations of the Baptists the percentage of youth constitutes 6 to 15% (Galitskaia, "K voprosu," p. 393). Among dissident Baptists, young people under 30 accounted for 14% of the congregations in one region of the Ukraine and for 5% and 7% in two others (Eryshev, "Instilling," p. 136).

People in their middle years account for a higher percentage of religious believers. Among the Baptists, people aged 40 and under have been found to account for 18.9% (Ignatenko, "Opyt," p. 252), for from 20.4% to 26.4% (Klibanov, *Religioznoe sektantstvo*, p. 88), or even for as many as 50% of some congregations.[10] Pivovarov found that of those who attended church, 13.2% and 23.6% were in the age group 20 to 40 in urban and rural churches, respectively (*Struktura*, pp. 17–18). Among Baptists in Kazakhstan, 43% were under the age of 50 (Klibanov, *Konkretnye issledovaniia*, p. 213). "In sectarian organizations, people of middle age (30 to 50) still constitute a significant part of the believers: in the urban groups of Baptists—42%, among the [True Orthodox Christians] Hidden Ones (town of Vozino, Troitsko-Pechorskii region)—36%, True Orthodox Christians—47%, and among the Pentecostals (76%) and Jehovah's Witnesses (66%) they predominate" (Gagarin, "Otkhod," p. 186). Ugrinovich found that 62.5% of an Orthodox congregation were aged 20 to 60, with 23.4% aged 21 to 45 (*Vvedenie*, p. 135). A general survey of Mennonites indicated that 70% were younger than 50.[11] Nor is this figure unprecedented: Cherniak's study of median ages of believing workers at three factories in Kazakhstan indicated that half of the religious workers were younger than 32.9, 34.3, and 36.0 (*Formirovanie*, pp. 134–35).

Most Soviet scholars agree, however, that the elderly predominate among religious people. According to some studies, superannuation among them is far advanced. Tepliakov's study of one Molokan congregation showed that all of its 49 people were elderly; while in another, the youngest member was 51 (*Problemy*, p. 154). In Tul'tseva's study, 32 of the 33 members (97%) were over 60 ("Evoliutsiia," p. 209). A Sabbatarian congregation "consisted exclusively of old persons over the age of 60 years."[12] Gurianov's study revealed that 90 of 97 believing collective farmers were over 60 ("Bogi," p. 16). According to one scholar, in general 82.7% of the believers are above 50 (Kozhevnikov, "Ateisticheskoe vospitanie," p. 2). "The Omsk congregation of Evangelical Christians-Baptists is composed of 76% retired and housekeepers, all of them people over 60 years of age."[13]

Figures below 70% for the elderly are not uncommon. Thus, among the 26 members of a village church board, 18 (69%) were over 60.[14] Among Baptists in the Tambov and Voronezh regions, 67% were over 60;[15] while a study of 675 believers in the Ukraine indicated that 69.6% were over 60 and that only 3.1% were under 30 (Duluman, *Sovremennyi veruiushchii*, pp. 33–34). Only 67% of two Baptist congregations in Alma-Ata were over the age of 50 (Klibanov, *Religioznoe sektantstvo*, p. 88). Ugrinovich's study of 89 Orthodox Christians in a village near Moscow revealed that 55% were over 60, 39% were between 45 and 60, and only 6% were younger than 45 (*Filosofskie problemy,* p. 125). Almost exactly the same age breakdown was found by Klibanov among non-Orthodox in one of the eastern regions of Belorussia (*Religioznoe sektantstvo,* p. 82). A field expedition in central Russia revealed that "the basic composition of Michurin Baptists is the people of advanced age. We gathered the following data on the composition of the current Michurin Baptists: 20–30 years old—1; 30–40—5; 40–50—18; 50–60—28; 60 and over—47. Those over 60 account for about 47% of their number; ages 50 to 60, almost 29%; 40 to 50—18%; and 20 to 40—in all, only about 6%."[16] The situation that obtained among Old Believers in Latvia in 1966/67 is shown in table 5.2. Among 200 members of a Baptist congregation in Astrakhan, near the Caspian Sea, 22.0% were under 50, and 55.5% were over 60 (Nikonov, "O nekotorykh tendentsiiakh," pp. 174–75). Table 5.3 shows the results of a study conducted in a village on the Volga River near Gorky. Nearly three-fourths of one urban congregation of Baptists were over 50 (Klibanov, *Religioznoe sektantstvo,* p. 74), and similar results were found among

TABLE 5.2

RESULTS OF A SURVEY OF OLD BELIEVERS IN LATVIA

Age	Number of Old Believers	Percentage of total
Under 40	43	8.2
41 to 50	98	18.8
51 to 60	140	26.8
Over 60	241	46.2
Totals	522	100.0

SOURCE: Podmazov, "Sovremennoe staroobriadchestvo," p. 182.

TABLE 5.3

RESULTS OF A STUDY OF A VILLAGE ON THE VOLGA RIVER

Age	Percentage of total (832 people)	Percentage of religious (196 people)
18 to 20	6.2	0.5
21 to 30	15.9	2.6
31 to 40	23.9	8.1
41 to 50	21.4	14.3
51 to 60	14.8	28.6
Over 60	17.8	45.9

SOURCE: Solov'ev, "O vliianii," p. 194.

Molokans in Armenia and Georgia (ibid., p. 90). In a Baptist congregation, 130 of 199 members, or 65%, were over the age of 40, and in an entire region, only 892 of 1,898 Baptists, or 47%, were over 60.[17] Observations in Moscow churches suggested that the percentage of those over age 50 who were attending services range from a high of 87 to a low of 55% (Pismanik, "O sostoianii," p. 215; cf. Pantskhava, *O nekotorykh osobennostiakh,* p. 7). According to Tepliakov, "People aged 55 and older constitute 59.0% of the rural and 56.6% of the urban believers and waverers" (*Problemy,* p. 163). According to Selivanov's survey of 30,000 inhabitants of the Penza region, more than 40% of the believers were under 55, and 25% were under 45 (*Partiinoe rukovodstvo,* p. 41).

Research results showing that the elderly constitute only half or less of the believers are not unknown. Saprykin found that only half of 618 members of various churches in Balkhash, Kazakhstan, were over 50 ("Ateisticheskaia rabota," p. 223). Sectarians in eastern parts of Belorussia were found to have 43 to 44% over the age of 50, with 12 to 15% between the ages of 20 and 40 (Klibanov, *Religioznoe sektantstvo,* p. 82). Baptists in a region of European Russia embrace a similar proportion of people over 60 (43%), but have somewhat more in the age group 20 to 40 (22%) (ibid., p. 74). Again with regard to Baptists, "of the Voronezh community, 5.3% are young people from 20 to 30; 13% are 30 to 40; 15.7% are 40 to 50; 25.3% are 50 to 60; and 40.7% are over 60."[18] Table 5.4 shows the composition of a Baptist congregation in Kazakhstan.

A number of studies have shown that old age is by no means the rule among religious people. In one Baptist congregation, 70% were under 60 (Malakhova, "Istoriki," p. 234). In another region, only 57% of the Baptists throughout the region were under 60, but 22% were between the ages of 20 and 40 (Klibanov, *Religioznoe sektantstvo,* p 74, and "Raskol," p. 92). Schismatic Baptists in one region showed similar figures, with 20%

TABLE 5.4

A Baptist Congregation in Kazakhstan

Age	Number of believers	Percentage of believers
20 to 30	1	1.5
31 to 40	11	16.4
41 to 50	11	16.4
51 to 60	19	28.4
61 to 70	11	16.4
Over 70	14	20.9

Source: Saprykin, "Ateisticheskaia rabota," p. 225.

aged 20 to 40 and 24% aged 40 to 60 (Klibanov, *Religioznoe sektantstvo,* p. 114). In a congregation of 246 Old Believers, the following age groups were noted: "Age 18–24—4 people (1.6%); [25–]30—22 (9%); 31–50—74 (30%); 51–60—55 (22.3%); and 61 and older—91 (37.1%)" (Tepliakov, *Problemy,* p. 144).[19] In Western Belorussia, which was annexed to the USSR during World War II, 40% of the non-Orthodox sectarians were found to be under 50 (Klibanov, *Religioznoe sektantstvo,* p. 82). Similarly, "as the Kiev researcher, A. A. Eryshev, writes, 'In the western regions of the Ukraine, in comparison with the eastern regions, there are more youth among believers.' A. A. Eryshev presents data acquired as a result of the research mentioned above: among sectarians in the western regions of the Ukraine, people aged 20 to 40 constitute 27%, from 40 to 60—41.9%, and over 60—29.9%. The Ukrainian researchers also separate out an age group under 19, which constituted 1.2% among the sectarians surveyed" (ibid., p. 77).[20] Adrianov found that 41.7% of the members of a Pskov church were under 50 ("Evoliutsiia," p. 171), while Paskov's study of 538 believers noted that only 230, or 42.75%, were over 50 ("K voprosu," p. 150).[21] In 7 Seventh Day Adventist congregations in Moldavia, only 25.6% were over 60 (Klibanov, *Religioznoe sektantstvo,* p. 101). Finally, one congregation of Baptists yielded truly astonishing figures: only 20% were over 60, and fully half of the congregation was under 40 (Malakhova, "Istoriki," p. 234).

Results such as these are atypical, however. By and large, Soviet researchers find that "among people who maintain a religious world view, the overwhelming majority consists of people of advanced age" (Cherniak, *Formirovanie,* p. 133). The elderly are found to predominate in most of the studies. The fact that some research projects have found otherwise, and particularly the wide variation that can be found among some of the more youthful congregations, may disturb one's confidence somewhat in the other, more normative studies. But Soviet scholarship is able to make a very persuasive case indeed that most religious believers are elderly.

Soviet scholars have not been so persuasive, however, in their analyses of these findings. The research demonstrates fairly convincingly that older people predominate; the question of why this pattern obtains has not been answered successfully.

With very few exceptions, Soviet scholars conclude that the preponderance of the elderly is a symptom of the decay of religion. It is axiomatic to the Soviet ideology that religion must disappear from the socialist society; the advanced age of the religious believers indicates that the process has progressed a long way and that as soon as these few remaining old people are gone, religion will vanish. Soviet scholars tend to utilize data regarding age to predict the length of time remaining to the congregation or religious group being studied (Ugrinovich, *Vvedenie*, p. 135).

The problem with this interpretation, however, is that Soviet atheists have been making similar observations and have been drawing the same conclusions for more than fifty years. From the 1920s onward, antireligious publications have noted the preponderance of the elderly in the churches and have been confidently awaiting the collapse of religion. In view of this history, it is difficult to remain satisfied with the facile assumption that the observed age patterns are harbingers of the demise of religion. It seems much more likely that some process of replenishment of the ranks of these elderly religious believers is taking place.

On very rare occasions, Soviet commentators have attempted to go beyond the simplistic interpretation. They are beginning to surmise that the preponderance of the elderly may be a common pattern in religion and that it may indeed be indicative of a normal, healthy congregation.

> From the data given above it is evident that there are almost no youth among the Old Believers, and people of retirement age constitute the strongest age group. But here it would be appropriate to make a minor reservation. As is evident from the Old Believer press at the beginning of the twentieth century, and especially from the period of the bourgeois regime in Latvia, even then (although not so sharply as now) the problem of the spread of atheism among the youth had arisen. However, despite the change of generations, Old Believers have not disappeared. As the leader of the Gaikovskii congregation (city of Daugavpils), Nesterov, says, the fact of the matter is that several who come from religious families, who in their youth considered themselves to have "fallen away," with the years returned to the bosom of the church. This once again recalls the vitality of religion and cautions against a revaluation of the process of "natural disappearance" of the Old Believers, which has its place among some propagandists. [Podmazov, "Sovremennoe staroobriadchestvo," pp. 182–83]

"Young people were always less subject to religion," according to the sociological researcher E. Duluman (*Sovremennyi veruiushchii*, p. 92), who formerly was an Orthodox priest.

> Science has long since established a peculiar tendency: *with age, somewhere after 35 or 40 years, people's religiousness begins to grow.* One is confronted by such facts even in our time in the field of concrete sociological research. The preachers of religion also love to emphasize this circumstance. Thus, the priest N., from the village of Lozovyi Iar in the Kiev area, said:

"Even in the twenties, many atheists asserted that the aged believers of that time would die, and then contemporary youth would not go to church. And now, look at my praying ones—old people, 60 to 75 years old. But in the twenties they were 14 to 25. Even contemporary youth, with age, will begin to go to church, to fill the houses of prayer. It is a law! I also was a Godless in my youth."[22]

Duluman's observation echoes the wry remark of his former professor, Pariiski, dean of the Theological Academy at Leningrad a decade earlier about "all those so-called grandmothers—who must be immortal, by the way, since we've been hearing about them for the past forty years" (quoted by Grunewald, *Churches,* p. 148).

According to Kobetskii,

one should not let the following fact slip by our attention: the level of religiousness among youth in the 20s and 30s was 15 to 20%, while the level of religiousness among the same generation after forty years, in the 60s and 70s, reaches 40%. This indicates cases of returning to religion by those people who in their younger years were considered unbelievers. The reasons for this are obvious: with the entry upon advanced age, going on pension, and the disruption of former professional ties, first of all connected with the working collective, and in the presence of unsatisfying conditions of life, a person sometimes may return to religion. Such a change begins with casual visits with believers or preachers, episodic attendance at a church or a sectarian congregation, and often ends in a complete transfer of the former unbelieving person into a position of a religious world view. There is no doubt that the lack of firm materialistic convictions on the part of the individual lies at the base of such cases. It is precisely on the strength of this that they seem to be unable to resist the influence of the religious surroundings and the religious ideology. [*Sotsiologicheskoe izuchenii,* p. 27]

While it is questionable that the pattern of elderly majorities always may be found in all denominations (the Baptists and Pentecostals would appear to have a considerable appeal among youth, as do some branches of illegal Orthodoxy),[23] it is certainly possible to make this case for Russian Orthodoxy.[24] The church offers a place where the socially unsuccessful can feel that he belongs. If he fails to attain the highest rewards of the Communist system, the church nevertheless accepts him.[25]

"But the moment comes," it was said in one of the sermons delivered by the priest V., from the Leningrad region, "when even the finest blessings of life begin to lose their value in our eyes: wealth no longer attracts us, glory does not move us, learning does not interest us, diversions do not amuse us. We who have dreamed of ruling the universe begin, little by little, to feel the weakening of life's forces. Instead of wealth we begin to notice the meager belongings of the coffin. A terrible melancholy lies upon our heart. We seek something higher, eternal, unlimited, and here, in the entire world, we do not find comfort for ourselves."[26]

Indeed, in view of the age pattern observed during the past half-century, one could make a good case that Russian Orthodoxy, at least, exercises its maximum influence after an individual has reached middle age and has begun to experience whatsoever crises and inner conflicts may occur then. But Soviet scholarship has yet to explore this possibility.

One further factor remains, which may exercise at least a contributing influence on the age patterns observable among religious people in the USSR. This is the existence, or threatened existence, of sanctions against those who are religious. As has been noted, there is ample evidence that discovery of one's religiousness can lead to the interception of one's career, expulsion from the educational system, and worse. In a society that is consciously organized against religion, there is every incentive for an individual to avoid or perhaps conceal an interest in religion, at least until he has achieved enough security to be able to tolerate whatever risk is entailed. Therefore, a younger person, who is still completing his education or is developing his working career, will tend to avoid the church, entering it only later on in life.[27] Thus, the existence of sanctions against religion tends to reinforce a relative absence of young people in the church. Soviet scholarship has yet to analyze this possible factor at all.

With regard to gender, Soviet scholars agree that women tend to be more religious than men. In the large-scale Penza study, 81% of the believers were women (Selivanov, *Partiinoe rukovodstvo*, p. 47). Results of Tepliakov's Voronezh study of 60,000 people are indicated in table 5.5. Almost certainly due simply to the greater longevity of women, "research on age composition of believers shows that believing women are older than their male fellow believers," with those over 60 accounting for 75.6% and 55.8%, respectively (Duluman, *Sovremennyi veruiushchii*, p. 38). Age relationships for men and women that were derived from a study of collective farmers are portrayed in the graphs in figure 5.1.

Almost without exception, Soviet researchers find that there are more women than men in the churches and congregations, and some of the reports suggest that an overwhelming majority are women. In one Moscow church, 97% of those in attendance at a Saturday morning service after

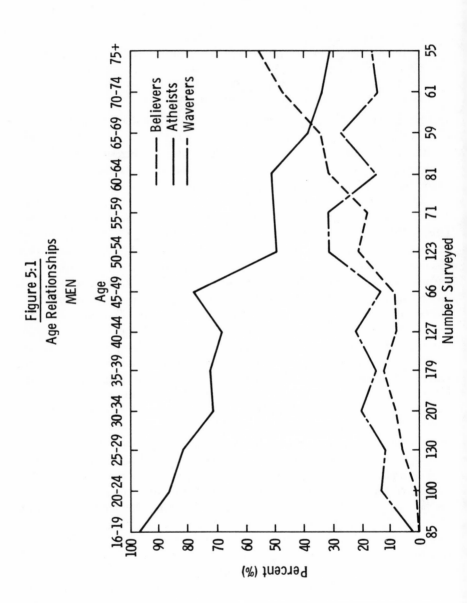

Figure 5:1
Age Relationships
MEN

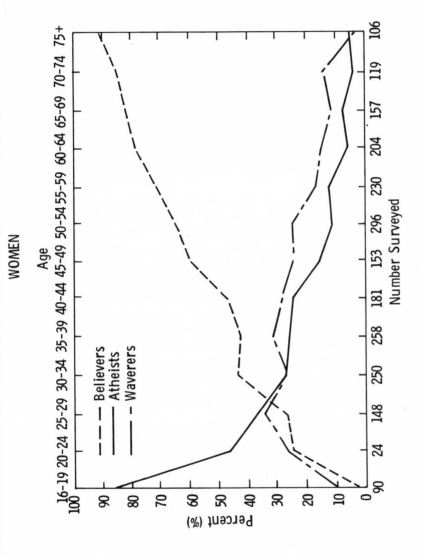

WOMEN

Age

Percent (%)

16-19 20-24 25-29 30-34 35-39 40-44 45-49 50-54 55-59 60-64 65-69 70-74 75+

Believers
Atheists
Waverers

Number Surveyed

90 24 148 250 258 181 153 296 230 204 157 119 106

Source: Kolbanovskii, _Kollektiv_, pp. 230-31.

TABLE 5.5

A Study of the Voronezh Region

Worldview	Men	Women	Total
Nonreligious:	*88.9%*	*69.0%*	*77.6%*
Atheists	15.3	9.2	11.9
Convinced nonbelievers	42.5	34.4	37.8
Nonreligious	31.2	35.4	27.9
Religious:	*11.1*	*31.0*	*22.4*
Waverers	7.1	16.8	12.7
Convinced believers	4.0	14.2	9.7
Totals	100.0	100.0	100.0

Source: Tepliakov, *Problemy*, p. 125.
Note: There are a number of discrepancies in these data.

Easter were women (Pismanik, "O sostoianii," p. 213). Observers in other churches discovered that from 89% to 93% of those in attendance were women (ibid., pp. 213–14; Iablokov, "Obshchenie," p. 52).

Such a high percentage of women among believers is not typical. Reports that women constitute 85% to 90% of the congregations are more frequent,[28] while reports ranging between 80% and 85% are perhaps most common of all.[29] Another large group of studies indicates that women constitute between 75% and 80% of the congregations.[30] Somewhat less frequently, Soviet researchers report a preponderance of women ranging between 65% and 75%.[31]

More nearly equal ratios between men and women are sometimes reported. Thus, Malakhova reported that a Baptist congregation consisted of 40% men and 60% women ("Istoriki," p. 233). The same ratio obtained in Tatar villages of the Gorky Region (Orlov, "Opyt," p. 94). In Belorussia, 54% of Baptists were found to be women (Ignatenko, "Opyt," p. 261), while a study of Pentecostals found a ratio of 47 men to 53 women (Gagarin, "Otkhod," p. 186). Finally, among Mennonites the ratio was found to be almost equal (Il'inykh, "Osobennosti," p. 205).

These last illustrative reports are significant, for they reflect a smaller preponderance of women than is to be found in the general population. According to M. Pismanik, population figures for the USSR during the late sixties consisted of 114,776,000 women (54.96%) and 94,050,000 men (45.04%); whereas in the general population over the age of 50, 65.11% were women ("O sostoianii," pp. 214–15). According to Klibanov, for the RSFSR, 44.4% were men and 55.6% were women (*Religioznoe sektantstvo*, p. 74), while the preponderance of women was even more pronounced in the RSFSR according to the 1959 census: men 41%; women 59% ("Raskol"

p. 93). Much of this disparity is due to male casualties during World War II. Thus, figures such as the above, although they show women to be in the majority, in fact are indications of the reverse, for they indicate that in these congregations or groups, the proportion of men is larger than in the general population. Particularly if the almost universal finding that the majority of the religious believers are elderly is valid, then some of the figures noted above will not indicate that religion exercises a greater appeal among women than men: in fact, some of them may indicate just the opposite.

The bulk of the evidence, however, does indicate that more women than men are attracted to religion in the USSR. Whether this is due to environmental factors (lower educational level among women, more isolation because fewer women are employed than men, less leisure time due to housework, etc.), as Soviet researchers suggest, or whether it is due to more subtle factors operating nearly universally—or at least in those societies throughout the world where a similar preponderance of women in the churches can be noted—is still problematical.[32]

6

EDUCATION
AND OCCUPATION

Nearly every Soviet practitioner of the sociological study of religion devotes a good portion of his attention to formal education, both from the point of view of the incidence of religiousness among those who have attained various educational levels in the population as a whole and, conversely, from the point of view of the educational levels attained by religious believers. There are two major reasons for this interest.

The primary reason is a function of the ideological position with regard to religion. Marxism is an avowedly rationalistic philosophy, a direct descendant of eighteenth- and early nineteenth-century rationalism. Marxism maintains that all things are subject to rational comprehension, and the greater an individual's intelligence is, the more likely it will be that he will discern the true structure of the universe. By definition, Marxism-Leninism is the truth, and one of the functions of any valid educational system is to lead the student to the truth. Religion, according to this theory, is error, a mistaken world view that has arisen from economic exploitation. Almost automatically, then, proper education will prove to be inimical to religious belief, and an inverse correlation should obtain between religiousness and the level of education. Soviet researchers have an intense interest in discovering and demonstrating this correlation, for it is axiomatic to the ideological theory that religion and intelligence, or at least education, are incompatible.

A second reason for the interest in education versus religiousness is more pragmatic. The Soviet government is immensely proud, in many respects justifiably so, of its educational system. The system has proven its effectiveness in equipping the rising generations to compete successfully in the complexities of the modern technological world. Having inherited an apparently moribund educational network that was controlled by the church, the fledgling Soviet state created a school system that has proven itself through the years. This creation was specifically oriented away from religion, and at various periods, attempts have been made to include atheism as a part of the standard subject matter. Particularly since the late fifties, the antireligious establishment has devoted considerable effort to ensuring that atheism will be taught in every discipline on every level. If such efforts, as well as the atheistic presuppositions of the educational system as a whole, have been successful, then an inverse correlation should be discoverable between education and religiousness. The longer a student has been exposed to the Soviet school system, the greater are the chances that he will have been led to the truth and that his religious presuppositions and superstitions will have been overcome.

Soviet researchers find that there is indeed an inverse correlation between religiousness and educational level in the general population: "Of those who have higher, incomplete higher, and secondary education, 88% are nonreligious. The number of nonreligious also predominates among people with primary education (67.8%)" (Korolev, "Rol'," p. 145). In a study of women collective farmers, Alekseev discovered that the incidence of religiousness fell from 30.8% among those with an incomplete secondary education to only 5.6% of those who had completed their secondary schooling ("Metodika," p. 150). The large-scale study in the Voronezh region disclosed the percentage relationships shown in table 6.1.

Conversely, the study in the Penza region yielded the percentages of educational level among believers and nonbelievers that are indicated in table 6.2.

Vasilevskaia, in order to elucidate the educational patterns observable among various religious categories in the population, devised a coefficient

TABLE 6.1
RESULTS FROM A STUDY OF THE VORONEZH REGION

Classification by amount of education	Nonreligious	Religious
Illiterate	30.7%	69.3%
Semiliterate	51.3	48.7
Primary education	73.9	26.1
5 to 6 years of education	80.7	19.3
7 years of education	90.7	9.3
8 to 9 years of education	97.4	2.6
Secondary education	98.6	1.4
Incomplete and complete higher education	99.85	0.15

SOURCE: Tepliakov, *Problemy*, p. 128.

of educational level by assigning arbitrary numbers to educational levels. "The following indices of educational level were accepted: primary—1, incomplete secondary—2, secondary—3, secondary special—4, incomplete higher—5, and higher—6" ("Opyt," p. 388 n.1). It should be noted that these value assignments give greater weight to secondary special than to secondary general education; actually the two are parallel, with the former having a greater vocational emphasis. Her findings are shown in table 6.3.

Cherniak, in a study of the distribution of those who approved of religion among workers at three factories, discovered that among workers with a primary education, from 8.8% to 23.5%, depending upon the factory, approved of religion; among workers with an incomplete secondary education, the range was from 4.5% to 11.8%; among workers with complete secondary general and secondary special education, 2.8% to 8.4%; and among those with incomplete higher and higher education, 3.5% to 8.5% (*Formirovanie*, p. 238). The last figures are surprising, for the expected inverse ratio between education and religiousness did not obtain

TABLE 6.2

RESULTS FROM A STUDY IN THE PENZA REGION

Level of education	Nonreligious	Religious
No primary education	11.5%	43.0%
Primary	39.7	43.0
Seven years	17.9	2.8
Incomplete secondary	11.5	2.8
Secondary general and special	19.4	8.4

SOURCE: Puchkov, "Vliianie," p. 107.

TABLE 6.3

RESULTS OF A STUDY MADE BY VASILEVSKAIA

Family's relationship to religion	Educational coefficient			
	Up to 1.1	1.2 to 2.5	2.6 to 3.5	3.5 to 6
Believers	47.5%	45.0%	7.0%	......%
Waverers	32.0	54.0	14.0	......
Indifferent	20.0	61.4	18.6	......
Atheists	13.4	39.5	23.6	23.5

SOURCE: Vasilevskaia, "Opyt," p. 388.
NOTE: One should use caution in assessing this analysis, for her finding that only among atheists are there people with higher education, with none at all in any of the other categories (including those who are indifferent to religion), is not supported by other researchers. (Only 99.5% of the believers are accounted for.)

in two of the three cases: in one factory a larger percentage of those with higher education than of those with secondary education approved of religion (3.5% vs 2.8%), while in the other the percentage of those in the higher education category who approved of religion exceeded the percentage of those in the categories both of secondary and of incomplete secondary education (8.5% vs 5.4% and 6.2%, respectively). While these results depart from the norm, the expected inverse ratio between education and religiousness was found to obtain at the lower levels. Speaking of the absolute numbers of workers, Cherniak concluded: "The relative density of those who relate approvingly to religion among workers with a full secondary education is nominally three times lower than among workers with a primary education. Considering the portion of workers with a primary education and the number of believers among the remaining educational group, one may conclude that with increasing education from primary to complete secondary, the number of those who relate approvingly to religion will decrease, on the average, 1.25 times, i.e., by 25%" (*Formirovanie*, p. 241).

To summarize, Soviet scholars discover a fairly consistent pattern that the incidence of religiousness decreases with increased levels of education. There are exceptions to this pattern, possibly frequently enough to raise doubts as to its universality; but by and large, Soviet scholars are able to produce results that confirm the theory that the incidence of religiousness should relate inversely to the educational level.

Soviet scholars devote considerable effort to ascertaining the educational level among believers themselves. In this sector, the theory requires that the higher levels of education should be sparsely represented among religious believers (or, ideally, be absent altogether), while the lowest educational levels should predominate. A great many studies show this to be precisely the case.

More than 90% of the religious believers are illiterate or semiliterate, according to some studies.[1] Other studies show that more than 85% are in this educational category (Osipov, "Priglashenie," p. 31). With regard to religious people who avoid all contact with atheists, one study discovered that "for believers of this group a low general educational level is typical. According to our data, of the general number of believers [301], 68 were illiterate, and 191 had completed literacy school or 1 to 2 years of church parish school at some time. Accordingly, 259 people, or 86%, even if they wanted to, cannot freely read scientific atheist literature" (Duluman, *Sovremennyi veruiushchii*, p. 170). Other studies indicate that 80% of the believers belong to this educational category (Stel'makov, "O sootnoshenii," p. 41; Klibanov, *Religioznoe sektantstvo*, p. 88), and still others find that the percentage approximates 75 (Tepliakov, *Problemy*, p. 144; Klibanov, *Religioznoe sektantstvo*, p. 101; Malakhova, "Religioznoe sektantstvo," p. 95). Findings that 60 to 70% are illiterate and semiliterate are not uncommon (Klibanov, *Religioznoe sektantstvo*, pp. 82, 90, 101; Murav'ev, "O konkretnosti," p. 64).

Not all results show such a preponderance of the poorly educated among believers, however. Some studies indicate that only approximately 50% of the believers are in the poorly educated category (Klibanov, *Religioznoe sektantstvo*, p. 82; Mamaeva, "O nekotorykh ob"ektivnykh i sub"ektivnykh faktorakh," p. 82), while other studies would suggest that only about 33% of the believers are illiterate or semiliterate: "When you think, for example, of the fact that in the Belorussian SSR, according to data from the 1959 census, the illiterate among men constituted 0.5% and among women 1.4%, and then that in the Brest region more than 30% of the composition of the Evangelical Christians-Baptists are illiterate, then the concepts 'sectarian' and 'illiterate' draw so close together that they become all but synonyms" (Klibanov, *Religioznoe sektantstvo*, pp. 82, 83).

Finally, some studies indicate that at least in some groups of believers the lower educational levels are not at all dominant. "As a result of the research we conducted, the following results were acquired: among believers one finds about 7% of the men illiterate, but among women, some 3.1 times more, namely 22.2% (Duluman, *Sovremennyi veruiushchii*, p. 38). In a study of factory workers, Cherniak found that not more than 18.2% of those who approved of religion had less than a primary education (*Formirovanie*, p. 124).

Some caution must be exercised in evaluating these results. The terms "illiterate" and "semiliterate" are not always to be taken literally. Obviously, when a Soviet researcher examines an urban congregation of one of the denominations that historically have placed a high premium on literacy and Scripture reading and discovers that "even in the Moscow congregation of Seventh Day Adventists, illiterates and semiliterates constitute about 80%" (Ugrinovich, *Filosofskie problemy*, p. 118; cf. Il'inykh, "Osobennosti," pp. 205–6), the results cannot be very credible if the terms are taken literally. In fact, Soviet scholars use these terms in a technical rather than literal sense, referring to levels of formal education. Thus, an individual who has not attended school at all is classified as illiterate, while one who has less than a 4-year primary education will be classified as semiliterate. Whether these individuals can read or not and the extent to which they have engaged in self-education are irrelevant to the classification. (In this regard, Nikita Khrushchev himself might have been classified as illiterate or, at best, semiliterate, inasmuch as his early schooling consisted of a few months of study with a village priest.)[2]

This usage can result in some confusion—and, indeed, in misleading implications—when the incidence of illiteracy and semiliteracy among believers is compared with census figures, which define literacy in functional terms (the ability to read) and which indicate general literacy levels of 98% and 99% for the population as a whole (Duluman, *Sovremennyi veruiushchii*, p. 38). In fact, the disparity between the educational level of religious believers and that of the general population is not nearly so great as some sociologists suggest. Thus, in one study of 2,904 employees at five Moscow factories, Kniasev discovered that 24% had from 1 to 4 years of formal education; 61.4% had between 5 and 9 years; 12.8% had a secondary education; and 1.8% had a higher education ("Sistema," p. 248). "In Belorussia less than 20% of the peasants had a secondary education, and the volume of knowledge of the basic mass of the toilers of the village is in the neighborhood of third to sixth grade."[3] General education statistics for women over 50 indicate that only 17.3% have received a primary or incomplete 7-year education, while 73.1% have received no education at all (Pismanik, "O sostoianii," p. 216). Soviet researchers have energetically demonstrated the preponderance of women and the elderly among religious groups, and hence their findings concerning the educational level may not indicate any radical difference at all between believers and nonbelievers.

When the comparison is made without weighing the results among believers for age and gender, a considerable disparity is evident. One study of 675 Ukrainian religious believers found that none of them had a higher education, vs. 2.3% of the general population; 1.8% had secondary and incomplete higher education, vs. 33.8% for the general population; with regard to primary and incomplete secondary education, the figures were 13.6% vs. 31.0%; 63.3% of the believers were semiliterate, as against 31.4% for the country as a whole; and 21.3% were illiterate, vs. 1.5% for the general population (Duluman, *Sovremennyi veruiushchii*, p. 35). Klibanov's study of 1,142 Baptists indicated that "illiterate, semiliterate, and those having a primary education constituted 87.2% by the end of 1963. People with secondary educations constitute 1% among them, and those with incomplete secondary educations, 11.6%. At the same time, according to data of the 1959 census in the RSFSR, for 1,000 people (adults aged 18 or over) there are 19 people with complete higher education, 263 with incomplete higher and secondary education, including incomplete secondary, and 235 with primary and incomplete 7-year" (*Religioznoe sektantstvo*, p. 75). Inasmuch as this study indicated that those who were classifiable as illiterate and semiliterate in the general population constituted 48.3% (removing the possibility of exaggeration due to the shift from percentage among the religious to per thousand among the general population), this would indicate an educational level among these Baptists of well over half that which prevails in the general population, and no attempt has been made to compensate for age and gender. That these factors should be considered is obvious: "Research data speak of the fact that Baptist congregations have in their composition 68.4% women, 81.1% of the believers are older than 40, 16% are aged 30 to 40, and 2.9% are under 30. Illiterate, semiliterate, and those with primary education constitute 74.9%, those with 5 to 6 years of education, 13.4%; 7 to 9 years, 4.8%; and those with secondary and higher education, 6.9%" (Ignatenko, "Opyt," p. 252).

A comparison of the educational levels of 13,310 religious people with those of 10,403 people who had renounced religion gave the percentages found in table 6.4. Among 538 religious believers, 0.74% had a secondary education; 8.18%, an incomplete secondary; 19.70%, a primary education; and 71.38% were classifiable as semiliterate (Iablokov, "Obshchenie," p. 61). A more detailed study gave the percentages for the religious distribution of men and women in each of the educational categories that appear in table 6.5. Finally, among the parents who baptize their children, the educational levels seemed quite compatible with those prevailing in the general population, with 74.7% having a primary education or less (Aptekman, "Vitality," p. 369).

Despite the research projects cited above, which indicated extraordinarily high levels of illiteracy, many studies have discovered that significant portions of the religious believers have received a primary education or

TABLE 6.4

RESULTS OF A STUDY OF EDUCATIONAL LEVELS

Educational level	Religious people	People who have renounced religion
Illiterate and semiliterate	66.8%	9.7%
Primary	18.8	12.0
5 to 6 years	6.7	6.2
7 years	5.0	12.8
8 to 9 years	1.7	19.9
Secondary	0.9	22.7
Incomplete and complete higher	0.1	16.7
Totals	100.0	100.0

SOURCE: Tepliakov, *Problemy*, p. 157.

TABLE 6.5
A STUDY OF EDUCATIONAL LEVELS AND RELIGION

Educational level	Believers		Waverers		Unbelievers	
	Men	Women	Men	Women	Men	Women
No formal education..	44.4%	79.3%	16.7%	13.1%	38.9%	7.6%
Semiliterate	33.5	65.0	25.9	23.5	40.6	11.5
Primary	17.0	50.7	20.6	28.1	62.4	21.2
Incomplete secondary	3.3	30.8	13.3	27.7	83.4	41.5
Secondary school	2.0	5.6	4.0	24.0	94.0	70.4

SOURCE: Kolbanovskii, *Kollektiv*, p. 241.

better. In the Voronezh Baptist congregation, "of 722 people, in 1967 there were 12 [*sic;* should read 120] people (16.6%) with secondary education" (Tepliakov, *Problemy*, p. 157). Among urban believers, 20 to 30% were found to have had more than a primary education (Gagarin, "Otkhod," p. 186), while among believing workers, 33.5% had completed 8 years or more of schooling (Andrianov, "Evoliutsiia," p. 172). In the Dnepropetrovsk region, 35% of the Baptists had had a primary education or better, while "among the replenishments entering into the congregations of Evangelical Christians-Baptists during the last several years (in 17 of the 25 regions of the Ukrainian SSR), women constitute 71% and people with a primary education—more than 94%," (Klibanov, *Religioznoe sektantstvo*, p. 81).

Particularly among younger believers, even higher educational levels can be found: "If among the adult population believers constitute a group of people, the majority of whom are not employed in socially useful labor— dependents and retired people (those among the adult believers who are workers are primarily people of semiskilled labor and, as a rule, semiliterate), believing young people have a higher educational and cultural level (some of them have higher and secondary education), high professional qualifications, and they work at large industrial enterprises" (Galitskaia, "K voprosu," p. 394). In a Baptist congregation in the Krasnodar district, "there is a significant percentage of comparatively young people having education from 7 to 10 years, and some believers have finished trade schools" (Stel'makov, "O sootnoshenii," p. 40). Ignatenko interviewed a young Baptist with a higher education ("Opyt," p. 262), while Kozhevnikov notes, with some dismay: "One cannot pass over in silence the fact that among believers there are young people. Our research showed that 1% are young, under 30. There are, it seems, believers with higher, incomplete higher, and secondary education" ("Ateisticheskoe vospitanie," p. 2).

Thus, while at first glance, Soviet sociological research would seem to support the inverse relationship between religious belief and educational level that is predicated by the ideology, there are enough exceptions to the rule, in the form of religious believers who have experienced the highest educational levels, to bring into question the hypothesis that there is a necessary inverse relationship. Furthermore, as has been indicated above, many of the less extreme findings of Soviet scholarship, on inspection, indicate a distribution of educational levels that may approximate very closely that which prevails in the general public among populations with a similar distribution of age and gender. Hence it would not seem that Soviet scholarship has established beyond all question an inverse relationship between religiousness and educational level, even though it does indicate that, by and large, the lower levels of education are dominant among religious people.

As has been indicated, if the inverse relationship does not obtain, Soviet sociologists are confronted with something of a theoretical problem. V. P. Bukin astutely points out, however, that the increasing specialization of Soviet society may, in part, lie behind this problem: as modern education becomes more specialized, a student may remain ignorant in non-technical areas, and hence increased education may not have an effect on the eradication of religion.[4]

Even were such an inverse ratio established, however, the reasons for this ratio are by no means self-evident. As was indicated above, Soviet ideologists feel that such a relationship must obtain both because of the incompatibility of religion and education and as an index of the success of the school system. However, because there have been so many reports of the interception of the educational careers of young people, whereby students are expelled when it is discovered that they harbor religious convictions, one can wonder whether the causation may not be the other way around. It may well be that if one wants to acquire more education, it becomes increasingly difficult, and finally impossible, to remain religious. It may also be that the maintenance of religious beliefs makes further education impossible, when it is known that the state will intervene and close all opportunities of formal education to students who refuse to renounce their religious beliefs.

The occupation of religious believers is another area of great concern to Soviet sociology of religion, and nearly as much effort is expended in collecting data about occupations as in the area of education. Directly or indirectly, much of this interest is ideologically inspired.

The ideology, as has been noted, requires that the intellectual, educational level of the religious believer be low. Consequently, it would seem only natural that religious believers would gravitate toward the lower occupational levels, inasmuch as occupational level is usually a function of either education or intelligence. More directly the Marxist ideology, which places great emphasis upon the working class, would suggest that under socialist conditions, those who retain their religious beliefs will be in the more backward sectors of the working class, rather than among the vanguard, which not only excells in working capacity but also recognizes the truth of Marxism and, hence, atheism. Furthermore, because Soviet Marxism emphasizes the collective, it would be expected that fewer individuals would retain their religious beliefs within the working collective than outside it, and hence a greater proportion of the religious population can be expected to be divorced from the working collective entirely, or else to relate to it only modestly in relatively undemanding occupations (Gaidurova, "Zavisimost'," p. 18). Finally, the ideological structure of society, to the extent that it properly reflects the conscious ideological design, will ensure that those who do not share society's ideological goals and ideals will be less likely to achieve success in society, whatever their professions.

For these and other reasons, Soviet researchers can expect that occupational data will tend to show that there is a concentration of religious believers toward the lower end of the spectrum. In large degree, their results confirm this prediction.

Soviet researchers note that a large proportion of religious believers do not work at all but instead belong to such nonproductive groups as the retired, the disabled, and those whose sole occupation is housekeeping. While such nonworking elements do loom large in the results of Soviet sociological research, the range of data regarding this category of religious believers is exceedingly broad, and no clear pattern emerges. By and large, the results depend on the population group that is selected. Thus, Gaidurova reported that 99% of the religious believers contacted were in this category ("Zavisimost'," p. 17); whereas Klibanov reported 83.1% (*Religioznoe sektantstvo*, p. 101). A large number of studies found that the proportion of nonworkers was in the range of 60 to 75%.[5] Other reports place this group in the vicinity of 50% of the total number of religious believers.[6] Percentages in the 30 to 40% range have also been reported (Klibanov, *Religioznoe sektantstvo*, p. 100). "Analysis of 521 questionnaires shows at a glance the special association between the relationship of believers to religion and occupation in the collective-farm industry. It seems that nonworkers were most numerous of all in the group of believers (35%). Among the wavering they were 27%, while among nonbelievers—21%" (Gaidurova, "Zavisimost'," pp. 17–18). Discoveries that only some 30% of the believers are nonworkers are not uncommon (Gagarin, "Otkhod," p. 186; Klibanov, *Religioznoe sektantstvo,* p. 79), while there have been reports of extraordinarily low percentages of nonworkers among religious believers: 16% and 18.6% in two cases (Klibanov, *Religioznoe sektantstvo,* pp. 79, 83), and 10.5% and 10.3% in two others (ibid., pp. 82, 101).

Thus, while the majority of the researchers report fairly large concentrations of the nonworking elements among religious believers, the range of data is so broad that no absolute pattern emerges. Within the nonworking category, several divisions may be found. "Among Baptists, 51% are not employed in social production, and of these 59.2% are retired, 29.1% are housekeepers, and 10.1% are invalids" (Ignatenko, "Opyt," p. 252). "Research showed that more than half of the believers of the Orthodox faith were not directly connected with social production but were severed from the working collective. Among them, housekeepers were 34%; retired, about 17%; dependents and helpers around the house, more than 5%; and unskilled people who do odd jobs, 14%" (Tepliakov, "Sostoianie," pp. 34–35). Comparing believers with nonbelievers, Tepliakov reported that among religious people, 24.3% were dependents, as compared with 5.3% of nonreligious, and that 27.8% were retired, as compared with 8.2% ("Pobeda," p. 144).

In the preceding chapter, it was noted that Soviet researchers have found that there is a preponderance of women and the elderly among believers. One can then expect, as a corollary, that there will be large numbers of believers in these categories of nonworkers. Inasmuch as most people retire from work and begin to collect their pensions between the age of 55 and 60, it is only natural that religious groups with large numbers of the elderly will also have large numbers of nonworking members (Tepliakov, *Problemy,* p. 163). The same reasoning will apply when a large majority of the religious believers are women, for in the general population, 89% of those who are occupied exclusively with housekeeping are women (Pismanik, "O sostoianii," p. 217). Gaidurova notes that

> the greater part of the women are occupied as housekeepers, which cuts them off from participation in collective-farm production. If one takes account of the fact that a substantial part of the believers are women and people of retirement age, then the connection between the nonparticipation of people in social production and the preservation of customary religious consciousness among them becomes more "tangible."

All of this speaks of the fact that nonparticipation in social production is at the present time a general peculiarity of the life of a part of the believers. Therefore, this peculiarity is not fortuitous if one considers that the basic mass of them consists of the retired and invalid—in the main, among housekeepers.

Of course, many of them stopped working because of advanced age (all the researchers emphasized that the majority of the believers are of advanced age and elderly). However, many of the elderly and even of the young believers in general never were connected with social production or were engaged in it for a period of time that was not prolonged.

A part of the believers, for example, have conducted and still do conduct private enterprise, or work at private handicrafts. ["Zavisimost'," pp. 18–19]

Tepliakov's survey of the Voronezh region indicated that the percentage of religious people among the population varied in the following manner: among white collar workers—1%; among workers—21.3%; among collective farmers—31.3%; among the retired—52.9%; among housekeepers —53.8%; and among invalids—70.7% ("Sotsial'nye issledovaniia," p. 109; "Pobeda," p. 137). In the Penza region, 30.8% of the workers on collective farms were religious, 25.1% of the workers at state farms, and 12% of the urban workers of Penza, which had the lowest percentage in the region.[7] In Novosibirsk and the Novosibirsk region in Siberia, 12.2% of the industrial workers and 20.3% of the agricultural workers were religious.[8] Among Baptists who are classified as socially productive, the ratio of urban workers to collective farmers was approximately 3:2 in the Voronezh region (Tepliakov, *Problemy*, p. 157).[9] The ratio was approximately 1:3 in the Astrakhan Baptist congregation, despite its urban location (Nikonov, "O nekotorykh tendentsiiakh," pp. 174–75). Occupational data for 675 religious believers in the Ukraine, broken down according to three age groups, are shown in table 6.6. In one region, among 3,568 Baptists, 1,151

TABLE 6.6
RESULTS OF A STUDY IN THE UKRAINE

Occupation	Number	Percentage	To age 30	Ages 30 to 60	Over 60
Workers and collective farmers ..	217	32.2	12	129	76
White-collar	9	1.3	2	4	3
Housekeepers	183	27.1	....	33	150
Retired	189	28.0	....	7	182
Dependents	71	10.6	6	7	58
Clergy	6	0.8	1	4	1
Totals	675	100.0	21	184	470

SOURCE: Duluman, *Sovremennyi veruiushchii*, p. 34.

(32.26%) were collective farmers, 297 (8.32%) were workers, 20 (0.56%) were white-collar workers, 803 (22.51%) were retired, and 1,297 (36.35%) were housekeepers and dependents (Duluman, *Sovremennyi veruiushchii,* p. 35).[10] A large-scale survey of various occupational categories in the Voronezh region during the period 1965 to 1967 yielded the percentage breakdowns among various occupational classifications that are given in table 6.7.

With regard to the rural population, Ugrinovich found that occupational data concerning an Orthodox village parish indicated that 55.8% were housekeepers and retired, 18.8% were employed at odd jobs on the collective farm, 7.8% were unskilled laborers, 7.0% were skilled workers (mechanics and the like), and 2.8% were office and administrative personnel (*Vvedenie,* p. 137).[11] Occupational categories of rural men and women were found to consist of the percentages of religious believers that are indicated in table 6.8.

In terms of the more highly skilled, in one study of the rural population, Kolbanovskii discovered that among believers, 34.4% possessed an occupational skill, while 65.6% did not; among waverers, the figures were 43.7% and 56.3%; and among unbelievers, 55.7% were skilled and 44.3% were not (*Kollektiv,* p. 238). In Gaidurova's study, the differentiation was much more pronounced: "Analysis of the questionnaires of 521 inhabitants of this town showed the following: if among unbelievers, about half (46%) have a specialization; among waverers—22%; while among believers, only 4.3%. The absolute majority of these last answered the question concerning type of work: 'It's all the same,' 'Wherever they send me'" ("Zavisimost'," p. 27). Conversely, among skilled collective farmers, 12.7% were found to be atheists; 60.8%, unbelievers; 11.1%, indifferent; 6.1%, waverers; and 9.3% were believers. Among those without skills, 2.8% were atheists; 38.6%, unbelievers; 19.4%, indifferent; 17.2%, waverers; and 22.0% were believers (Puchkov, "Vliianie," p. 119). This pattern is not atypical. "Among men employed at odd jobs, believers constitute 13.4%, while among machine operators, only 3.9%. Among women collective farmers employed at odd jobs, 50.3% are believers, while among animal herders, whose labor is more skilled and less highly paid—35.7%; the educational level and median age of these production groups are approximately the same" (Alekseev, "Metodika," p. 150).

With the possible exception of collective-farm administrators, those who work with equipment and machinery enjoy the highest occupational status in the normal collective-farm population. In this occupational group, religiousness is encountered much less frequently than in many of the other levels: "Among machine operators whose work is connected with complex

TABLE 6.7
Some Results from Tepliakov's Study of the Voronezh Region

Occupational category	Number surveyed	Convinced atheists	Convinced non-believers	Nonre-ligious	Wavering believers	Convinced believers
Graduate specialists	7,703	42.05%	40.3%	17.4%	0.13%	0.12%
White-collar, without diploma	2,944	19.8	51.6	26.0	1.8	0.8
Secondary school, technicum and higher-education students	4,234	20.7	44.4	30.6	1.4	0.9
Skilled workers	8,590	9.2	54.4	30.8	4.0	1.6
Semiskilled workers	5,814	1.8	40.6	34.1	14.3	9.2
Rural mechanics and masters of animal husbandry	5,847	9.4	49.1	35.2	3.2	3.1
Unskilled collective farmers	8,485	4.3	24.3	40.4	16.0	15.0
Housekeepers	3,727	0.6	28.0	18.4	29.4	23.6
Retired people	9,069	2.5	23.6	20.3	25.3	28.3
Invalids, adult dependents	2,080	0.4	13.4	14.9	31.8	39.5
Private farmers, workers at home, clergy	33	......	......	......	39.3	60.7

SOURCE: Tepliakov, *Problemy,* p. 128.

NOTE: There is an apparent inaccuracy in the third occupational category ("Secondary . . . students"), for the percentages total 98 rather than 100.

technology, there are comparatively few religious people. Of 468 tractor drivers, combine operators, truck drivers, and other machine operators, only 1.3% were believers in god, 5% were waverers, 23.1% were nonbelievers, and 70.6% were atheists. In terms of the percentage of nonbelievers, machine operators on collective farms stand alongside highly qualified workers in industrial enterprises" (Tepliakov, "Pobeda," p. 136). Tepliakov continues by citing studies which showed that only 4.7% of 336 machine operators were religious and that the percentage of nonreligious among machine operators varies from 78.5 to 95.8.

With regard to nonrural workers, many Soviet researchers differentiate according to the level of skill of the workers. Thus, table 6.9 shows what Puchkov found to be the distribution of religiousness among four general levels of occupational skill. As a general rule, more religious people are

TABLE 6.8
Some Results of Kolbanovskii's Study of Collective Farms

	Men			Women		
Occupation	Believers	Waverers	Atheists	Believers	Waverers	Atheists
Housekeepers and retired people	40.4%	17.2%	42.4%	77.1%	13.7%	9.2%
Odd jobs	13.4	20.6	66.0	50.3	28.1	21.6
Animal husbandry ..	16.5	28.4	55.1	35.7	28.1	36.2
Construction and office personnel ..	17.9	25.1	57.0	33.3	21.1	45.6
Mechanics, chauffeurs, technicians	3.9	11.8	84.3	......	......	......
Administrative personnel	5.6	4.2	90.2	14.3[a]	14.3[a]	71.4

Source: Kolbanovskii, *Kollektiv*, pp. 239–40.
[a] The indication that 28.6% of female administrative personnel are either believers or waverers is surprisingly high. It may be atypical, in view of the widespread policy of not allowing religious individuals to hold responsible positions.

TABLE 6.9
Results of a Study of Religiousness and Occupational Skills

Category	Atheists	Unbelievers	Indifferent	Waverers	Believers
High qualifications	11.7%	68.0%	11.7%	5.2%	3.4%
Middle qualifications..	9.3	70.5	11.6	3.2	5.4
Low qualifications	5.2	63.0	12.8	10.8	8.2
Unqualified	6.7	45.8	14.8	14.1	18.6

Source: Puchkov, "Vliianie," p. 104.

found at the lower levels of industrial skill. "Materials of the Penza region research testify that among unskilled workers, the level of religiousness is 32%, while among skilled, it is only 7.8%" (Korolev, "Rol'," pp. 133; cf. *Gertsenovskie chteniia* 1 [1970]: 16). In one study of 2,887 believers and waverers Tepliakov discovered that only 267 (9.2%) possessed an occupational skill (*Problemy*, p. 164). Not all researchers discover such extreme results: Andrianov found that 35% of the believers were qualified specialists ("Evoliutsiia," p. 172). Cherniak, referring to believers, concluded that "by level of qualification these are workers of the second and third rank (59.7%), or are employed as assistants and do not possess their own qualifications" (*Formirovanie*, p. 124). Andrianov, at least, thought that there was a trend away from this concentration of believers in the unskilled ranks:

> Six or seven years ago, workers in unskilled labor were dominant in the composition of believers, but with time this situation has changed somewhat. Industrial differentiation causes significant displacement in the professional preparation of the believing element among Soviet citizens, facilitating the stimulation of their varied aids and the broadening of their horizons of life and the development of social activities. Thus, for example, almost 20% of physical laborers who consider themselves believers belong to the category of skilled workers. They carry out technological operations requiring not only industrial practices but also theoretical knowledge. ["Evoliutsiia," p. 172]

The range of occupations included in the unskilled (or, at best, semi-skilled) category is fairly broad, according to Gaidurova: "For example, among believers (Orthodox and sectarian) of the Orenburg region, knitters and darners of down kerchiefs (often at home), seamstresses, stokers, watchmen, yardmen, practical nurses, guides, grooms, and so forth and so on, predominate" ("Zavisimost'," p. 25). Also included in this category are maids, janitors, and other domestics, hospital attendants,[12] storekeepers, some grades of carpenters, draymen for horses, and the like (Ugrinovich, *Filosofskie problemy*, p. 126; Saprykin, "Ateisticheskaia rabota," p. 233; Tul'tseva, "Evoliutsiia," p. 209).

In the highly skilled occupations, religious people are to be found relatively infrequently. "Religious people are fewest of all among workers in intellectual labor. Of 10,647 surveyed representatives of the intelligentsia and white-collar workers without diplomas, religiousness was expressed by 91 people, which constitutes less than 1%. In the composition of believers, representatives of the intelligentsia constitute only 0.6%" (Tepliakov, *Problemy*, p. 129). Ugrinovich discovered that only 4% of the scientific-cultural intelligentsia and that only 3% of the technical-economic intelligentsia were waverers between belief and unbelief; there were no believers in either category (*Vvedenie*, p. 182). Tepliakov discovered only 0.6% believers and 0.9% waverers among intellectuals in the labor force ("Pobeda," p. 135). The percentage of religious workers tends to increase with decreasing levels of qualification.

Of 572 workers questioned who have a higher qualification (metal-work repairmen, automatic machine operators, electricians, machinists, etc.), 56.3% were atheists, 42.1% were indifferent to religion, 1.5% were waverers, and 1% were convinced believers. Consequently, in the group of highly skilled workers, those who are free from religious survivals constitute 97.5%.

Among workers having middle qualifications for work, religiousness is somewhat higher. Among 3,313 lathe operators, planers, molders, and other workers questioned who have [skill] ratings of 3 to 5, 10.9% were waverers, 5.4% were convinced believers, 26.9% were nonreligious, and 56.8% were atheists. As is evident, nonbelievers in this group constitute 83.7%.

Among 1,257 workers at odd jobs and people having low labor skills, 20.4% were atheists, 35.7% were indifferent to religion, 21.7% were waverers, and 22.2% were convinced believers.

As a whole among workers, nonbelievers constitute 78.7%; waverers and believers, 21.3%. [Tepliakov, "Pobeda," pp. 135–36]

Even within occupational subcategories, the level of religiousness is not a constant but is affected by other variables. Thus, for example, a higher rate of religiousness may be found in small industrial enterprises than in large ones.

Another peculiarity in the life-style of believers consists of the fact that those among them who work are employed, not at substantial industrial enterprises, but at small factories, in small workshops of light industry, in domestic service industries and construction organizations, or in cooperative artels.

Thus, in the three congregations and groups we mentioned (Baptists, Pentecostals, and Khlysty) of the Orenburg region, of 86 workers, only a few people were employed at large factories, with the remainder at brickworks, railroad crossings, down-plucking factories, in collective farms, hospitals, sanatoria, etc. . . .

In the Kropotkin congregation of Baptists, altogether there was not a single believer who worked at a large industrial enterprise. The same can be said about fringe members of this congregation. [Gaidurova, "Zavisimost'," p. 24]

A higher incidence of religiousness in small industry than in large was also observable among working youth, although they can be found in the large factories as well (Galitskaia, "K voprosu," p. 394). This is particularly true of the more vigorous sects, such as the Baptist schismatics (Klibanov, *Religioznoe sektantstvo*, p. 114). In addition, the rate of religiousness for a given occupational category varies from unit to unit within the same industrial enterprise (Cherniak, *Formirovanie*, pp. 121–22).

Bichany noticed an exception to the general rule that workers in skilled occupations show a lower incidence of religion. Those employed in high-risk occupations, such as professional drivers or those working in high-rise construction, are much more likely to be religious ("Rol'," p. 109).

With regard to performance, although there have been many reports that religious people are good workers,[13] some Soviet sociological researchers have demonstrated otherwise. Thus, Cherniak found that only 1 to 2.47% of those who make innovative suggestions to improve industrial production were convinced believers (*Formirovanie*, p. 219). The following results were derived from Korolev's study of three factories: "Among rationalizers and inventors, unbelievers constitute 98.8%, while believers only 1.2%, or 3% of the number of all believers and waverers, while among the atheists, rationalizers are 43%. In all, 19.3% of the workers in the factories participate in rationalizing" ("Rol'," p. 133). The differentiation would not appear to be so distinct with regard to productivity. The same study found that 15.2% of the believers, as contrasted with 22.8% of the unbelievers, overfulfilled the norm by 110% (ibid., p. 134). Among the believers, 35.9%, as against 65.9% of the unbelievers, were trying to increase their job qualifications (ibid.). Vasilevskaia discovered that "in 20% of the believers' families there is a front-rank worker in industry. Among the members of such families, 17% are constantly raising their qualifications. Events of social life and matters of industry are observed here with a high degree of interest from the position of citizens of socialist society" ("Opyt," p. 397).

With regard to the various kinds of productivity competitions that are introduced from time to time, Soviet researchers find that the overwhelming majority of the competitors are atheists (Korolev, "Rol'," p. 135). The percentage of such competitors who think that religion is harmful is nearly twice as high as among the general mass of workers (ibid., p. 136). Interestingly enough, a very high proportion of former believers find it expedient to engage in such competitions. "Thus, in 1966/67, among religious people engaged in social production, 7.1% participated in socialist competition and in the movement for a Communist attitude toward work, while among former believers engaged in social production, it was 46%" (Tepliakov, *Problemy*, p. 135). However, in one region, 31% of the working believers participated in competition for a "Communist relation-ship to labor," compared with 55.6% of 10,625 nonbelievers (Tepliakov, "Pobeda," pp. 150, 153). The percentage of believers who join such com-petitions apparently is growing (Andrianov, "Evoliutsiia," p. 177).

The examination of tenure in a particular job yields interesting insights. According to Cherniak, "It is evident that for all the age groups here investigated, there is one and the same trend: the longer the experi-ence of work at one undertaking, the lower the percentage of those who approve a religious world view" (*Formirovanie*, pp. 207–8). The corollary is that religious workers tend to be more transient than the nonreligious. Soviet scholars find two reasons for this, the first being the success of anti-religious influences within the factory.

> Prolonged work of one believing worker or another at a single undertaking permits the collective to know him better and to apply more effective means of atheistic education, thus bringing about his gradual departure from religion. There is also great significance in the fact that for an industrial worker who works for a prolonged period in a single industrial collective, the interests and affairs of the latter acquire primary significance. Therefore, as a rule, among people who have great experience of work at a single undertaking, the portion of those who relate approvingly to religion at a single enterprise is important, as is the preservation of close ties between people who retire and the industrial collective. [Cherniak, *Formirovanie*, pp. 208–9]

Unfortunately, this is a counsel of perfection. The stigma attached to the discovery that there are religious believers within an industrial enter-prise—as well as the fact that the instituting of antireligious measures to counteract their influence is not only nonproductive, it is even, to some Marxists, a questionable effort ideologically—leads many plant managers to seek the easier solution of discharging the religious workers. "It should be noted that the administration and society, as a rule, not only do not undertake measures to retain the workers at one and the same plant, they consciously do not say anything against their discharge and even sometimes facilitate it, since they thus 'free themselves' from the necessity of conduct-ing systematic educational work with them" (Cherniak, *Formirovanie*, p. 209). Thus, the hypothesis that the inverse ratio between the incidence of religious believers and tenure at a given job is due to the working collective's success in winning them away from religion may not be entirely credible in all circumstances.

The second hypothesis to explain this relationship may be more tenable. This hypothesis ascribes the transiency of religious believers, at least in some cases, to their desire to proselyte.[14] "Certain believers often change their place of work in order to extend the possibility of disseminating their faith" (Cherniak, *Formirovanie*, p. 208). Some religious workers, at least, achieve notable results in their attempt to win others to their point of view.

> At the time of the study of the relationship to religion of workers at the "Kauchuk" factory in Moscow, which was organized by the Department of the History and Theory of Atheism of Moscow State University, the attention of the researchers was drawn to one participant's sharp deviation from the average index of the percentage of those who called themselves believers (the portion of those who called themselves believers was two times larger). At first this evoked astonishment: the demographic and social composition of the workers and the level and salary of the work for those assigned to this participant were identical with the demographic and the social composition of the workers and the level and the salary of the work for other participants. Supplementary research discovered that in the group that concerns us, two fanatically inclined Orthodox believers work. The active religious persuasion of comrades at work which they practiced explained the relationship to religion of the workers of this group. [Iablokov, *Metodologicheskie problemy*, p. 130]

Similarly, "at the down-plucking factory of the city of Orenburg during the period of the expedition's work, there was a group of believers from the Khlysty sect; their brigadier was also a sectarian woman" (Gaidurova, "Zavisimost'," p. 26).

To summarize, it would appear that the inverse relationship between religiousness and job tenure would be explained by effective antireligious influences, management's attempt to get rid of religious workers, or the fact that religious workers themselves move on to other jobs to increase the effectiveness of their proselyting after they have accomplished as much as can be done at the given position.

Whatever the causation behind the various parameters, the intensive efforts of Soviet sociologists to discover relationships between religion and occupational categories have yielded fairly consistent results. "Research has shown that the attitude toward religion among workers is in functional connection to the degree of their qualifications" (Tepliakov, "Pobeda," p. 135), and this relationship is inverse: the higher the occupational qualifications, the fewer the believers. The reasons for this inverse relationship have not yet been clarified. Certainly, it is not demonstrable that this is entirely due to such ideological reasoning as was described at the beginning of this section, such as increased social consciousness of the proletariat, and so forth. Just as in the case with education, the question must arise as to whether the active measures of job discrimination that are covertly and indirectly encouraged are not in large measure responsible for this phenomenon. The danger of job discrimination, for example, may be directly responsible for such peculiarities as the virtual absence of workers among those who are willing to register their names on the board that is responsible for the local church (e.g., Gaidurova, "Zavisimost'," p. 17).

In short, while it may be claimed that religious belief tends to prevent the believer from acquiring advanced work skills, it may also be that it is not his religious belief that impedes his advancement but rather that state policy and the society as a whole prohibit his advancement in the ranks of the workers, whatever his skills and qualifications may be.

7

URBANIZATION
AND LIVING CONDITIONS

Sociological study of religion in the USSR has consistently demonstrated that different results will be obtained in urban conditions than will be found in the countryside. As a general rule, the rural population will tend to be more religious than the urban. This is not a new discovery; Soviet observers of religion have long since noted the diminished religiousness of the urban population.[1] Contemporary scholars examine this differential between rural and urban populations, but by and large, they have not drawn sweeping conclusions concerning the urbanization process as yet.

In one fairly large-scale study, Tepliakov discovered that of 21,557 rural inhabitants, 32.7% were religious, while of 15,962 city dwellers, only 15.1% were religious ("Pobeda," p. 134). Similar figures (35% and 15.5%) were obtained by Selivanov in the study of more than 30,000 inhabitants in the Penza region (*Partiinoe rukovodstvo*, p. 46). For Belorussia, the figures were that 39.6% of rural inhabitants were religious, and 15% of urban ones (Duluman, *Sovremennyi veruiushchii*, p. 32). According to Ugrinovich's study,

In village localities of the Orenburg region, for example, there are 16 times more Orthodox congregations and groups than in the cities, while the relationship between urban and rural population of the region is 48:52%. Selective data on the religiousness of the population of the Moscow area also support the conclusion concerning greater religiousness of the rural population. Thus, for example, in the village of Pavshino in 1962, in 109 families, there were 89 believers, i.e., 17.4% of the total number of members of the families observed. At the same time, among 235 working

113

women living in one of the dormitories of a Moscow suburb, those who attend church numbered only 20 (8.5%), and even they attend church in most cases 1 or 2 times a year, on Christmas and Easter.[2] [*Filosofskie problemy,* pp. 118–19]

This is a fairly significant difference, to be sure; but it should be noted that Ugrinovich is comparing dissimilar sorts of data. After surveying religious belief in rural conditions on the basis of what would appear to be family units, he presents data limited to working women who live in dormitories in a city (among whom one might expect a lower incidence of religion than among many other population groups) and examines these women, not on the basis of religious belief, but on the basis of their actual church attendance. This being the case, one would hesitate to draw conclusions as to whether his statement is, in fact, especially instructive.

According to Duluman, "Research demonstrates that in rural localities, believers, as a rule, are more numerous than in cities. In the Ukraine, in the cities and urban settlements, there are only 11% of all the active churches and houses of prayer, but in the villages, 89%" (*Sovremennyi veruiushchii,* p. 32). It should be noted that the imbalance between the number of churches, in which rural churches predominate by a wide margin, and the number of believers, in which the rural predominate but by a margin that is not nearly so wide, is not necessarily as incongruous as it might seem. Because of geographic factors, urban churches can provide services for the needs of a larger number of religious believers than can rural churches, especially those that are in fairly remote locations with low population density. As a case in point, in one region, "despite the fact that all the active [sectarian] preachers come from villages, 47.7% live in the cities and suburbs, 29% in the three district centers closest to [the city of] Kustanaia, and the remaining rural locales have a total of only 5%" (Filimonov, "Sotsiologicheskie issledovaniia," p. 82).

Thus, geographic factors tend to influence the results acquired by Soviet sociological studies. The location of the study, whether in urban or rural environs, must be taken into account. Indeed, even within a given city, the location of the study influences the results. "Thus, within the boundaries of two selected districts of the city of Cherkassy, which are located in the distribution area of a heavy machinery plant, only 4.9% of all people who were questioned called themselves believers. But in two regions located on the periphery of the city, adjoining a recreation zone and the borders of collective farms, 18.4%. As we see, in one and the same city there are regions in which the level of religiousness of the population is different" (Duluman, *Sovremennyi veruiushchii,* p. 33). The same, of course, applies to rural districts, where the actual location that is selected for the study in large measure influences its results.

The increased incidence of religiousness in the rural population is generally reflected in other parameters as well. Thus, the age of rural believers tends to be higher, with the elderly more numerous (e.g., Klibanov, *Religioznoe sektantstvo,* p. 100; Podmazov, "Sovremennoe staroobriadchestvo," p. 182). It should be noted that at least one scholar, Pivovarov, finds this pattern to be reversed, with the urban environment having the higher concentration of the elderly (*Struktura,* pp. 17–18). Even among youth, a higher percentage of religiousness has been found in rural areas (Galitskaia, "K voprosu," p. 394). With regard to gender, there may be more women among rural believers, but the difference is not always very great. "Sociological research testifies that in the Belgorod region, women constitute about 80% of the believers; in the city of Gorky, 78 to 80%; and among Evangelical Christians-Baptists, 84.4%; in the Orlov region, among believers living in rural localities, 86%" (Lisavtsev, "Rukovodiashchaia rol'," pp. 102–3). The educational level in urban areas is usually higher (Gagarin, "Otkhod," p. 186), and the number of nonworkers tends to be lower (Pivovarov, *Struktura,* p. 18).

Some data begin to challenge this accepted pattern of the country's being the bastion of religiousness, whereas city dwellers, by comparison, are less religious. "True, N. S. Zlobin established that the urban congregation of Baptists in Riazan' is more active and greater in numbers than the village [congregations]. His conclusion, as he himself recognizes, is in contradiction with facts established by expeditions in Tambov, Lipetsk, and other regions. But in the last analysis, N. S. Zlobin concludes that a great part of contemporary urban Baptists in the Riazan' congregation are either those who were transferred during the period of collectivization of the inhabitants of the villages or are collective farmers on suburban collective farms" (Gaidurova, "Zavisimost'," p. 26 n.18). Others find that although the percentage of the population who are religious may be lower in the cities, urban believers tend to be much more vehemently religious than are their rural counterparts (Tepliakov, *Problemy,* p. 84). To some degree, this may be explained by the relative isolation of many urban inhabitants, as contrasted with the more intimate atmosphere of village environs: in their isolation, urban believers, according to ideological theory, may be deprived of the influence of the collective, which otherwise might counteract their religiousness (Mering, "Konkretno o samom vazhnom," p. 40).

On close inspection, the difference between urban and rural churches may be less important than might initially be thought. Many of the urban believers are not all that far removed from the countryside; they come from rural families (Gaidurova, "Zavisimost'," p. 26). "At the present time the gravitation of sectarians to the strong congregations and their migration, which is related to it, from rural localities to suburbs of cities and to district and regional centers have become so widespread that some researchers qualify contemporary sectarianism as one of the negative phenomena of urban life. This is absolutely incorrect, because in their own time the basic mass of sectarians were inhabitants of villages and towns" (Klibanov, *Religioznoe sektantstvo*, p. 88). The migration to the city from the countryside has influenced many of the parameters discovered in the study of urban believers (Andrianov, "Evoliutsiia," p. 171).

The problem is complicated still further by the conscious migration of religious believers to the cities for the primary reason of gaining access to a church. Particularly in the aftermath of the antireligious campaign, which caused approximately half of the churches in the USSR to be closed during the early sixties, the fact that there may be an active church in a given city may act as a powerful attraction for the deeply religious among the rural population.

> Cases are known in which Baptists have purposely moved to where there is a more active and systematically working congregation. Thus the Baptist I., who at one time moved from the Krasnoiar district to Chimkent, says, "A brother came to us who said that in Chimkent there is a congregation and a house of prayer [church]. I sold my farm and came to Chimkent. Apparently our brothers and sisters are still arriving from there." Analogous statements are found among a number of Evangelical Christians-Baptists who have moved to Alma-Ata. The large, actively working Alma-Ata congregation attracts them. [Klibanov, *Religioznoe sektantstvo*, p. 87, quoting V. A. Cherniak, Kazakh SSR]

Such migration for religious purposes is fairly commonplace in the USSR; it has a long history among the Russian people (ibid.). Indeed, such migration may be a major reason for the fact that some denominations, such as Baptists[3] and Pentecostals,[4] are predominantly urban in the USSR.

Thus, there are considerable differences, as may be expected, in the results of sociological research conducted in the cities, as against that which is conducted in the countryside. While some of the differences may be predictable, on closer inspection the process of urbanization in the USSR contains so many complexities that a great deal of further study will be needed before a detailed elucidation of the differences between urban and rural religiousness can be derived with any degree of confidence.

Similarly, a great deal of research is still needed with regard to the actual living conditions and the life styles of religious believers. This promises to be a fruitful avenue of research, because whatever the reasons for interest in religious believers, whether from a detached desire to learn or for more utilitarian reasons such as devising more effective antireligious measures, how these people live will structure a great deal of their interior approach to life. Such studies as have been made of the living conditions of religious believers have suggested highly interesting dimensions of the problem of religion in the USSR.

Studies of the income of religious believers yield some fairly surprising results. Initially, one might expect their per capita income to be relatively low, either for ideological reasons—if religion is an attribute of the most backward sectors of the society—or because the society is consciously structured so as to handicap the religious believer. Furthermore, the data indicating that religious believers congregate towards the lower levels of occupational skill, where remuneration is lowest, would suggest that the income of religious believers should also be significantly lower than the norm. To date, studies of income in relation to religious belief have not proven these assumptions to be correct.

The large proportion of nonworking elements among religious people naturally assures that, at least for these people, income will be relatively low. "Inasmuch as when they reach age 55 to 60, the basic mass of the population leaves active work, naturally, for this category, people receive a diminished monetary income. There is no monetary income for housekeepers (and they constitute almost 15% among the religious); monetary income is lacking among the 11.4% of other adult dependents" (Tepliakov, *Problemy,* p. 163). The relatively generous social-security provisions in the USSR tend to ameliorate the income differential between the workers and the nonworkers, but still the higher proportion of the latter among believers tends to reduce the average income. "Analysis of data on the sources and level of material security shows that those who live as dependents of relatives constitute among nonbelievers 5.3%, but among the religious, 24.3%; among nonbelievers, 8.2% live on a pension; while among believers, 27.8%; 45% of the nonbelievers have personal earnings from 50 rubles a month and higher; and only 17.1% of the believers; 72.6% of the believers and waverers live either on income from personal agriculture and receive help from their relatives, or on a pension and earnings up to 30 rubles a month" (Tepliakov, "Pobeda," p. 144). Among workers, however, the distinction between the religious and the nonreligious tends to disappear, at least insofar as income is concerned. Cherniak discovered that the average monthly earnings per family member were 53.13 rubles among those who relate negatively to religion, 48.59 rubles among those

117

who are indifferent, and, surprisingly, 51.19 rubles among those who approve of religion. "All this together substantiates the conclusion that the relationship is very weak between level of real income and such an index of world view as relationship to religion" (*Formirovanie*, p. 191). According to another study, by Andrianov ("Evoliutsiia," p. 172),

a convergence of the level of prosperity both for groups of the religious and for the nonreligious population is definitely revealed. The following table can serve to support this in an obvious degree:

Income per family member[5]	Believers	Unbelievers
225 rubles	17.9%	4.6%
250 rubles	55.6	50.7
275 rubles	14.3	18.1

One of the reasons that has been suggested in order to explain the relative equality of income among religious and nonreligious workers is the willingness of the former to seek overtime work. "As a whole, those who relate approvingly to religion are somewhat less materially secure, and therefore the desire to utilize their free time for overtime work is greater than among unbelievers" (Cherniak, *Formirovanie*, p. 193). While this explanation does not go so far as to suggest the Weber hypothesis, it would be consistent with a suggestion that religion tends to reinforce habits that lead to economic success (e.g., frugality, diligence). Certainly, for religious people to achieve material success regardless of the relative poverty of their starting point is common in history and is even true of some branches, at least, of the Russian Orthodox tradition (Fletcher, *Russian Orthodox Church*, pp. 6–7, 222–24).

Whatever the reason, Soviet researchers cannot be confident that levels of religiousness can be determined simply by observing economic levels, as though there were an inverse relationship between the two. In one rural study, Alekseev says that

the larger part of the researchers of our team assumed that the religiousness of the population of collective farm A will not be high, inasmuch as the economic development of this farm is relatively high in comparison with that of the others. In fact, this was not so. To draw a conclusion from this that the economic circumstances of the collective farms exercise no influence on the formation of the world view of the peasants on collective farms is impermissible. One can only draw the conclusion that its influence is not rectilinear, not mechanical. Apparently, those differences in the level of economic development of the collective farms, and consequently the material well-being of the collective farmers,

exercise less influence on overcoming religiousness and its reproduction than the activity of religious organizations and the local
traditions connected with them. ["Metodika," pp. 147–48]

Living accommodations are a very important consideration in the
USSR (Cherniak, *Formirovanie*, p. 193). For a number of reasons, the
provision of living space remains a neglected sector, and despite the considerable energies that have been devoted to the housing industry in recent
decades, conditions are still overcrowded for most Soviet citizens. Acquisition of adequate accommodations continues to be one of the chief concerns
even among religious people (see above, p. 46).

Different kinds of living space (e.g., a rented room, dormitory, apartment, private house) are associated with different levels of religiousness
(Cherniak, *Formirovanie*, p. 191). This is doubtless because these various
kinds of living arrangements attract different sectors of the population,
as was suggested above in the case of urban women who live in dormitories
as contrasted with the suburbs, where some of the people have private
houses and where a higher degree of religiousness is observable (Aptekman,
"Vitality," p. 373). Within a single type of dwelling, however, the relative
spaciousness (e.g., as measured by the number of square meters per individual) apparently has no relation to the incidence of religiousness. "Groups
of workers distributed by their relationship to religion have nominally the
same structure in the living space provided them. . . . This underlines the
fact that as a whole, the level of material provision in a socialist society does
not show any substantial influence whatsoever on the preservation of religious survivals" (Cherniak, *Formirovanie*, pp. 192–93).

With regard to family situation, a great portion of the religious
believers are women who live alone. In part, this is a natural result of
woman's greater longevity, but to a much larger degree this is one of the
enduring legacies of World War II. A large sector of the Soviet male
population was decimated by the war, and as a result, the number of
women who do not have spouses is very high. "Among believers, one meets
many whose personal lives are irregular. This phenomenon most often
can be explained by the direct or indirect consequences of the late war,
which left millions of widows and deprived many women of the possibility
of raising a family. One should also be aware of the survivals of an incorrect attitude toward family obligations on the part of some men and,
furthermore, of the irresponsible approach of a certain part of the youth
to intimate relations" (Pismanik, "O sostoianii," p. 220). It is not un-
natural for such unfortunates to gravitate toward the consolations of
religion.

Thus, Gur'ianov found that among believers with irregular family situations, 53.6% were believers who lived alone; 17.5% were aged couples who lived alone; 19.5% were mothers who were living with unmarried children; and 9.4% were grandmothers and grandchildren who were living together, with the middle generation, the parents, missing ("Bogi," p. 16). In 1971, according to Tepliakov, widows and single women constituted more than 70% of the Baptist women (*Problemy*, p. 157).

If one considers the Moscow congregation of Evangelical Christians-Baptists, which is the strongest one in the country, among women, who make up 80% of the composition of this congregation, 67% are widows or single. Of the number of Evangelical Christians-Baptists coming to Moscow in 1962 for various reasons from various places, women constituted more than 70%, and of them 73% were widows or single. We studied the composition of the newly baptized in 1962 in this Moscow congregation of Evangelical Christians-Baptists. Among them, women constituted 90%, and of this number, 70% were widows or single. . . . I. L. Lebedeva points out the "effect of difficult individual psychological factors, and first of all of misfortunes in personal life, which lead to the religious congregation." According to data gathered by her, "the percentage of women who resort to the sect as a consequence of these reasons is significantly higher than among men (women—62.5%, men—37.5%)." [Klibanov, *Religioznoe sektantstvo*, pp. 96–97]

Similarly, Pismanik notes that of 645 Orthodox women who had their children baptized, 269 (42%) were the sole parents ("O sostoianii," p. 221).

Pismanik's study of religiousness versus marital status yielded the percentages in table 7.1. Among Baptists, it was found that 67.5% lived in families, 10.5% were single, 20.2% were widowed, and 1.8% were divorced. "About one-third of the families of Baptists do not have a single

TABLE 7.1
RESULTS OF A STUDY OF MARITAL STATUS AND RELIGION

Marital Status	Convinced atheists	Convinced unbelievers	Nonreligious	Wavering believer	Convinced believer
Single	18.9%	41.2%	33.5%	3.9%	2.5%
Married	11.6	41.1	28.7	11.2	7.4
Widowed	2.5	18.6	14.5	32.7	31.7
Divorced	7.4	35.2	26.5	16.3	14.6
Unmarried mothers	4.2	13.9	23.0	36.4	22.5

SOURCE: Tepliakov, *Problemy*, p. 127.

unbelieving member in the family" (Ignatenko, "Opyt," p. 252). In a study of 13,310 believers in the Voronezh region, Tepliakov discovered that 50.8% were married, 6.8% were single, 37.0% were widowed, 2.1% were divorced, and 3.3% were unmarried mothers (*Problemy*, p. 127).

In part because of crowded living conditions, but probably in larger measure due to custom and tradition, the extended family that embraces three or sometimes four generations is not unusual in the Soviet Union. Vasilevskaia differentiated some of the types of family groups found in various categories of religiousness, as shown in table 7.2. "Among families with a religious inclination, families consisting of one married couple with children and without children, with parents of spouses· and other relatives, were dominant. One-third of all believing families related to this group, while these families constituted only 11.2% of all the families questioned." Vasilevskaia further explains that not more than 1.5% of all the families include more than 6 people, while families consisting of a single person constitute 14% ("Opyt," pp. 385, 387).

The significance of the extended family, of course, is to be found in the fact that religion may be transmitted directly from one generation to the second succeeding generation, especially as grandparents interact with their grandchildren.

One may suppose that in the process of the production of religious-

TABLE 7.2
RESULTS OF A STUDY OF RELIGION BY TYPES OF FAMILIES

Composition of family	Position on religion			
	Believer	Waverer	Indifferent	Atheist
Married couple, with or without children	3.8%	2.6%	14.8%	11.5%
Same, with one set of parents or other relatives	33.3	34.2	7.4	16.0
Two or more married couples, with or without children, and with or without one set of spouse's parents or other relatives		10.5	14.8	4.6
One parent with children	14.8	5.3	11.1	9.9
Same, and with one set of parents and other relatives	33.3	21.1	22.2	28.2

SOURCE: Vasilevskaia, "Opyt," p. 386.

ness in the family the main role belongs to the parents of the couple, or other close relatives of the older generation. The truth of this conclusion is indicated by the circumstance that among families of believers, only 3.8% consist of completely separate families (Footnote 1: A completely separate family is the designation for a family consisting of father, mother, and children. In the absence of any of them, the family in its composition becomes incompletely separate), which are most representative in the total mass of families studied—49.8%. This is also observed in families of waverers. Here the married couples with or without children, but with parents of the spouses and other relatives, constitute 34.2%, while the completely separate family—2.6%. [Vasilevskaia, "Opyt," pp. 385–86]

Because of this factor, the attitude and influence of the head of the family, generally the main breadwinner, who is the male parent, not the grandparent, becomes significant. When certain types of religious conduct were observed in families whose heads belonged to four basic religious categories, Vasilevskaia discovered that the percentages of them who were engaged in various kinds of conduct were as shown in table 7.3.

The extended family may have an even larger significance in the religious climate of the USSR than the above data suggest. At least in some of the sectarian denominations, ties of kinship permeate the local congregation. "If one turns to the characteristics of the older forms of Russian sectarianism, it appears that 'sisters' and 'brothers' in the belief among the Molokans and Sabbatarians (to be sure, among the Sabbatarians such forms of address are not used) living in the Tambov, Lipetsk, and Voronezh regions, in the overwhelming majority are brothers and sisters

TABLE 7.3

RESULTS OF A STUDY OF FAMILY PRACTICES AND RELIGION

Religious practices of family	Attitude of head of family			
	Believer	Waverer	Indifferent	Atheist
Keep religious norms of conduct in the family	68.4%	47.4%	22.2%	......%
Have icons	59.3	36.8	11.1	4.5
Attend church	42.6	23.7	7.4	......
Take part in religious rites ..	80.0	33.3	42.0	4.2
Observe religious holidays	81.5	71.0	37.0	9.2
Practice religious education of children in the family	50.0	33.3	5.0	......

SOURCE: Vasilevskaia, "Opyt," p. 392.

122

in the direct sense: brothers, first cousins, second cousins, nephews and nieces, aunts and uncles, etc." (Klibanov, *Religioznoe sektantstvo,* p. 100). Among Seventh Day Adventists, one-quarter of the Kiev congregation, and four-fifths of seven congregations in Moldavia, consisted of people who were related to one another (ibid., p. 99). At various times, as many as three-fourths of the Baptists in Moldavia were found to be related (ibid., pp. 99–100).

From the few studies that have examined the family structure and living conditions of religious people in the USSR, it would appear that a great many interesting and significant insights might be derived from such an approach. However, to date, Soviet researchers have devoted relatively little energy to studying these parameters. A great deal remains to be done before a clear picture of the personal and family environment of religious believers in the Soviet Union can be established.

8

RECREATION
AND SOCIAL ALIENATION

The use of leisure time has attracted some attention from the Soviet sociologists of religion, although purely recreational aspects are much less important to the researchers than certain other ways of utilizing leisure time. In particular, reflecting the deep pedagogical aspirations of Marxism, Soviet researchers are concerned with the use and the effectiveness of the various informational media to which people turn outside of working hours. Since the Soviet state has traditionally invested heavily in using the media to disseminate instruction and propaganda that is designed to mold the Soviet people into productive citizens, the interest of sociology in the use of these media is only natural.

Table 8.1 indicates the percentages of the people who took part in a number of activities, according to Korolev's study in the Penza region. The greater percentage of urban believers who utilize free time for satisfying their religious needs may be explained by the relatively easier accessibility of churches for the urban inhabitants.

Table 8.2 gives data from a Moscow factory indicating percentages of believers and unbelievers who participate in various recreational activities. It should be noted that identical percentages for believers who watch television and those who listen to the radio seem intrinsically improbable; the latter may be a misprint (one would normally expect a higher figure for those who listen to the radio).

Adrianov found that nearly three-fifths of the believers had resorted to the mass media.

Radio, television, newspapers, and magazines have entered into their lives in a big way. Every second believer, one way or another,

125

satisfies his social interests through the system of communication. . . .

Furthermore, many citizens who call themselves believers are not satisfied with channels that are necessary for primary information but increasingly often are turning to more fundamental sources. The fact of the increase in the number of books, including those on socioeconomic themes, at their disposal speaks to this. ["Evoliutsiia," p. 173]

Among the various forms of mass media, the least effective in reaching

TABLE 8.1

A STUDY OF RELIGION AND THE USE OF LEISURE TIME

Uses of free time	Rural		Urban	
	Atheists	Believers	Atheists	Believers
Read books, newspapers, magazines	84.2%	12.8%	74.7%	18.9%
Attend movies, clubs, other cultural institutions	53.8	5.4	66.9	21.3
Sports, tourism, hunting, fishing	13.7	0.4	36.6	3.1
Music, painting, amateur talent	11.0	0.4	12.9	0.9
Technical creation, film, photo	1.3	0.1	10.1	0.2
Satisfying religious needs	......	7.9	......	10.1
Other activities	4.0	14.4	8.7	8.3
Have no free time	5.1	27.6	3.2	14.8

SOURCE: Korolev, "Rol'," p. 150.

TABLE 8.2

A STUDY OF RECREATION AND RELIGION IN MOSCOW

Recreation	Believers	Unbelievers
Go to movies	47.0%	84.4%
Attend theater	18.7	55.0
Visit clubs	20.6	44.5
Watch television	83.5	86.5
Listen to the radio	83.5	94.3
Read artistic literature	17.6	47.4

SOURCE: R. A. Lopatkin, "Vzaimodeistvie sredstv, form i metodov ateisticheskogo vospitaniia" [The interaction of means, forms, and methods of atheistic education], in Voprosy nauchnogo ateizma [Problems of scientific atheism], ed. A. F. Okulov, vol. 9 (Moscow: "Mysl'," 1970), p. 183.

believers would seem to be that favorite of the convinced atheist—and, indeed, of the large army of professional propagandists in the Soviet countryside—the lecture. Bairamov discovered that even though atheistic lectures are often given at factories, only 10% of the workers said that they had attended any of them.[1] In one town, only 5% of the believers attended lectures (of all types), although 48% of the waverers and 58% of the nonbelievers did so (Gaidurova, "Zavisimost'," p. 30). In the Voronezh region, only 2,411 (18.1%) of 13,310 religious believers attended lectures (Tepliakov, *Problemy*, p. 139).[2] In a rural survey of 538 religious believers, Pashkov discovered that 462 of them (85.9%) did not attend lectures, or the cinema, for that matter ("K voprosu," p. 150). Nor is this atypical: in Selivanov's large-scale survey of the Penza region, 85% of the believers and 67% of the unbelievers said that they did not attend antireligious lectures (*Partiinoe rukovodstvo*, p. 126).

With regard to the performing arts, in one study of rural Orthodox believers, Klibanov found that 26.1% attended concerts, 17.0% attended the theater, and nearly 40.5% patronized the cinema ("Veruiushchii," p. 71). A comparison of urban versus rural believers revealed that 18% fewer of the latter attended the movies (Pivovarov, *Struktura*, p. 24). In one town, 72% of the nonbelievers attend the cinema, but only 34% of the waverers and 13% of the believers did so (Gaidurova, "Zavisimost'," p. 30). According to Iablokov's study, only one out of seven believers attended the cinema ("Obshchenie," p. 52). "Sociological research conducted in the village of Rochatnika, Mikhailov district, Riazan region, shows that of 88 believers, 30 regularly attend the cinema. They were given the question: 'What sorts of movies do you like most of all?' and here are the answers received: 4 liked popular science, 18 liked history, 20 liked films about contemporary life, and 21 liked comedies" (Kozhevnikov, "Ateisticheskoe vospitanie," p. 4).

Much more important than cinema from the point of view of ubiquity and the propaganda impact are radio and, more recently, television. Korolev discovered that there were more than 1.5 radio speakers, radio receivers, and television sets per capita among atheists, and even among believers there were more of these instruments than there were believers ("Rol'," p. 146. (A radio speaker is a remote station that carries programing received by a central receiving apparatus which serves an entire district or community.) According to Kolbanovskii's study, 86.3% of the believers listened to the radio, as compared with 94.6% of the waverers and 95.2% of the unbelievers (*Kollektiv*, p. 251). Tepliakov reported that of 2,280 families, 1,954 (85.7%) had radios and radio loudspeakers, and "personal questioning of 13,310 representatives of the religious part of the population showed that of them, . . . 9,675 (72.7%) listened to the radio (*Problemy*, pp. 138–39).[3] A detailed study of ownership yielded the percentages shown in table 8.3. It should be noted that the higher incidence of the possession of radio speakers among the religious people may reflect that they are relatively disadvantaged economically, for this type of equipment, which gives the owner much less freedom of choice than a radio receiver, is the least desirable of the three.

On one collective farm, 92% of the religious believers listened to the radio, and 1 out of 6 watched television (Mamaeva, "O nekotorykh . . . faktorakh," p. 82). Perhaps this farm was atypical in its enjoying such a relative abundance of television when the survey was taken (in the late 60s), for at that time only half as many rural believers watched television as their urban counterparts (Pivovarov, *Struktura*, p. 24). In the Penza region, however, the number of television sets doubled between 1969 and 1972 (Selivanov, *Partiinoe rukovodstvo*, p. 125), so figures concerning the role of television in the use of leisure time may be presumed to be changing rapidly.

Of particular interest to Soviet sociological researchers is the question of whether antireligious programing reaches the believer through these media. According to Tepliakov, "of 13,310 believing citizens of the region surveyed, 9,675 people, or 72.6%, listened to radio programs, and 7,320 people, or more than half of those surveyed, also listened to programs on atheistic themes. Cases are known in which leaders of local religious organizations transcribed radio programs on tape recorders, and then in conversations with fellow believers they tried to refute their content" (*Problemy*,

TABLE 8.3

A STUDY OF RELIGION AND THE OWNERSHIP OF RADIO AND TELEVISION SETS

Population groups	Radio speaker	Radio receiver	Television
All questioned	54.4%	49.3%	38.7%
Nonbelievers:	54.6	56.4	45.4
Convinced atheists	53.5	59.3	51.6
Nonbelievers	53.9	57.7	46.3
Indifferent	58.5	49.2	36.5
Religious:	61.7	35.2	20.4
Waverers	60.1	42.8	27.4
Believers	62.3	31.6	17.2

SOURCE: I. P. Severchuk, "Sredstva massovoi informatsii i propagandy v sisteme ateisticheskogo vospitaniia" [Mass information media and propaganda in the system of atheistic education], in *Voprosy nauchnogo ateizma* [Problems of scientific atheism], ed. A. F. Okulov, vol. 13 (Moscow: "Mysl'," 1972), p. 200.

p. 102). In another study, Rogov found that half of the believers and two-thirds of the waverers were regular listeners to atheistic broadcasts.[4] "A study conducted in the Moletsk district [of Lithuania] a few years ago showed that 4% of the adult population listened to atheistic broadcasts; now this figure has grown to 59%."[5] Severchuk found that 12.6% of the audience for atheistic broadcasts and publications were believers and waverers ("Sredstva," p. 207). It should be noted, however, that he did not specify whether he included in this figure only regular listeners or whether he included anyone who has ever listened to such a broadcast.

Traditionally, the press has played the central role in the Communist Party's persuasion techniques, and vast resources have been allocated to newspapers and magazines since the Party's accession to power in 1917. The press is the key form of communication between the leadership and the populace. Accordingly, it is of great interest to the Soviet researchers to discover the extent to which newspapers and magazines reach religious citizens. There are wide variations in the data regarding this question.

In one study of rural believers in Latvia, Mamaeva discovered that 75% read newspapers ("O nekotorykh . . . faktorakh," p. 82). According to another study, 60% of the families of urban believers were regular subscribers to newspapers and magazines (Vasilevskaia, "Opyt," p. 397). In a study of 2,280 families in which all the adults were religious, Tepliakov found that 1,154 (50.6%) subscribed to newspapers and magazines, and although of 13,310 believers only 2,331 (17.5%) were found to read newspapers and magazines themselves, another 5,021 (37.7%) listened when such publications were read aloud—thus 7,352, or 55.2%, had access to the press (*Problemy*, p. 138).[6] Not all researchers have found such widespread utilization of the press among believers. According to Korolev's study, only 31% of the believers read newspapers and journals, although 54.5% of the waverers did so ("Rol'," p. 146; cf. Selivanov, *Partiinoe rukovodstvo*, pp. 13–14). Similarly, in one village, only 16% of the believers read newspapers, but 65% of the waverers did so (Gaidurova, "Zavisimost'," p. 30). According to Pashkov, "It is enough to state that of 538 believers who gave an answer to the question about education, 71.4% are semi-literate and do not read newspapers or books" ("K voprosu," p. 150). Not unexpectedly, there are likely to be significant differences in this regard between the Orthodox and the denominations that traditionally have emphasized Bible reading by individuals and, hence, literacy. "Thus, according to data collected by Belorussian researchers, among the Orthodox, 19.4% read newspapers and magazines, but among Baptists, 62.7%. Furthermore, the number of readers of religious literature constitute among them 68.7%, which is only a little bit more than those who follow newspapers. In practice, this means that almost all literate Baptists read newspapers and magazines" (Klibanov, "Veruiushchii," p. 71).

The number of religious people who have recourse to books as one of their forms of recreation is, naturally, a great deal smaller than the number who utilize the daily and periodical press. Considerable differences are found between urban and rural believers; Pivovarov found that only one-fourth as many of the latter read works of literature (*Struktura*, p. 24). In one rural town, 11% of the believers and 41% of the waverers, compared to 68% of the nonbelievers, read works of literature (Gaidurova, "Zavisimost'," p. 30). At the other end of the spectrum, Andrianov discovered that only 16% of the believers who were surveyed did not own any personal books; 14.5% had up to 10 books, 44.0% owned 10 to 50 books, 16.5% owned 50 to 100, and 10% owned more than 100 books ("Evoliutsiia," p. 174). Surely these figures are atypical; in the Penza region, by way of contrast, only 3.7% of the believers and 6.5% of the waverers owned a personal library, although 45.7% of the atheists, 22.8% of the nonbelievers, and 14.7% of the indifferent also owned books (Severchuk, "Sredstva," p. 200). It should be noted, however, that among 280 students who had formerly been religious, 80% cited the influence of books in helping them to overcome their religious views.[7]

Conversely, some researchers express doubt about how much weight should be attached to such data. "Aside from quantitative analysis, these data yield very little and insignificant information, for one may have books and not read them, one may take magazines but read only narrowly prescribed subjects in them, one may watch television only for sports programs, one may have a radio but not listen to broadcasts, etc." (Baltanov, *Sotsiologicheskie problemy*, p. 138).

Broad variations are also found with regard to the use of public library facilities. In a study of 2,280 religious families, Tepliakov discovered that "in 703 of them there was a home library, and in 389 there were books from the public library; i.e., there were books in the homes of almost 48% of the religious families" (*Problemy*, p. 138). Vasilevskaia found that 37% of the believers were constant readers at libraries ("Opyt," p. 397), while Mamaeva found that one-third of the believers in the collective farms borrow library books ("O nekotorykh . . . faktorakh," p. 82). According to Korolev, 10.9% of the believers surveyed, 23.3% of the waverers, and 59.7% of the atheists availed themselves of the public libraries ("Rol'," p. 146). Similarly, Selivanov found that 11% of the believers used the library (*Partiinoe rukovodstvo*, pp. 13–14).

Very little information has been gathered regarding the use of religious literature. According to Ukrainian researchers, sermons are the source of religious knowledge for two-thirds of contemporary believers, although religious literature is also used by some of them (Iablokov, *Metodologiche-skie problemy*, p. 129). According to Duluman's report,

> In the research we conducted, we questioned 675 believers. Their answers to the questions presented were as follows:
> 1. Does the believer read religious literature?
>   a. Reads only the Bible and prayer book—126 people
>   b. Reads various religious literature—157
>   c. Reads no religious literature—355
>   d. Unclear—37. [*Sovremennyi veruiushchii*, p. 107]

Thus, 42% of these believers utilize religious literature, which indicates that it occupies a fairly important place—quite possibly a more important one than secular books—in their lives. Religious literature has a surprising impact among the youth. In a 1972 survey of students, in which religious-ness was typically found to be virtually nonexistent, Ulybin discovered that 24.8% of these students had nevertheless read the Scriptures at one time or another ("Iz opyta," p. 103).[8] According to Galitskaia's study,

> Research conducted by the Brest branch [of the Institute of Scientific Atheism] showed that 11.5% of the young people questioned are acquainted with religious literature. No small part of religious literature is especially intended for youth, for example, *Youth Edition of the Herald of Salvation, Kindergarten, Childhood Friend, Children's Hymns, Friend, Prodigal Son, Biblical Conversations with Children,* and other literature disseminated in manuscript form, and also theological dissertations that have a special audi-ence—namely, the younger generation—pamphlets, compositions addressed to children, and prayers. The compositions of the ideal-ist philosophers M. Berdiaev, V. Solov'ev, and S. Bulgakov, which, according to the opinion of theologians, excellently perform an evangelizing function, are also vigorously used as propaganda among youth. ["Izuchenie," p. 67]

One reason for religious literature's not playing a larger role in the free time of believers is that for a very large proportion of the religious people in the USSR, such literature is virtually unobtainable. Religious literature has been vigorously proscribed for a half-century, and the few religious journals that are permitted to appear in very small numbers, together with the extremely limited editions of Scriptures and other reli-gious literature that have appeared from time to time, are utterly inade-quate. Compared with the vast need for religious literature, to all intents and purposes these provisions have no effect whatsoever in alleviating the problem. It is significant that all of the titles listed above are produced illegally and are circulated from hand to hand and that no works of the three theologians are printed in the Soviet Union; if they are available at all, it is only because copies have been illegally smuggled into the country and copied by hand (a process known as *samizdat* or "self-publishing"). Were it not for this almost insuperable problem of the lack of religious literature, such materials would certainly play a much larger role in the leisure-time activities of religious believers in the USSR.

One option for the use of free time is church attendance or other forms of worship, which, broadly speaking, sometimes quite accurately, can be considered recreational. Most Soviet researchers tend to ignore this option when they study the use of free time among religious people. Nevertheless, Gaidurova notes that religious believers are aware of the recreational aspects of religious meetings: "They emphasize that prayer meetings are nothing other than hospitality, tea, and conversations with people you are close to, i.e., a form of recreation, amusement, and fulfillment of intellectual needs which is satisfying for them" ("Zavisimost'," p. 20). Puchkov discovered that among workers "only 10 people of 1,793 surveyed wanted to utilize free time for satisfying religious needs" ("Vliianie," p. 113). Such a low figure might be due to the fact that, given the tension of the times, many religious people may have considered that it would be wiser not to volunteer information about this way of using free time. Furthermore, with the exception of activities that can take place in a legally functioning church—if one is available at all—gatherings for religious fellowship are technically illegal, and hence Soviet researchers would be unlikely to achieve great success in attempting to elucidate this area. In large measure this may explain why such a use of free time generally does not appear at all in many Soviet studies of recreational patterns among religious believers.

Finally, there remains one form of recreation that is widely indulged in but appears only very rarely in the research data. Gusev refers in passing to the problem of alcoholism; but his only comment is that thanks to medical and other lectures against drunkenness in one locale, observance of the major Christian festivals has fallen off ("Konkretnost'," pp. 26–27).

Turning from recreational patterns to the larger topic of social alienation among religious believers, Soviet researchers have found a comparatively fruitful area of study. Though the concept seldom receives a rigorous definition, it is generally used to indicate either a feeling of estrangement from normative Soviet social life or a failure to participate in society's activities. In seeking to delineate the degree and directions of this alienation from society, Soviet researchers have devised a number of approaches that yield useful insights into the problem.

One index of alienation is the attitude of the religious believer towards people who do not share his faith. Particularly under Soviet conditions, where militant atheism receives official support and the treatment that is meted out to believers is discriminatory at best and often includes the sternest measures, the believer might well feel that his interests will be best served if he avoids contact with the rest of society. Adding to such motivation is the centuries-long tradition of many of the more extreme religious groups of cutting themselves off completely from society. Even among the Baptists, there are elements in their doctrine and tradition that admonish believers to shun the sinful world.

> But even these people are far from uniform in the degree of their social contacts. Among them one may find "nonaccepters," fanatics whose relationship to their surroundings is not simply negative but often hostile. Among "those with no contacts," this group constitutes approximately one-tenth, while among Baptists in general, 6.6%. As regards the remaining "noncontactors," they can be divided into two subgroups, the one (46.2% of the Baptists as a whole) is characterized both by the presence of unbelieving members of the family and by relationships, albeit not close, with neighbors and fellow workers. The other subgroup has a greater number of unbelievers in the composition of the family and broader and more intensive relations with comrades at work and with neighbors in the place of residence. However, in both groups, prejudice against unbelievers exists. [Klibanov, "Veruiushchii," p. 72]

According to two other studies, 6.7% of the Baptists avoid all contact with unbelievers; 60.4% are ambivalent towards them; and for 23.9%, religion has no relevance to their relations with the nonreligious (Ignatenko, "Opyt," pp. 257–58; Ugrinovich, *Vvedenie*, pp. 220–21).

As a rule, the Russian Orthodox tend to be less alienated from society than the Baptists. Andrianov found that 57% of the Orthodox, as compared with 42% of the Baptists, were tolerant of other faiths, and 52% of the Orthodox and only 31% of the Baptists were willing to evaluate atheists positively ("Evoliutsiia," p. 179). To the question "Can an unbeliever be moral?" 9.4% among the Orthodox and 28.9% among the Baptists answered no, 67.7% of the Orthodox and 60% of the Baptists answered yes, and the remainder either gave no answer or claimed ignorance (Iablokov, "Transformatsiia," p. 131).

Several researchers have found a rather high degree of tolerance among believers. "To the question of how a person relates to other religions, only 20% of the believers we questioned gave a negative answer" (Sytenko, "O nravstvennom oblike," p. 122). In Vasilevskaia's study, the responses of waverers gave almost exactly the same results: 38% related to atheism with good will, and 42.5% were indifferent ("Opyt," p. 399). Pismanik found that

> among believers, general mutual labor with unbelievers removes the fixed idea of the "sinfulness" of unbelievers. It is significant that 73.6% of those studied named both believers and unbelievers among their friends and close friends. This entire group did not accept the idea of the "uncleanness" of atheists, related to them in a friendly way, and even included them in their "small groups." Some alienation toward atheists was expressed by 21.8% of the believers, and only 4.6% of the believers try insofar as possible to refrain from "sinful" contact with atheists.[9]

Other researchers have found that this form of alienation from society is practically nonexistent among the Orthodox; the only possible index is that the Orthodox tend to have a narrower range of social contacts than have unbelievers (Klibanov, "Veruiushchii," p. 72).

Using a more concrete approach to this form of social alienation, Sytenko asked members of advanced work brigades whether they would help others at work or not. Among the believers, 76.4% answered affirmatively and 14.8% negatively; the figures for waverers were 76.6% and 6.6%, respectively, the remainder in both groups answered ambiguously ("O nravstvennom oblike," p. 126).

A second approach to the question of social alienation is simply to ask believers about their view of society's progress. Among Baptists, "for example, only 6.3% of the believers admit moral progress in our society, while at the same time, material and technological progress is evident to the overwhelming majority (81.5%) (Ignatenko, "Opyt," p. 256). In another project, only 3% expressed dissatisfaction with the results of the scientific, technological, and cultural progress of society (Sytenko, "O nravstvennom oblike," p. 123).

The social alienation of religious believers is reflected most vividly in studies of attitudes toward civic activities and obligations. Cherniak found that "those who fulfill social commissions, as a rule, relate negatively to religion, while among them, of course, there may also be those who do not fulfill social commissions" (*Formirovanie*, p. 269). Korolev found that only 3.6% of the total number of participants in civic activities were believers ("Rol'," p. 140).

Studies of believers generally reveal that only a very small portion of the believers are willing to undertake civic activities. Tepliakov found that only 0.36% of the believers fulfilled social obligations (*Problemy*, p. 135). Of 198 believers, only 7 (3.5%) took an active part in such groups as apartment-house committees, trade unions, and the like (Iablokov, "Obshchenie," p. 51). Ugrinovich discovered that "according to research data, among the inhabitants of the city who were surveyed, 60% of the nonbelievers and 10% of the believers take part in socio-political activities; among the rural inhabitants, 66% and 8%, respectively" (*Vvedenie*, p. 214). Andrianov found that the percentage of believers who were active in civic affairs increased from 10% in 1965 to 14% in 1970 ("Evoliutsiia," p. 180). Among the Orthodox, "only 11% of the parents who have baptized their children take a systematic part in civic activity" (Aptekman, "Vitality," pp. 369–70). In Belorussia, 20% of the Orthodox but only 10.5% of the Baptists were active in public affairs (Klibanov, "Veruiushchii," p. 72). "Only 10.5% of those studied fulfill any sort of social commission. In this regard, what Baptists think about their social obligations is also typical. Only 3.4% stated their obligations to the collective and to society at all fully and consciously; 39.9% reduced them to some single obligation, basically of a moral character ('to work, to be peaceable, to be gentle'); 8.8% were not able to name a single social obligation of a person, while 1.4% categorically did not accept for themselves any sort of obligation towards society" (Ignatenko, "Opyt," p. 262). Another study yielded the figures shown in table 8.4 regarding attitudes toward civic obligations.

Not all studies are in agreement that believers are so uniform in their avoidance of civic activities. "In our research, 11.8% of the believers who do not participate in social work are motivated to this by the fact that it is 'sinful' to do so" (Pismanik, "Religioznaia," p. 151); presumably, the remainder do not share this theological hostility toward public affairs. In one case, 23.4% of the believers who were questioned remarked that civic organizations had failed to ask them to assume responsibilities (Korolev, "Rol'," p. 143). And in some types of public activity, religious believers, along with all other strata in Soviet society, display a high degree of fulfillment of civic duty: "For example, about 80% of those approached by our questionnaire were direct or indirect participants in protests directed against American aggression in various regions of the world. Every third believer, by voluntary initiative, works gratis for part of his free time in the aid of Vietnam. Almost all religious Soviet citizens participate in Communist Saturdays and other social measures" (Andrianov, "Evoliutsiia," p. 178).

TABLE 8.4
RESULTS OF A STUDY OF MOTIVES REGARDING RELIGIOUS ATTITUDES

Motives	Atheists	Unbelievers	Indifferent	Waverers	Believers
Develops feeling of collectivism	25.8%	32.8%	36.2%	23.5%	31.8%
I receive moral satisfaction	25.8	20.8	19.0	29.4	22.7
Helps to master habits of leadership by social affairs	25.8	19.9	15.5	11.8	9.1
Broadens intellectual interests	12.9	11.2	6.9	17.6	13.1
Fulfills obligations without wanting to	8.1	11.2	17.2	5.9	9.1
Other opinions	1.6	4.1	5.2	11.8	13.7

SOURCE: Korolev, "Rol'," p. 140.
NOTE: It seems curious, at best, that identical percentages of atheists selected each one of the first three options. The percentages given for the believers total only 99.5%.

Another approach to the question of alienation is the question of where one turns in time of trouble. "Answers to the question: 'If the necessity should arise for you, to whom would you go for advice?' give evidence of the changes in the rural worker's views on authority. They resolved to turn for advice first of all, not to the priest or other clergy, but to agitators, propagandists, teachers, and people who are wise in life's experience. And only individuals among those questioned, 15% of the people in all, would tolerate advice from churchmen" (Safronov, "Chto," p. 68). Andrianov's somewhat more exact study showed that in time of trouble, 30.2% turn to Soviet organizations, 32.5% seek the help of a collective, 15.2% rely only on themselves, and 22.1% consider God to be their sole defender ("Evoliutsiia," p. 181). One curious study was conducted among workers at a factory employing only blind people. "To the question: 'To whom do you turn in life's difficult moments?' the answers were thus: 41% work through their difficulties themselves, 21% turn to friends and relatives for help. And only 1.5% of the workers seek consolation in religion. These, as a rule, are elderly people, who were brought up in a religious spirit."[10] It might be well, however, to reserve judgment on such data, for this approach of asking individuals to whom they would turn in time of crisis would seem to be open to influence by the researcher rather more than some other approaches. To a considerable degree, the answers might depend on precisely how the question is phrased and what the circumstances and environment were in which the question was asked.

Another approach to the problem of social alienation, which was utilized by at least one research project, was to measure the degree of job satisfaction. Thus, among deeply religious workers at two factories, attitudes ranged from intense satisfaction with their work (22–27%), through satisfaction (52–68%), to intense dissatisfaction (0–2%). Unfortunately, this approach did not prove to be very instructive, for the percentages in each category of job satisfaction among those who were negative towards religion contain only insignificant variations from the results obtained among believers (+7 to —6 percentage points) (Cherniak, *Formirovanie*, p. 178).

It would seem to have been demonstrated fairly conclusively, at least with regard to data presented in Soviet sociological research, that a degree of alienation from society is present among religious believers in the USSR. It is difficult, perhaps even impossible, to measure this aspect of the religious situation. However, such approaches as the above provide insights suggesting that, at least under contemporary conditions, religious believers do not tend to fit comfortably into their society in every respect. At best, more religious believers will tend to be indifferent to society than will be involved in it (Klibanov, "Veruiushchii," pp. 72–73). How much of this social alienation is due to tensions caused by Soviet religious policy is still unclear; however, according to Tepliakov, 90% of the believers "do not know or poorly understand" that policy (*Problemy*, p. 76).

By and large, it would not seem that the alienation is necessarily a desideratum of the individual who chooses religion. "Research has shown that the absolute majority of people who join themselves to the religious are honorable Soviet people. They are, in the main, representatives of the older generation, who have passed through the rich school of life. Many of the believers, in their time, did a sufficient amount of work, and then they began to receive a pension. Those who are able, however, as a rule work conscientiously" (ibid., p. 37). In large measure, what appears to be alienation against society may primarily be due to interests in other matters, rather than to a hostile attitude on the part of the believer. "Our research shows that it is not so much direct prohibition as the religious world view that hinders taking an interest in books, theaters, cinemas" (Bograd, "Opyt," p. 138). The question of alienation from society is a complex matter, and does not yield to simple answers and approaches. "In our literature, it is usually shown that the religious convictions of believers prevent them from participating in social life. This is true. But one should also take into account other circumstances that prevent it. First of all is the fact that work in society is work with people, requiring special customs, abilities, and a particular minimum education. A person acquires this not only in school and in the family but most of all in production. Since many believers do not participate in social labor, naturally the possibility for conducting social intercourse is very limited among them" (Gaidurova, "Zavisimost'," p. 21 n.13).

In summary, it is clear that many religious people are in one degree or another alienated from society. It would be strange if it were otherwise, in view of the tensions of the times. Soviet scholarship has made a good beginning at exploring this phenomenon, using imaginative approaches and gaining interesting insights into many aspects of the alienation of religious believers. However, a great deal of work remains to be done, both in ascertaining the extent of social alienation among the religious population of the USSR and in defining and determining its characteristics and the causes for it.

9

CONVERSION AND
RELIGIOUS EDUCATION

Soviet researchers are naturally concerned with the question of how an individual becomes religious. This is a difficult question, because of the intensely personal nature of religious faith; ultimately, there is an unlimited variety of reasons that may induce the individual to accept the religious way of life. To attempt to classify these motivations is a formidable task. "But nevertheless, to differentiate various groups of believers according to the motives of religiousness is fully verified. It makes it possible to differentiate believers, and this, in its turn, has great significance for carrying out concrete work for atheistic education" (Duluman, *Sovremennyi veruiushchii*, p. 82).

It should be noted that Soviet sociologists may not be especially well equipped to explore the problem of how and why an individual becomes religious. The extreme, indeed, often exclusive, emphasis of the Marxist ideology on society and social causation may blind the researchers to other factors, if any, which may be operating. Even without any appeal to the supernatural, there are many psychological, personal, and other states of the mind which a pure appeal to the environment finds difficult to handle. Nevertheless, some, at least, of the researchers adamantly insist on social causation exclusively: "We think that the attempt to find even one individual whose religiousness does not derive from his living conditions is equivalent to trying to discover a result without a cause" (Nikitin, "Dialektika," p. 54). In a way, this seems odd, for much of the Soviet effort against religion concentrates, not on changing the environment, but on propaganda, which is precisely an appeal to the mind and the emotions.

Most studies agree that parental influence looms large among the influences that lead people to religion. At two factories, 39.7% and 22.7%

of the believing workers cited parental influence; other motivations were misfortunes, loneliness, difficulties, visions, clerical influence, and, finally, religious literature. "One should note that for each of these conditions, there were not more than 2 to 6% of the given group (Cherniak, *Formirovanie*, p. 321).

Unfortunately, the more precise the differentiation, the more likely it is that primitive, simplistic conclusions will be reached by the researchers.

We studied 1,443 people—675 members of religious congregations and 768 former believers. It was established that the determining influence on their religiousness was:
1. Brought up in a religious family: 1,194 (82.7%)
2. Preachers of religion: 62 (4.2%)
3. Came to faith in god by himself: 165 (11.6%)
4. Not clear: 22 (1.5%). [Duluman, *Sovremennyi veruiushchii*, p. 82; the percentages are not precise]

If one makes such sharp distinctions as these, there is a real risk of misinterpreting the complexity of religious phenomena. When the authors conclude confidently that "the concrete social research we conducted shows that only 4.2% of the believers surveyed became members of religious congregations because of the influence of some preacher or other of religion" (ibid., p. 87), certainly a simplistic approach to the influence of the clergy is implied. A more realistic assessment might at least entertain the hypothesis that the influence of the clergy is a great deal more pervasive, operating in many cases even where it is not identified as the sole or determinative influence.

Other attempts to probe the factors leading to conversion are no less perplexing. "According to data from a study conducted in the Sumskoi region of the Ukraine, 77% of the Orthodox believers became religious as a result of religious education in childhood, 25% as a result of missionary and charitable activity of sectarians, and 6% under the influence of religious literature" (Kobetskii, *Sotsiologicheskoe izuchenii*, p. 32). Surely there is room for some doubt concerning this report (other than that the percentages total 108; this may indicate multiple answers on the part of some respondents). First and most astonishing is the report that proselyting activity by sectarians led people to Orthodoxy, for while ecumenism may be laudable, very few sectarians in the USSR proselyte for Orthodoxy. Second is that religious literature led 6% to religion; in view of the extreme dearth of religious literature in the USSR, this is a surprising figure.

Among the 768 former believers in the study mentioned above, 197 had turned to religion in search of truth or answers to questions; 168 had sought emotional release, peace, and joy; and 403 had claimed that no personal initiative had motivated their acceptance of religion (Kobetskii, *Sotsiologicheskoe izuchenii*, p. 92). The last figure probably refers to those who were religious from earliest childhood, although it might indicate that some of these former believers felt it prudent to be less than candid about their earlier errors. The same scholars note, however, that "according to the testimony of the Atheism Department of the Institute of Philosophy of the Ukrainian Academy of Sciences, which has conducted work studying sectarian believers, about 60% of those surveyed stated that religion attracts them in its moral-ethical aspect" (ibid., p. 78). This seems intrinsically more credible than Sofronov's study, which suggested that some people are religious for materialistic reasons and that they sever their church relationships as soon as they begin to receive government pensions ("Ateisticheskoe vospitanie," pp. 239–40). A detailed analysis of motivations for religious profession may be found in table 9.1.

One of the most common reasons cited for acceptance of religion is difficulty encountered along life's way (Mamaeva, "O nekotorykh . . . faktorakh," p. 81). While it may be true that such difficulties can work in either direction, often facilitating faith but in some cases undermining it (Duluman, *Sovremennyi veruiushchii*, p. 90), a large percentage of religious believers were impelled to seek consolation in religion because of such difficulties. "As research conducted among members of the Baptist sect of the city of Anapa showed, 19% cited 'the need for comfort, personal adversities' as reasons that led them to religion" (Galitskaia, "Izuchenie," p. 60; cf. Galitskaia, "K voprosu," p. 403).

The devastation suffered during World War II led many to religion. "One of the reasons for revival of religious attitudes was the burdens of the war with Hitler Germany. In 187 families (of 407) there are people who either became invalids of the war or who lost very close people in the war" (Tepliakov, "Sostoianie," p. 35). Among women, the loss of their husband or of children was often "the fatal fact determining their final choice between god and 'the world'" (Klibanov, *Religioznoe sektantstvo*, p. 96). According to one study, published by Pismanik in 1969, "The following typical answers were received: 'My husband left me. After some time I trusted another man, but he also dropped me. My faith in people was shaken. I suffered.' (P.N., born 1915, housekeeper). 'If I did not receive consolation at the prayer meeting, then I would not have come here. And where else can you receive it? four children, my husband dropped me.' (V., born 1923, housekeeper)" ("O sostoianii," p. 220). The

TABLE 9.1

RESULTS OF A STUDY OF MOTIVES FOR RELIGIOUSNESS

Motives for religiousness	No. of believers	Age			Education		
		To 30	30-60	Over 60	None	1-4 years	5-8 years
Religion satisfies questions of the mind	5	....	3	2	....	4	1
Religion promises salvation of the soul	18	....	6	12	4	11	3
Religion gives emotional peace and delight	14	1	7	6	3	7	4
Religion is the path to moral maturity	5	....	2	3	....	5	....
Believe "just in case"	10	....	5	5	4	6	....
Appeal to tradition	44	....	22	22	9	27	8
Totals	96	1	45	50	20	60	16

SOURCE: Duluman, *Sovremennyi veruiushchii*, p. 72.

fact remains, of course, that the religious congregations do provide very real aid and mutual support for such unfortunate people (Sukhov, *Religiia*, p. 112).

Many of the believers returned to religion only later in life. "Of the believers, 23% said that 15 to 25 years ago they did not pray at home, they did not go to church, and they did not fulfill the rites. Therefore, externally these are as it were 'returnees' into the bosom of the church; but in substance? Conversations with them, first of all, emphasized that they had considered themselves more or less godless, and at one time they even broke with the faith; but in fact, they were not completely liberated from religious impressions. In any case, many of such 'unbelievers' returned to contact with the church with the grief of war years, and others with their retirement from laboring activities" (Gur'ianov, "Bogi," p. 16). This phenomenon may serve to support the observation made earlier, that at least in Orthodoxy, religion's persuasiveness increases after the individual has reached middle age. It also suggests the pervasive, enduring influence of religious attitudes that have been acquired during childhood.

(TABLE 9.1—*continued*)

Denomination		Degree of Religiousness			Attends Church		
Ortho-dox	Bap-tist	Convinced believer	Habitual believer	Wavering believer	Regularly	Rarely	Never
2	3	2	3	....	2	2	1
3	15	12	4	2	12	5	1
7	7	4	6	4	8	5	1
1	4	4	1	....	4	1	....
6	4	5	3	2	5	5	....
34	10	2	6	36	2	28	14
53	43	29	23	44	33	46	17

Among the Baptists, for example, the great majority apparently had become religious early in life, whether or not they were recent converts to the denomination. "In our case, only 51 contemporary Baptists, of 107 believers surveyed, are offspring of Baptist families. The remaining 56 came to the sect from the outside. Incidentally, the most believers of all convert to the Baptists from Orthodoxy. The entry into a Baptist congregation of people who formerly did not profess any religion, as became clear in the course of conversations with believers, is exceedingly rare" (Duluman, *Sovremennyi veruiushchii,* p. 86). "Analysis of the former religious profession of Baptists is interesting: 74.6% in the past were Orthodox, 19.1% came out of Baptist families, and only 4.5% had not in the past experienced religious influence" (Ignatenko, "Opyt," p. 252). According to Klibanov's study, 38.8% of the Ukrainian sectarians had formerly been Orthodox, 8.2% had been Catholics, 22.5% had been Uniates, 1.2% had been Reformed, and 4.1% had belonged to other sects (*Religioznoe sektantstvo,* p. 78). In many cases, those who came from families that were already within the religious group are the primary source for younger believers: converts from Orthodoxy or other religions tend to be elderly (ibid.).

Some researchers have found that a very high proportion of the believers had become religious during childhood. Galitskaia, in a study in Uzbekistan, concluded that 85% of the contemporary believers had been believers since childhood ("Izuchenie," p. 69). According to Tepliakov, 80% of the believers gave continuous religious education to their children (*Problemy*, p. 40), and "from detailed conversations with those who were revealed to be believers, it was established that 93% of them became such in childhood, under the influence of adult members of the family who were believers (Lisavtsev, "Rukovodiashchaia rol'," p. 103; Tepliakov, "Pobeda," p. 139). According to one study, "of the 1,443 surveyed, 1,145 (79.3%) began to believe in god in early childhood, 153 (10.6%) in youth, 139 (9.6%) as adults, and only 6 (0.4%) in old age. Thus, 90 percent of those surveyed (1,298 of 1,443)—regardless of whether in their youth they defied it with atheism or for their entire life were humble sheep in the flock of Christ—were already religious people before attaining maturity" (Duluman, "Vosproizvodstvo," p. 12).[1] In Latvia, among 280 students who had renounced religion, 96% cited the influence of parents and other adults in explaining their earlier adherence to the faith (Ignatenko, "Opyt," p. 267). In the Voronezh region, "97.7% of contemporary believers acquired their religiousness precisely in the family" (Tepliakov, "Sotsial'nye issledovaniia," p. 111).

A study of two Baptist churches in Alma-Ata yielded some strange results. In determining what percentage of adults who were baptized each year had come from families that were already in the church, the results shown in table 9.2 were acquired. It will be noted that in the second church in 1961, more than three-quarters of the newly baptized were from families that were already in the church, while thereafter the percentage dropped back to its earlier figure. In the first church, however, there was a radical decline in the number of people who had been brought up in the church who received the rite of baptism. This is almost certainly due to the "Letter of Instructions," mentioned earlier, in which the denomina-

TABLE 9.2
PERCENTAGES OF ADULTS BEING BAPTIZED WHO CAME FROM CHURCH FAMILIES

Congregation	1959	1960	1961	1962	1963
First church	70.5%	90.0%	76.0%	18.0%	31.0%
Second church	54.0	40.0	76.0	54.0	53.0

SOURCE: Klibanov, *Religioznoe sektantstvo*, p. 88.

tional headquarters in Moscow ordered that the minimum age for baptism be raised from 18 to 30. In the case of the first church, at least, compliance with this order would account for the adrupt diminution in the number of progeny of church families who were baptized.

Naturally, this pattern of replenishing the ranks from the offspring of religious families is not confined to the Baptists; it obtains in other groups as well (Klibanov, *Religioznoe sektantstvo*, p. 99). The inevitability that religion will be transmitted to the children is evident when one considers that approximately half of the urban and one-third of the rural children have baby-sitters during the day because their parents work (Pivovarov, *Struktura*, p. 63). Traditionally, grandmothers serve as baby-sitters, and in view of the high incidence of believers among elderly women, it is only natural that young children should acquire religiousness from their grandparents. And it is significant, perhaps, that at least in the Penza survey, "about half of those questioned in the region stated that there are believing relatives in their families" (Selivanov, *Partiinoe rukovodstvo*, p. 51).

It should not be inferred that religious influence during childhood, which is fairly ubiquitous in Soviet society, necessarily has a lasting effect. Galitskaia's study showed that "67.6% of the young people who call themselves atheists were brought up in families where the parents are believers" and that only approximately 1 in 10 children from believing families continue to be religious ("Izuchenie," p. 70).

Religious upbringing in the home, however, remains the primary means by which individuals become religious. In one study of 1,443 religious believers, 1,298, or 90%, acquired their religiousness before they were 18 years old (Duluman, *Sovremennyi veruiushchii*, p. 93). In another study, "for the overwhelming majority (93%) of the number of believers surveyed, religious views were acquired in childhood as a result of education in the family" (Tepliakov, "Sostoianie," p. 34). To some degree, as has been indicated, the distribution of the patterns of age and, especially, of gender among believers ensures that religious education in the family will continue to take place. According to Kozhevnikov, the predominance of women "cannot but disturb one, especially because women are primarily occupied with educating children" ("Ateisticheskoe vospitanie," p. 2). In the Voronezh region, 80% of the believers who were studied were raising children (Tepliakov, "Sotsial'nye issledovaniia," p. 111).

Soviet sociologists have not been especially successful in exploring the problem of religious nurture. In one study, which included 112 believers and waverers, Safronov made the following discovery: "To the question 'Do you consider it essential to teach religion to children?' the answers were distributed thus: 135—'No,' 21—'I do not know,' and only 11—'yes'" ("Chto," p. 71). Okulov found that only 16.4% of the believers thought that religious education in the family was useful ("VII . . . kongress," p. 328). According to another survey, 23.3% of the families of believers engaged in religious education (Duluman, *Sovremennyi veruiushchii*, p. 97), while Ignatenko found that only 30.4% of the Baptists advocated it, and 69.6% asserted that they themselves did not have any religious influence on their children ("Opyt," p. 252). Such conclusions as these are scarcely credible, in view of the weight of evidence that religious education is widely practiced in religious families. The refusal of believers to admit to such practices almost certainly is a reflection of the tension of the times. As has been noted, the antireligious campaign has expended great effort in combating the religious education of minors. There have been many highly publicized cases of the denial of parental rights: children of religious parents have been forcibly removed to atheistic boarding schools when parents have been convicted of giving religious education to their own children.[2]

From inquiry into the degree to which families attempt to bring up their children religiously, the results shown in table 9.3 were derived. Although this study seems to have been done meticulously, on closer inspection it is no more credible than the others. In terms of percentages, only 62% of the convinced believers practice religious education in the home, while 93% of the habitual believers and 89% of the waverers do so. Surely this is the opposite of what one would expect. One must wonder whether the convinced believers, who perhaps have a greater awareness of the history of sanctions against parents who teach religion to their

TABLE 9.3

PRACTICE OF RELIGIOUS EDUCATION IN THE FAMILY

	Does family practice religious education?		
	Yes	No	Total
Total number of families surveyed	423	127	550
Religiousness of parents:			
Convinced believers	163	99	262
Habitual believers	69	5	74
Waverers	191	23	214
Denomination of parents:			
Orthodox	332	64	396
Baptist	49	45	94
Other	42	18	60

SOURCE: Duluman, *Sovremennyi veruiushchii*, p. 93.

children, might be exercising more prudence in their answers, while those who are less profoundly attached to religion are giving a more candid (and a more dangerous) answer. Alternatively, one can wonder whether the classification scheme used by the authors is correct. If, in fact, those who are in the first category are less likely to bother with teaching the faith to their children, one wonders whether it is indeed accurate to rate their degree of religiousness higher than that of people in the other two categories.

Secondly, the denominational distribution is equally peculiar. It will be noted that 84% of the Orthodox and 70% of those belonging to the "other" denominations practice religious education, but among the Baptists, only 52% do so. Again, one would have expected the opposite, inasmuch as Orthodoxy is likely to be much more traditional and less articulate than the Baptist faith. Here again, one can hypothesize that because the majority of the cases of deprivation of parental rights have been levied against sectarian parents, the Baptists would tend to be more aware of the risks and hence more circumspect in their answers. In short, one can only conclude that the reliability of this study of practices concerning religious education is questionable at best.

Studies of the observable effects of a religious upbringing seem to be on firmer ground. Duluman's team (*Sovremennyi veruiushchii*, p. 97) found that

> all believing school children, without exception, are products of those families in which religious upbringing exists. With regard to the results of the influence of religious upbringing on the world view and behavior of children in the 127 families we studied, one can judge from the following table.

RESULTS OF INFLUENCE OF BELIEVING PARENTS ON THEIR CHILDREN

	Quantity		Parents' denomination		
	No.	%	Orthodox	Baptist	Other
1. Children became believers	15	11.8	4	8	3
2. Children avoid social life	10	7.9	1	4	5
3. Religious influence of parents is not evident	90	70.9	78	3	9
4. Children not influenced by religion, in time became atheists	12	9.4	8	2	2
Total	127	100.0	91	17	19

One curious but interesting study to determine the attitudes toward religious education among those who do and do not read antireligious literature produced the results shown in table 9.4.

Studies of the degree of religious knowledge among young children give persuasive evidence of the effectiveness of religious nurture in the home. One study of preschool children aged 6 and 7 indicated that 55% were well informed on religion (Tepliakov, *Problemy*, p. 193). A study of religion among schoolchildren on three collective farms indicated that the percentage of believing students was from 1.4 to nearly 2 times greater than the percentage of believing adults. Among preschool children, on Easter, 1965, in Moscow, "almost every fortieth child received the eucharist."[3] On one of the collective farms, 43.5% of the adults were religious believers, but 84.0% of the school children were religious; on the second, the figures were 38.1% and 56.0%, and on the third, 33.2% and 46.0%, respectively (Alekseev, "Metodika," p. 146). These are astonishing results; they probably reflect the influence of grandparents. Large numbers of the parents may be nonbelievers, thereby accounting for the lower percentages of believers among adults; but a high proportion of the grandparents may be expected to be religious, and in the extended family, which is the norm in the USSR, their influence might be reflected in the schoolchildren.

The secular school system apparently serves as an effective counteragent to religious education in the home. "In our research, of 348 who had departed from religion, 104 people stated that they had been freed from the influence of religion while still of primary school age" (Solov'ev, "O vliianii," p. 191). In the entire student body, the level of religiousness reverts to the very low levels discussed earlier, for the students who have been in school for several years counterbalance the predominantly reli-

TABLE 9.4

EVALUATION OF RELIGIOUS EDUCATION FOR CHILDREN

	Person interviewed	
Opinion	Read	Did not read
Absolutely harmful and impermissible	64.5%	31.9%
Simply not necessary	25.8	34.5
Neither harmful nor useful	3.4	10.7
Might be useful	1.1	3.1
Absolutely useful and essential	0.5	2.2
Difficult to answer definitely	4.7	17.6

SOURCE: Korolev, "Rol'," p. 149.

gious incoming pupils. In one typical example, out of 2,386 pupils, only 144 (4.8% [6.03]) were religious, which generally supports other research that only 3 to 5% of schoolchildren remain religious believers (Duluman, *Sovremennyi veruiushchii,* p. 97).

In summary, Soviet sociological researchers have not enjoyed marked success in dealing with the subject of religious education. While the attempts to delineate the various motivations that have led people to become religious—childhood influences or the effects of subsequent catastrophes, and the like—may seem acceptable enough, at least on the surface, the ways in which religious education is treated are seldom very credible. The complicated process of providing a religious upbringing for children does not seem to have been well elucidated in contemporary Soviet sociological writings. Certainly one of the chief reasons for this deficiency is the extreme tension that surrounds any discussion of attempts to communicate religion to minor children. Quite possibly, Soviet sociologists will have to wait for some future relaxation of tension in this regard before they can hope to achieve results that are more persuasive.

It should be noted that the above discussion relates primarily, perhaps exclusively, to those areas of European Russia where Christianity is the dominant religion. The problem of transmitting religious practices and points of view to children in non-Christian families is considerably more complex, because the religious tradition exercises a far more pervasive influence than may be encountered elsewhere. In Islam, for example, the intimate identification of religion with the national culture of the peoples contributes to a far stronger religious influence within the family. In one study, for example,

> the first group of 36 (13%) advocated a duty of blind acceptance by children (especially daughters), including adult children, of the unlimited authority of the parents. They expressed the sense of duty in the simple formula: "I said it thus, which means that is how it should be." Proceeding from such an understanding of duty, the parents consider that the right to choose a profession, bridegroom, bride, and the entire form of life belongs to them, not to the children.
>
> The first group of parents held the following to be important elements of a son's or a daughter's duty: belief in god, strict observance of religious rites and customs, *tukhum* mutual responsibility, defense of the honor of the *tukhum,* vengeance for blood relatives, loyalty to parental ties, material support of parents, and the obligation of children, including those with families, to live with their parents. Of these they selected as the main ones:

belief in god, strict observance of religious rites, material support of parents, and the obligation of children to live with parents.

The second group of those who were questioned considered that the formula "I said it, which means that is how it should be" had become obsolete to a significant degree. They considered the following to be established elements of a son's or a daughter's duty: belief in god (especially for girls), observance of religious rites, mutual aid of relatives in case of need, acceptance by minor children (especially daughters) of the superior right of parents in questions of selecting a bridegroom or bride. This group of those who were questioned accepted as basic elements of duty: material support of believers, and the children living, if possible, in the same region or city where the parents live. Such opinions were expressed by 113 people (40%) of those questioned. In the families of this group, they do not pay attention to the education of children in religious dogmas.[4]

Obviously, religious education is practiced differently in these environs.

Thus far, the study of religious education has dealt exclusively with informal religious upbringing in the home. The reason for this is simple enough: at least since the late fifties, formal religious education conducted by the church or any other agency has been strictly illegal. Prior to possible matriculation in the handful of theological schools that remain—or, in case of the Baptists, in the correspondence course—at the age of 18, no religious education, other than that provided by parents (or grandparents) for their own children, is legally permitted. This absence of formal religious education for children, together with the great dearth of religious literature, makes it all but impossible to exert any sort of institutional control over what is transmitted from one generation to the next. As a result, no mechanisms are available to ensure that what is transmitted is the pure faith without any admixture of folk elements.

Soviet scholars refer to these folk elements as superstitions—thus risking some confusion, for according to the ideology, religion itself is superstition. "Despite the fact that superstitious impressions in the contemporary collective farm village are gradually disappearing, in a number of cases they are much more alive than Christian beliefs. Thus, for example, belief in prophetic dreams, according to the data of our questionnaire, is the most widespread superstition, rivaling even belief in god" (Kolbanovskii, *Kollektiv,* p. 235). Belief in superstition is particularly pronounced among Russian Orthodox. One study of 603 Orthodox Christians discovered that 462, or 77%, believed in various magical phenomena, and only 89, or 15%, disclaimed superstition (Pashkov, "K voprosu,"

p. 159). Apparently, superstition is most prevalent among the young: "Belief in fortune-telling is connected with a person's age: it is characteristic, in the main, for a certain part of the youth; by and large, people who have lived 25 to 30 years do not experience the need to turn to fortune-tellers, because the life experience that they have undergone already contradicts this form of superstition."[5] A survey of ninth-grade students indicated that although only 0.2% believed in god, 1.9% believed in the existence of supernatural powers (Galitskaia, "K voprosu," p. 405). In a study of two rural villages, Sukhov discovered that 11.07% of the unbelievers, including some atheists, believe in one superstition or another (*Religiia*, p. 48). The believers in these two towns "explained their attitude towards 'unclean powers' in the following way: of 538 people, 200, i.e., a little more than one-third of all those answering the question, specifically recognized them; 292 people said they do not know; and 44 people stated that they do not believe in their existence. Among believers living in the cities, the attitude toward 'unclean powers' was specified in the following manner: of 37 people who answered the question, 24 believe, 6 do not know, and 7 do not believe in their existence" (Pashkov, "K voprosu," p. 157).[6] Even more disturbing was the discovery that of 87 girls aged 17 to 19 who were students in a medical school near Moscow, 26 (or 30%) believed in fortunetelling, prophetic dreams, and auguries, even though none of those students believed in God (Tazhurina, "Mistifikatsiia," p. 73; cf. Bukin, "XXV C"ezd," p. 11). Table 9.5 indicates the percentages of belief in various superstitions that Kolbanovskii found. It should be noted that not all Soviet scholars consider such beliefs to be totally fantastic: Tazhurina, at least, recognizes that belief in fortunetelling is a logical extension of the natural ability to predict on the basis of reasoned analysis ("Mistifikatsiia," pp. 84–85).

Apparently the critical factor in the incidence of superstition among

TABLE 9.5
A STUDY OF BELIEF IN VARIOUS SUPERSTITIONS

Belief	Men	Women	Total
Evil eye	17.6%	45.3%	35.4%
Prophetic dreams	20.8	49.6	40.5
Sorcery	11.1	30.3	23.3
Divination	2.8	9.8	7.2
Superstitious signs	6.6	15.2	12.1

SOURCE: Kolbanovskii, *Kollektiv*, p. 235.
NOTE: These data may be misleading, for the figures suggest that the ratio between men and women is not the same for all of the categories.

believers is whether or not a church is available. In the two villages mentioned above, there are no churches, and the majority of the believers are able to attend church no more than once or twice a year (ibid., p. 79). By contrast, Baptists in the same region, who are generally able to make satisfactory arrangements for fulfilling their religious needs informally when a legally operating church is unavailable, seemed much less prone to turn to superstition (ibid., p. 75). The conclusion seems obvious: "On the basis of the data of our expedition, one can definitely say that a direct link exists between frequency of attending church and one relationship or another to 'superstition.' Approximately 70% of the Orthodox surveyed adhere to all the superstitions condemned by the church; these same people, when asked how often they attend church and consequently hear the sermons of the priest, answer: 'When it is convenient,' 'When I take the time,' 'I don't have time to go'" (ibid., pp. 76–77). Thus, there is considerable evidence that when institutionalized religion is not available, syncretism with folk beliefs and even with outright superstition is likely to take place. In the absence of institutional correctives, superstitious beliefs tend to spread (ibid., p. 63).

> The results of the church being far away and the lack, in fact, of an Orthodox influence or of a Christian ideology in general are as follows: the absolute majority of the believers do not read the Bible and do not know its contents, nor the basic positions of the Christian faith. . . . All this raises the supposition that in fact, what is disseminated in these towns is not so much Orthodox Christianity as a synthesis of several aspects of the Christian religion with remainders of the ancient pagan faith in the guise of superstition. This synthesis, as it seems to us, is also a form of religious consciousness in these localities. In this there is nothing surprising. The forms of the appearance of religious consciousness are dependent on a whole series of factors. In our case, the distance to the church, the specific village conditions, and the preservation of traditions of the ages, including remaining pagan aspects, established the conditions in which religious beliefs appear in the form of a synthesis of Christian aspects and superstition in the narrow sense of the word. [Ibid., pp. 79–80]

After having established this intimate relationship between the religious views that are transmitted in the absence of institutional correctives and the autochthonous superstitious belief, Soviet scholars then must answer the question as to whether religion and superstition are merely two different aspects of the same thing. After much analysis, Tazhurina, at least, concludes that the two are not different aspects of the same phenomenon,

152

because in the life and conduct of the individual, the influence of superstition is by no means as all-pervasive as is belief in God (ibid., p. 84).

In conclusion, it seems fairly clear that religious upbringing in the family continues to be the major channel for the transmission of religious belief from one generation to another. Because this is the sole form of religious education available and because for a very large portion of the religious believers the influence of institutionalized religion is virtually nonexistent, it would appear that syncretism with folk beliefs and superstitions is a very real concomitant to the present patterns of religious education in the USSR.

10

THE WORLD VIEW

Soviet scholars are not content with measuring the outward, observable aspects of religiousness. Operating on the assumption that a genuine understanding of the contemporary believer requires that his interior world be investigated, they embark on bold—indeed, overbold—attempts to penetrate to the world view of the religious believer. This is an elusive subject, and to date, at least, it would not appear that Soviet sociological researchers have enjoyed convincing success in ascertaining the outlook of religious believers, particularly in matters involving their belief system.

Because the official ideology prides itself on being scientific, Soviet researchers have a considerable interest in exploring the attitudes of religious believers toward science. Theoretically, the ideology demands that religion and science be incompatible: the more the individual accepts a scientific world view, by definition the less religious he will be. Religious people, to the extent that they are truly religious, should shun science and its achievements, preferring the comfortable myths of their religious prejudices.

It would appear that Soviet researchers have not been very successful in demonstrating the validity of this presupposition. From a study in the Voronezh region, Tepliakov found that 8,763 of 11,768 believers, or 74.5%, deeply appreciated the achievements of the secular world ("Sotsial'nye issledovaniia," p. 109). When "speaking about the 'importance of religion,' many believers (92%) simultaneously emphasized the necessity for science and its role in making labor easier and the life of the people better" (Sytenko, "O nravstvennom oblike," p. 21). From a study of factory workers, "it was clear that among those who relate approvingly to religion, 30.6% wished to study questions of contemporary politics and international relations, 38.6% were interested in the origin and development of life on earth, 20% in the questions of the origins of the planets and stars, etc." (Cherniak, *Formirovanie*, p. 363). During a study of the Baptist congregation at Alma-Ata,

> one of the preachers, for whom statements about the relationship of religion and science are especially characteristic, said, "Unbelievers say about us that we are people who have been left behind, that we do not utilize the achievements of science and technology. This is a lie! We use all the achievements of contemporary as well as previous unbelievers, only we believe in god. In contrast to them, we bring good to the world, love of humanity, peace."
>
> It is typical that he concludes that the very existence of science is due to the necessity to study "god's creation." "We should know and study the creation of god," he preaches, "for we wish to know, for example, the course of all sorts of research. We wish to know what it has discovered. Thus should we understand what god has created!"
>
> He even places believing science in opposition to unbelieving science, and states that more is "revealed" by believers than by unbelievers. "Many researchers believe in god, and god helps them to understand what unbelievers cannot understand." [Nikonov, "O nekotorykh tendentsiiakh," pp. 196–97]

In Siberia, 85.7% of the Baptists consider science to be useful and essential (Kharakhorkin, "Kritika," p. 46), which would scarcely seem to indicate that they are indifferent to the world of science, much less fear it, which the ideology predicts.

Indeed, it would appear that some believers are not at all impressed by the alleged incompatibility between religion and science that atheist practitioners claim. One middle-aged Baptist told a researcher, "Neither learned papers, nor conversations, nor even those experiments that not long ago they demonstrated in school, will destroy my faith" (Duluman, *Sovremennyi veruiushchii,* p. 168). In a study of atheistic consciousness among waverers (no convinced believers were included in the study), 45% denied that science refuted religion, and 56% denied that natural laws, in the absence of any supernatural influences, were adequate for explaining the existence and development of society (Lebedev, "Studencheskaia molodezh'," pp. 202–3). Among 867 Russian Orthodox, 103, or nearly 12%, considered science and religion to be parallel phenomena (Onishchenko, "Tendentsii," p. 97).

Even in the Soviet Union, churchmen and sectarian preachers in their sermons and in the religious press make statements that religion and science cannot contradict each other, since they are concerned with different spheres of the life of man. More than that, they assert that science and religion mutually complement each other, that they are partners. See the statement, for example, of Professor L. N. Pariiskii, of the Leningrad Theological Academy: "Religion does not contradict science and cannot contradict it. The Christian religion bases itself on the Holy Bible; science, on the study of nature. The Bible and nature are two books that were written by god and were predestined for the teaching of man. As works of one and the same author they cannot contradict each other."[1]

Even among Jehovah's Witnesses, who are portrayed by Soviet propaganda as among the most benighted and alienated from modern society, 54% of those who were surveyed "consider that science is from god and does not contradict faith."[2]

In one study of 800 sermons delivered in a Baptist church, Iarygin found that a significant place was given to the topic of science and religion, while in two others, 16% and 14% of the sermons were devoted to this theme ("Baptistskaia propoved'," p. 55). Another study of six Baptist churches showed that the proportion of sermons devoted to this theme in five of the churches ranged from 4.0% to 16.8%.[3]

Soviet researchers become especially annoyed when preachers use science for religious ends:

The Baptist leaders in their preaching try to present the doctrine of god's trinity as three various conditions of one world spirit, able to come forth as "god the father," "son," and "holy spirit," but the point of view expressed in one sermon was much more typical: "It is difficult for people to imagine god's trinity. It is difficult to understand how this triad lives in unity. But look: water at normal temperature is a liquid; but if we heat it, it changes into vapor; if we cool it, it turns into ice, which can support a great weight. This means that water, in its normal condition, consists of three forms, as it were. So also, the lord is thrice one." The Baptist preacher tries to establish a façade of scientific erudition. He tries to explain one of the central doctrines of the faith by a primitive example, counting on a semiliterate, biased audience. . . .

Here is an example from the assertions of a preacher who attempted, by vulgarizing scientific evidence, to maintain the concept of a certain divine goal, harmony, and order in nature and to prove by this means the necessity of the existence "of the creator of this harmony." "Think, brothers and sisters! Every successive day will be something unlike its predecessor, but every time, the day and the night change places regularly. Each successive day now will be a little bit longer than the former, and the night will be a little shorter. And this language is understood by all people, even though we speak in various tongues and speeches. Think how many fish exist, how many types, how many colors, how many different birds there are on earth! Can it be that all this arises simply by chance, as the unbelievers claim? For all of this we owe only the lord god!" [Nikonov, "O nekotorykh tendentsiiakh," pp. 180–82]

There is considerable disagreement in the data concerning the persistence of a nonscientific view of the environment. Tepliakov found that 74.3% of the religious people ascribed weather conditions to God's mercy. Conversely, 83.5% of 13,310 believers did not believe in using prayers in order to obtain greater agricultural yields. And 25.1% of them gave an incorrect (religious) explanation of the weather (*Problemy*, pp 164–65, 139, 142).

Selected observations from a number of Belorussian towns showed that not less than 50% of the toilers of the village are unable to give a correct answer to elementary questions dealing with the world view. "To the survey question: 'How did man appear on earth?' of 38 questioned in the town of Leplevka, Brest district, only 12 people answered: 'From the ape.' Almost one-third of those questioned in all the towns answered in the questionnaire: 'I do not know.' Peasants aged over 55 in all observed towns answered this question, as a rule, 'From god.'" [Lensu, "Differentsirovannyi podkhod," pp. 136–37]

Thus, it would seem that the evidence does not demonstrate conclusively that all believers agree with the ideological tenet that religion and science are necessarily incompatible.

It could scarcely be otherwise. The Marxist thesis that religion and science are incompatible, however compelling it may seem to be from a theoretical or formal point of view, has certainly not been borne out historically. Just as it is far from true that all scientists have been atheists, it has never been true that the Christians have rejected science categorically. Depending on the times and circumstances, conflicts between religious authorities and one branch or another of science have been very bitter indeed—for example, astronomy in the case of Catholic Poland during Copernicus's time, or biology in the case of fundamentalist United States during the post-Darwinian period—but not even during the most severe of these conflicts have all branches of science been rejected by the religious authorities. Thus, the Soviet attempt to prove the ideological presupposition that religious believers have to categorically reject science must inevitably fail, at least if history is any index.

In their examination of the world view of religious believers, Soviet researchers have not found that there is an impressive level of theological development. According to one study, only 5% of the religious believers, when asked what was their primary reason for adhering to religion, answered that it "satisfies questions of the mind" (Duluman, *Sovremennyi veruiushchii*, p. 72). One young Orthodox believer said to a researcher: "And who created the world, and man? From whence was it taken, after all? The Bible, in my opinion, gives reliable answers to these and similar questions" (ibid., p. 73). But it would not appear that such intellectually oriented individuals are especially common among the religious believers. In this same study of 675 believers, only 204 were found to be well acquainted with the fundamentals of the faith, 167 were only moderately acquainted with them, 267 knew them poorly, and 37 knew nothing at all about the faith (ibid., p. 107). Iablokov found that when asked what they considered basic to their faith, nearly 60% of the believers who were questioned could only point to the necessity of following the example of older generations ("Obshchenie," pp. 63–64).[4]

Lack of knowledge about the faith is not due to neglect of theology on the part of clergy. Studies of Baptist sermons, for example, consistently show that doctrinal matters occupy anywhere from 56% to 60% or 70% of all sermons delivered (Iarygin, "Kharakter," p. 152; Galitskaia, "Izuchenie," p. 59). Iarygin found that Biblical and Christological themes predominated in the more than 800 sermons that he studied ("Baptistkaia propoved'," p. 53). "Therefore, trust in 'saving grace,' the redeeming mission of Christ, and conviction of the necessity of man's constantly turning to god became not only the central dogmas of the Baptist faith but also the practical aspiration of systematic teaching activity. More than half of the sermons speak precisely to this theme. In the Uriupinsk congregation of Baptists, they constitute even more than 70%, and in the Frolovskii and Volgograd congregations, 70% of all sermons on matters of the faith. This tendency seems to be typical for all Baptist congregations" (ibid., p. 54). Soviet researchers find that even though relatively small numbers are actually converted to religion by preachers, the clergy have a profound influence on the formation of the world views of the members of their congregations (Duluman, *Sovremennyi veruiushchii*, p. 88).

Soviet researchers have not enjoyed especially impressive success in attempting to discern the concepts of God that prevail among believers.

"According to our data, among the Orthodox, people who believe in an abstract god constitute 11.8% in all. True, it is necessary to bear in mind that we studied Orthodox believers only in the villages. If one considers that the educational level of believers in cities is higher than it is in villages, one can suggest that for urban people, the percentage will be significantly higher" (ibid., p. 132). In one study among Baptists, Ignatenko found that 28% held that God was spirit, 17% had anthropomorphic ideas about God, conceiving him in human form, and the other concepts were mixed: God is power, spirit, love, and anthropomorphic all together; God is spirit and anthropomorphic simultaneously; God is love; God is the good; and various other answers (God is nature, light, something indescribable, an indefinable being, etc.); however, nearly 20% could not answer the question at all ("Opyt," p. 254).

Rather inconclusive results were derived from another study, which explored the concept of God among Orthodox, Baptists, Jehovah's Witnesses, Pentecostals, Seventh Day Adventists, and Uniates. The answers were similar to those listed above, with such additional concepts as that God is the prime mover, God is truth, etc. (Onishchenko, "Tendentsii," p. 93). The Voronezh study produced the data shown in table 10.1.

In a study among Old Believers, Podmazov found that 27.6% had an indeterminate concept of God, while 23.5% conceived of Him in anthropomorphic terms:

> The data from concrete sociological research state that among contemporary Old Believers, the number of believers who represent god in the form of a concrete anthropomorphic being is comparatively large (23.5%). For believers in this category, such answers as the following were characteristic: "God looks the same as he is pictured on the icon"; "In the scriptures it states

TABLE 10.1

CONCEPTS OF GOD

Concept of God	Number	Percentage
God is trinity (orthodox)	1,973	14.9
God is concrete substance (anthropomorphic)	2,580	19.4
God is holy spirit (abstract)	2,096	15.7
"Something is there"	2,435	18.3
Have no impression	3,943	29.6
Avoided answering	283	2.1
Totals	13,310	100.0

SOURCE: Tepliakov, *Problemy*, p. 141.

that god created man in his image and likeness. This means that god has the image of man." Incidentally, even to this day, a few of the old people are motivated to prohibit cutting the beard because one must not, if you please, spoil the "image of god." ["Sovremennoe staroobriadchestvo," p. 186]

The results of a fairly elaborate study to measure the concept of God against a number of other variables are presented in table 10.2.

A second approach to the problem is to categorize arguments that are given in favor of the existence of God. One study found that of 380 answers, 24% utilized traditional theological proofs, 7% appealed to uncertainty, 23% argued from the soul's salvation to the existence of God, 20% cited sermons or the Bible, and 25% gave no concrete proof of God's existence (Duluman, *Sovremennyi veruiushchii*, p. 137). Another study discovered the arguments listed in table 10.3.

Finally, some attempts have been made to ascertain the believer's attitude toward God, but with conflicting results. According to one study, "about 40% of them do not feel love toward god; the answers of 65% of the believers testified that they fear god more than love him, and about a third no longer even have 'the fear of god' " (Tepliakov, *Problemy*, p. 132). However, according to Iablokov, "Profound changes are taking place in the emotional sphere of believers. These changes even involve the main religious feeling—the feeling of love toward god. Research shows that the majority of the believers do not experience love to god in that form in which the clergy tries to teach it. According to the research of D. V. Pavliuk, 30% of the Orthodox who were investigated stated that they do not perceive the feeling of love to god, and 17.5% of the believers did not know whether they love him or not" (*Metodologicheskie problemy*, p. 121).

Such conflicting results are not surprising, however. The attempt to explore this dimension through sociological procedures has not been well conceived. Certainly the attempt to examine and comprehend rationally, much less to articulate, so complex a phenomenon as one's emotive relationship to the Deity is so difficult and so subject to variant expressions of what may be the same attitude that it would seem strange if there were any agreement in the results from such an examination. Without a long, detailed, involved, and exceedingly time-consuming attempt to examine the individual's attitude in depth and in detail, such studies as these can only provide misleading results at best.

Similar criticisms can be leveled at the other attempts to explore the concept of God through sociological means. If professional theologians can struggle for a lifetime without achieving a succinct single

TABLE 10.2
RESULTS OF A STUDY OF CONCEPTS OF GOD

Impression of god	Number	Age			Education				
		To 30	30-50	Over 50	Illit-erate	Pri-mary	5-7 yrs	8-10 yrs	Higher
Concrete physical	45	5	11	29	9	26	7	3	....
Abstract	113	14	50	49	13	71	21	6	2
Mixed (vague)	96	4	33	59	15	57	20	4	....
No answer	45	4	24	17	5	30	8	2	....
Totals	299	27	118	154	42	184	56	14	2

SOURCE: Duluman, *Sovremennyi veruiushchii*, p. 126.
NOTE: It should be noted that there are errors in this table. The column for "Education, 8-10 years" totals 15, which would bring the total for the "Education" category to the

definition of divinity, surely it is vain to expect rank-and-file believers to do so. In fact, some definitions would insist that no single concept can be adequate but that a number of analogies (God is spirit, love, a person, etc.) must be used together.

Nor has any single proof of God's existence ever been found to be satisfactory; instead, almost without exception, theologians have utilized a battery of related proofs. For Soviet researchers to expect to isolate an individual believer's approach to so complex a subject as this betrays a very poor understanding of the subject. Since the believer's answer necessarily must be so dependent on the mood and circumstances of the moment and will be so subject to the researcher's influence, what is presented as the results of this part of any sociological survey probably will have no meaning at all with regard to the believers.

A fairly considerable number of studies have touched upon one particular aspect of theology, the belief in life beyond the grave. In part this may be due to the peculiar and exceedingly primitive interpretation of the ideology, which states that religion serves the exploiters by offering a future reward to the exploited if they are patient in enduring their present sufferings. Theoretically, at least, if this belief in a future reward should weaken, religion's hold on the people should weaken correspondingly. Thus, an examination of this particular doctrine will, according to the ideology, provide an excellent index of the inevitable collapse of religion.

The results acquired by Soviet researchers have been exceedingly dis-

(TABLE 10.2—*continued*)

Religious denomination					Church attendance				Conducts religious propaganda	
Bap- tist	Pente- costal	Jeho- vist	Adven- tist	Ortho- dox	Regu- lar	Peri- odical	Does not attend	Not estab- lished	In family	Outside family
8	3	....	12	22	17	9	7	2	14	7
60	22	21	....	10	59	36	4	14	31	14
37	7	7	9	36	32	42	14	8	17	4
17	6	4	1	17	17	22	4	2	6	2
122	38	32	22	85	125	119	29	26	68	27

requisite 299. The first entry in the column for "Church attendance, Periodical" should be 19.

parate. According to Iablokov, "Only one-fifth of the believing collective farmers who were investigated in the Orlov region accepted the existence of life beyond the grave. According to the data of R. A. Lopatkin, who conducted research in the Ivanov and Tambov regions, 12.88% of those who believe in god reject belief in life beyond the grave. Analogous data were acquired by the Department of the History and Theory of Atheism of Moscow State University in the course of the work of the Orlov expedition" (*Metodologicheskie problemy*, pp. 120–21). Vasilevskaia found that among members of the families of wavering believers, only 9.5% believed in the existence of heaven, while 71.5% were in doubt ("Opyt," p. 398).

Tepliakov found that belief in immortality was apparently stronger under urban conditions, where 50% of the believers adhered to this doctrine, than in the countryside, where only about 40% expressed the idea of immortality (*Problemy*, p. 140). It should be noted, however, that his study may have measured only the greater success of the more sophisticated urban believers in articulating this somewhat complex concept. In a study of 2,057 convinced Orthodox and sectarian believers, he found that fewer than one-third did not doubt the existence of "eternal life beyond the grave," while 36.6% did not believe in it at all ("Pobeda," p. 154). Iablokov concluded that "belief in the immortality of the soul and life beyond the grave is gradually dying out. The results of selective interviews conducted by participants of the Orlov expedition testify that of 96 Orthodox Christians, 63 (65.62%) believe simply in life beyond the grave. The remainder either do not believe in it at all or are in doubt" ("Trans- formatsiia," p. 140).

TABLE 10.3
REASONS GIVEN AS "PROOFS" OF GOD'S EXISTENCE

"Proofs" of god's existence	Men	Women	Total
Appeals to tradition	112	901	1,013
Examples of miraculous help to people	6	109	115
Inexplicable phenomena of nature	27	40	67
The ontological proof	7	33	40
The moral proof	5	13	18
Indicating how widespread religion is	4	12	16
Appeals to the Bible	5	13	18
Consider proof impossible	3	30	33
Gave no proofs	43	159	202
Totals	212	1,310	1,522

SOURCE: Kolbanovskii, *Kollektiv,* p. 228.

In the Voronezh region, of 13,310 believers 5,800 (44%) believed in an immortal soul, whereas 4,395 (33%) did not (the remainder were in doubt) (Tepliakov, *Problemy,* p. 140). Curiously enough, Lebedev found that exactly the same percentage (33) of wavering believers among students in higher education did not believe in the immortal soul ("Studencheskaia molodezh'," p. 202). Surely this must indicate that the procedures that were used in deriving these data were not comparable, for it would be exceedingly unlikely, at least in the framework established by Soviet sociologists, that a large sample of the general population, including a great many elderly and uneducated rural inhabitants, would display the same attitude towards one of the central theological doctrines as would a much smaller sample from such a highly sophisticated and rigorously selected group as university students. In a study of rural believers, Pashkov found that "of 538 . . . who believe in god, only 208 people believe in life beyond the grave, 308 people do not know, and 22 people do not believe. Of 59 urban people who believe in god, 43 believe in life after death, 11 do not know, and 5 do not believe in it" ("K voprosu," p. 158). In another study of rural inhabitants, Iablokov found that only 36.8% accepted this doctrine without doubt ("Transformatsiia," p. 140).

Soviet researchers have not been unanimous in finding that a significant portion of the believers doubt the doctrine of immortality. According to Ignatenko, "Among Baptists we did not meet a single believer who would deny the existence of the world beyond the grave" ("Opyt," p. 255). And Iablokov found that "among Baptists, belief in the immortality of the soul and life beyond the grave has more vitality. Of 90 Baptists questioned in the Orlov region, 81 (90%) accept the existence of life beyond the grave" ("Transformatsiia," p. 140). It should be noted, however, that many of the believers have only a most impressionistic, unformed concept of immortality (Andrianov, "Evoliutsiia," p. 180). According to one study, more than 10% of the believers adhere to religion more or less as a form of insurance (Duluman, *Sovremennyi veruiushchii*, p. 72). "People of this group, if one can express it thus, are afraid 'just in case' " (Kozhevnikov, "Ateisticheskoe vospitanie," p. 2).

It is hardly surprising that Soviet sociology has not succeeded in finding or even approaching any widely acceptable profile with regard to this aspect of the religious world view. By its very nature, the doctrine of the afterlife cannot be approached on the basis of concrete, empirically verifiable knowledge, and many religious believers will approach the subject with a greater or lesser degree of uncertainty. Detailed descriptions of the afterlife are patently impossible, and hence a great deal of mystery almost inevitably surrounds the subject. As a case in point, Kobetskii found that only 9.6% believed in life after death and in the eternal soul; 52.4% either had difficulty in answering this question or gave no answer at all (*Sotsiologicheskoe izuchenii*, p. 38). Surely a sociological survey that poses a question that more than half of the respondents cannot answer is suspect, and its results must be used with great caution, if at all.

In this matter, a great deal, again, will depend on the moods and circumstances prevailing at the time of the survey, and the investigator himself can influence the answer greatly—for example, by pressing the point, he will be able to lead a large proportion of the believers to express doubt on one point or another, no matter how firmly they may be convinced about the existence of the afterlife. In this case, oddly enough, the careless or unconcerned respondent may in fact give a more accurate answer, one that corresponds more nearly to his actual belief, than a respondent who, in sincerely trying to give a detailed, exhaustive answer, becomes hopelessly entangled in the many logical dilemmas inherent in the subject.

Traditionally, religion and morality have been widely identified with one another. Soviet researchers have taken some interest in the question of the relationship between religiousness and morality, in part because the ideology suggests not only that there is no necessary connection between the two but that, in fact, the intelligent human being who has freed himself of such superstitious prejudice is more truly able to understand and live according to genuine morality than is the benighted religious believer. However, under Soviet conditions, the fact remains that the moral vigor of many religious people exercises a powerful attraction. Among Baptists, for example, from one-fifth to one-third of the sermons emphasize this highly attractive aspect of the Baptist way of life (Iarygin, "Kharakter," p. 152). "The smallest inadequacies in the life of our country and its people are emphasized in order to draw biased antisocial conclusions. 'Look at these atheists! At youth brought up on an atheist way, without god. They are depraved. For them nothing is holy. They believe in nothing. Think of it, on the streets of our cities, young guys curse with the name of god, with the most disgusting words, interweaving the name of god to them. Why? They were brought up that way' " (Nikonov, "O nekotorykh tendentsiiakh," p. 196).

Among believers, city dwellers tend to be more concerned with morality than are their rural counterparts (Tepliakov, *Problemy*, p. 85). Among students in higher education who are wavering believers, 43% rejected the ideological assertion that religion has a negative influence on an individual's moral level (Lebedev, "Studencheskaia molodezh'," p. 202). "Unfortunately, the majority of believers (including 'traditional believers') uncritically accept the preaching that religion supports good morals, that faith and 'the fear of god' preserve one from wickedness" (Pismanik, "Religioznaia konseptsiia," p. 150).

> Many convinced believers, under the influence of preaching on "sinfulness," consider that breaking with the cult and atheism are most serious transgressions, and sometimes they condemn the joy of living and happiness. Some expressions of the idea of "sinfulness" are also found among "believers by tradition." The latter (the most numerous group) are ignorant of the most reactionary assertions, but all the same, the idea of "sinfulness" distorts some of their moral assertions and understanding. Thus, many "believers by tradition" more or less explicitly deny "original sin," the supernatural nature of the conscience, the "prophylactic significance" of dreading the wages of "sin" after death, and heavenly punishment for departure from religion. [Ibid.]

Many believers, when asked to name the desirable traits in those around them, listed ethical traits of character rather than religiousness (Andrianov, "Evoliutsiia," p. 179), and indeed, some believers, when asked to name the single most important reason for their belief, indicated that "religion is the path to moral maturity" (Duluman, *Sovremennyi veruiushchii*, p. 72). In 1965/66, 94% of the Orthodox who were questioned saw in religion the hope for the preservation of the moral foundations of society; and in 1970, "78.5% of those questioned gave a positive evaluation of its significance for the moral education of people" (Andrianov, "Evoliutsiia," p. 174–75).

Despite this emphasis on morality, Soviet reesarchers have found disappointing levels of awareness of the state's attempt to formulate its own moral code to replace the religious approach. "As is well known, the Program of the CPSU formulated the Moral Codex of the Builder of Communism, which is an important step on the path of moral progress. During the course of the interview, a question clarified the believers' knowledge of this code and their relationship to it. According to the data of the Orlov expedition, 41.67% of the Orthodox and 34.48% of the Baptists know nothing at all about the Moral Codex" (Iablokov, "Transformatsiia," p. 128). However, "an absolute majority of believers who were acquainted with the Moral Codex of the Builder of Communism approved of it" (ibid., p. 129).

In some areas, Soviet researchers have found a disturbing persistence of local customs which are offensive to the moral sensibilities of the Russian majority. A small percentage of criminal convictions in some areas continue to be related to religion—for example, the exacting of a bridal price, exercising tyranny over women on the basis of Islamic tradition, and the like.[5] To balance such discouraging tendencies, Soviet researchers are gratified to find that among those who read atheistic literature, less than 2% continue to feel that religion has a positive influence on morality (Korolev, "Rol'," p. 148).

Only occasionally do Soviet researchers turn to other components and doctrines of the theology of religious believers. Ignatenko, for example, found that 94.9% of the Baptists believed in original sin ("Opyt," p. 256). According to Tepliakov, only 22% of the Orthodox and sectarians were convinced believers in miracles, while 53% did not believe in them at all ("Pobeda," pp. 154–55). Among the Fedoseevtsy (a sect that is related to the Old Believers), only 7.1% still consider that it is a sin to use a utensil that a nonbeliever has touched (Podmazov, "Sovremennoe staroobriadchestvo," p. 195). "From a questionnaire that was circulated in one of the eastern districts of the Latvian SSR on the holiday of the Intercession of the Blessed Virgin, a curious picture emerged: of 100 people who had gathered around the church, only a half knew what the celebration for which they had come to the temple was called, and in all, only 10 people had an idea of its contents. People were attracted by the very fact of the holiday, the beauty of the rite, and, if you please, respect for the old tradition."[6] Eschatology continues to exercise an influence over some believers (Podmazov, "Sovremennoe staroobriadchestvo," p. 192). Among one group of Old Believers, for example, "only 40 (34.2%) know the substance of the teaching of the priestless Old Believers on the nature of the anti-Christ and the end of the world, while 15 of them emphasized that they do not share these views. Consequently, only 21.4% of the believers know the substance of Old Believer eschatological ideas and allow for the possibility of their coming true. Meanwhile, in the past, especially among the Fedoseevtsy, these ideas received the greatest dissemination, as various sources testify" (ibid., pp. 193–94). Finally, in one study of 700 upper-class pupils, "we did not receive a single answer indicating a divine source of beauty."[7]

On the whole, it would not appear that Soviet sociological scholars have been especially successful in discovering and describing the theological dimensions of the religious world view of contemporary believers. In part, this is certainly due to a failure to understand this world view, as witness the many occasions when poorly formulated questions lead to unexpected—and intrinsically improbable—results. In part it is due to ideological preconceptions which lead Soviet researchers to place a great deal of emphasis on certain aspects (such as, for example, belief in an afterlife) that may not, in fact, receive much attention in the overall world view of religious believers. In large measure, however, the failure of Soviet sociologists to present a clearer, more detailed picture of the theological world view is simply due to their lack of interest: Soviet researchers are much more interested in parameters other than the theological convictions and speculations of the religious believers.

Soviet sociologists are much more interested in the influence that religion has on daily conduct. The relationship between the religious world view and the individual's behavior receives somewhat more attention than do purely theoretical theological dimensions of the world view.

Soviet researchers have attempted to establish what are the dominant motivations in the conduct of religious believers. In examining the motives for productive labor, Iablokov found the distribution shown in table 10.4. Material stimuli would seem to be dominant among a considerable group

TABLE 10.4

A STUDY OF MOTIVES FOR CARRYING ON PRODUCTIVE LABOR

Motives	Orthodox		Baptists	
	Number	Percentage	Number	Percentage
Religious motives	6	6.25	25	27.78
Nonreligious motives	79	82.29	50	55.55
including material	54	56.25	28	31.11
material and spiritual	25	26.04	22	24.44
Other	5	5.21	1	1.11
No answer	6	6.25	14	15.56
Totals	96	100.00	90	100.00

SOURCE: Iablokov, "Transformatsiia," p. 144.

of the believers: "56.3% of the Orthodox and 31.1% of the Baptists expressed this motive" (Iablokov, *Metodologicheskie problemy*, p. 122). Andrianov found that only 30% were primarily interested in material benefits, while the rest were seeking more elevated intellectual-spiritual values ("Evoliutsiia," p. 176). Such lofty aspirations may seem surprising; another study, however, presented findings that were truly astonishing. Tepliakov found that only 3.3% were motivated by material rewards; the rest worked in order to achieve "intellectually high moral qualities" ("Pobeda," p. 153). This is scarcely a credible result; if true, it would represent a startling breakthrough in the search for the "New Soviet Man," one that has not elsewhere been reported.

This is not to imply that such motivations are not present among a significant portion of the Soviet population. "Attention is drawn to the fact that for a significant group of believers, together with material stimuli, other spiritual but nonreligious stimuli to labor are of significance. In the number of spiritual stimuli, believers not infrequently cite such things as the joy of work, the desire for respect from society, the good of the coming generation, etc. Among Orthodox people, this group constitutes 26.04%, and among Baptists, 24.4%. For believers of this group, working activity is not only a means of satisfying the elementary requirements of life, but also a means of satisfying the need for labor" (Iablokov, *Metodologicheskie problemy*, p. 122). Believers are coming to recognize the social significance of labor; more than 85% of the rural inhabitants were found to be aware of this aspect of their endeavors (Tepliakov, *Problemy*, p. 142). In one group of Baptists, one in five indicated that among his reasons for working was the desire "to bring a better life for society" (Ignatenko, "Opyt," p. 261).

With regard to purely religious motivations, Soviet researchers present conflicting reports. Andrianov found that 95% of the believers who were questioned did not connect their labor with theological motivations ("Evoliutsiia," pp. 175–76). On the other hand, in a study of Baptists, Ignatenko found that "90.9% see the major goal of their life in receiving future salvation, and they consider that the earthly life of a man has no independent value" ("Opyt," p. 262).

With regard to the broader issue of the meaning of life itself, a considerable range of results has been acquired. A young Baptist man with a higher education responded simply, "For me life is a way to death, and death is gain" (ibid.). Another study, however, apparently received almost exclusively secular responses. "We received answers from 400 believers to the question: 'In what do you discern the meaning of your personal life?' 38 people, or 9.5% of the number of all those questioned, answered: in turning their children 'into people,' in seeing them happy in their 'earthly welfare.' Among these believers there were 30 Orthodox, 4 Baptists, and 4 representatives of other religious denominations. And only three believers—0.75% of all those questioned—answered that they find the meaning of their life in 'bringing to Christ' their children or the children of their close [relatives]. These believers were people of retirement age, two Orthodox and one Baptist, one of whom had no children of his own" (Duluman, *Sovremennyi veruiushchii*, p. 101). Similarly, in a study of believing factory workers, Cherniak found that nearly 64% at one factory and 38% at another considered that the welfare of society was the goal of life or one of its goals, combined with personal welfare (*Formirovanie*, p. 176). "Of 1,645 believers we surveyed, only 30% connected their answer to the question on the meaning of life with 'blessedness in the afterlife' " (Sytenko, "O nravstvennom oblike," p. 121). According to another study, only 16.7% of the Orthodox who were questioned gave a distinctly religious answer to the question about the meaning of life, while 57.8% of the Baptists did so (Iablokov, "Transformatsiia, p. 141). "In the official theology, the necessity to fulfill earthly tasks is not denied; however, it is considered that this fulfillment bears real meaning only when there is a relationship to god in it. When believers say that the meaning of life is in service to god and in fulfilling earthly tasks, one may not draw the conclusion from this that they support a purely religious understanding of the meaning of life. Their answer testifies to a bi-level orientation with regard to this question" (ibid.).

In approaching essentially the same matter from a slightly different direction, the large-scale study in the Voronezh region discovered the responses shown in table 10.5 when people were asked what were the sources of the good.

Similarly, when the concept of happiness was explored, a significant

TABLE 10.5
SOURCES OF THE GOOD

Sources of the good	Number	Percentage
God	1,730	13.0
God and people (god acting through people)	5,324	40.0
Only people	3,461	26.0
Do not know	1,879	14.1
Avoided answering	916	6.9
Totals	13,310	100.0

SOURCE: Tepliakov, *Problemy*, p. 141.

number of believers indicated no relationship between religion and happiness. "We have an especially large number of representatives of this group among the Orthodox (42.71% of all Orthodox questioned). Among Baptists, representatives of this group are fewer (8.89% of all Baptists questioned). In the consciousness of this group of believers, a nonreligious concept of happiness prevails. To these believers, moral satisfaction and joy belong first of all to labor for the good of the people, care for people around one, for children, etc." (Iablokov, "Transformatsiia," pp. 143–44). Only 6.2% of the Orthodox who were questioned by Iablokov connected happiness with communion with God, while the percentage of Baptists who did so was ten times as high (ibid., p. 143). "It is typical that more than one-fourth (25.7%) of the believers who were questioned consider that happiness is possible only beyond the grave, and only less than one-fifth (19.7%) feel that they are happy" (Pismanik, "Religioznaia konseptsiia," p. 150). Ignatenko, however, found the opposite to be the case: "Acceptance of the idea of salvation exercises its influence on the psychological situation of Baptists, which is expressed in a tranquility bordering on indifference to surroundings. Curious data testify to this also: 95.4% of those questioned expressed satisfaction with their lives. The reason for satisfaction was, for the overwhelming majority, religious. 82.1% connected their satisfaction with assurance of personal salvation" ("Opyt," pp. 255–56).

Apparently only a very small proportion of believers feel that a person's fate is predestined by God (Cherniak, "Nuzhen nauchnyi podkhod," p. 26); indeed, in the Arkhangelsk region, 151 respondents held that fate might exist, which was 84 more than believed in God (Kobetskii, *Sotsiologicheskoe izuchenie,* p. 39).

> In the research that we conducted, the following question was included in the proposal for carrying out the survey: "Which of the following assertions about a person's fate expresses your opinion?"—with the following variant answers: "A person's fate depends entirely on himself; it depends on him in part; a person's fate does not depend on him at all; it is ordained by god; I do not know; I have another opinion (specify)."
>
> As the survey at the [factory] and light-industry enterprises of Alma-Ata demonstrated, only 1 to 2.5% of the workers considered that a person's fate was ordained by god, while a substantial majority considered that a person's fate was either entirely or partially dependent upon himself. [Cherniak, *Formirovanie,* p. 115]

Finally, regarding the relationship between religion and behavior, a fairly broad range of opinions has been presented. In a study of Baptists, "to the question of what, in the last analysis, determines human conduct, 66.4% answered: 'the will of god,' 43.3% pointed to personal interest, and only 9.1% also cited social along with personal interest" (Ignatenko, "Opyt," p. 262). Ugrinovich found that 23% of the believers thought that religion played no role whatsoever in a person's life (*Vvedenie,* p. 109). More pragmatically, Vasilevskaia's study of the families of wavering believers found that "71.5% of the members associate their religiousness with family traditions and consider it an attribute of family life; they do not transfer religious ideas and norms of conduct to professional and social life" ("Opyt," p. 398).

Summarizing, it would appear that these attempts to discern such general aspects of the believers' world view are not especially convincing. The parameters selected by these researchers are highly amorphous and, indeed, scarcely deal with commonplace matters on which one would expect broad agreement. Raising such unexpected questions as these can only cause a degree of confusion in the respondent, and he will be likely to select an answer that may not, on reflection, correspond to his actual point of view. Particularly if the respondent is hostile, or even if he gives less than his most enthusiastic cooperation in the research, he is not likely to spend a great deal of time in examining the ramifications of the question before he gives an answer. Hence the way in which the question is presented, together with the atmosphere that prevails at the time the question is raised, will be likely to determine the answers. Consequently, such findings as have been described above may not actually be descriptive of anything at all other than the interview procedures that were used. As a result, great care must be exercised when one utilizes the data acquired by Soviet sociological researchers in such exotic areas as these.

11

RELIGIOUS LIFE

Soviet sociologists do not spend much effort on the purely religious aspects of contemporary religiousness—church attendance, observance of ceremonies, participation in the rites, and so forth. In part, this relative neglect may seem strange, for from an institutional point of view and from a social point of view as well, such overt behavior might be considered to be much more important than an individual's interior thoughts. However, Soviet researchers rightly consider that these overt expressions of religious faith by no means exhaust the problem of religiousness and that, indeed, from society's point of view, many other parameters are more important. Nevertheless, because activities relating to worship constitute a recognizable part of the religious way of life, many Soviet researchers do devote some attention to it.

Icons are among the most widespread phenomena in traditionally Russian Orthodox areas of the USSR. Apparently a very high proportion of the population, far in excess of those who would classify themselves as believers, keep icons in their homes. Indeed, for a large portion of the religious people, keeping icons and participating in a small number of ceremonies is the extent of their observable religiousness (Duluman, *Sovremennyi veruiushchii*, p. 31). No data are available concerning how many of the general population keep icons, but a very large proportion of the religious people do so. According to one study, 95% of the believers keep icons at home, even though only half of them do so for religious purposes.[1] "Icons, which, incidentally, the majority of those surveyed possess, are not infrequently kept in the homes by tradition. Here is how the statements themselves illustrate this: 24 people [of 177] say that they keep icons 'for personal prayers,' and 17 'because of the believing members of the

173

family.' And the remainder? 'It is customary,' say 77 people; 'To beautify the apartment,' answer 22 people. Thus, 99 inhabitants of the village keep icons because of tradition" (Safronov, "Chto," pp. 70–71).

Interestingly enough, in a study in two villages where there were no churches at all, Pashkov discovered that, with very few exceptions, there were icons in every house. This was true not only where there were believers in the family but even in the completely nonreligious families ("K voprosu," p. 151). In a study of three collective farms, Alekseev found that there were icons in 90%, 90.6%, and 62.8% of the homes, respectively ("Metodika," p. 146). Kolbanovskii found that 90% of the rural homes had icons, but they were present in only 35% of the town homes and 14% of the city dwellings (*Kollektiv*, p. 244). "In families whose heads are employed in state institutions, only 21% of the families have icons; families of workers and business employees, 30%; and of collective farmers, 47%. We are not talking about pensioners and the unemployed, among whom the major part (60% and 75%, respectively) adorn the red corners of their huts with icons. Thus the huts of collective farmers are 1½ to 2 times more 'saturated' with icons than are the homes of other families and workers and employees."[2]

What is of greater concern to Soviet researchers is that it would appear that not even atheists—including members of the Communist Party—are free from this religious tradition. According to Vasilevskaia, among the homes where the head of the family is an atheist, 4.5% have icons ("Opyt," p. 392). Some Party members keep icons at home, including one whose wife was serving as a counselor to the Young Pioneers (*Pravda*, 13 December 1961). In a survey of 5,559 members and candidate members of the Communist Party and 11,165 members of the Komsomol (Communist League of Youth), Tepliakov discovered that more than 17% of the Communists and 45% of the Komsomol members kept icons at home (*Problemy*, p. 59). On one collective farm, it was discovered that 28 of the 52 members of the Communist Party had icons in their homes (Safronov, "Ateisticheskoe vospitanie," p. 238).

With regard to church attendance, there are wide variations in the data. Some studies find that a high proportion of the religious believers are exceedingly faithful about church attendance. "Conversations conducted with believers in Orel testify to the fact that each rank-and-file Baptist relates extraordinarily seriously to attending the meetings, trying not to miss a single service" (Tazhurina, "Mistifikatsiia," p. 74). In the large-scale Voronezh study, Tepliakov found that 75% of the believers attended church and prayer meetings more or less regularly (*Problemy*, p. 167). Of the urban believers, 72% did so (ibid., p. 85). Ugrinovich found that 55 to 60% of all believers attended regularly, 30 to 35% attended less regularly, and only 2 to 5% attended once in a while with relatives or friends (*Vvedenie*, p. 135; cf. Klibanov, *Religioznoe sektantstvo*, pp. 121–22). It should be noted that in some studies, at least such high percentages of regular church attendance among the believers may not, in fact, indicate that the believers who were studied were more diligent about attending church than were those studied by other researchers; in some cases, these results may indicate that a definition of "believer" was utilized that would tend to include only those who were active and faithful in such external attributes of religious life as church attendance, while relegating the remainder to another category, such as "waverers." Thus, these findings may be more indicative of the definitional schemes that were used than of accurate indices of patterns of church attendance among all Soviet believers.

Other researchers have found that regular church attendance is not so common among the believers. "As became clear in the course of the Penza research, in the composition of the Orthodox, one may separate out a group of convinced believers who are distinguished by their activity in fulfilling the basic prescriptions of the faith and cultus. To this category may be ascribed not more than 30 to 40% of the Orthodox, while among the Baptists it constitutes not less than 63%" (Klibanov, "Veruiushchii," p. 73). Among Old Believers, only 21.6% attended regularly, while 57.4% only came to church on major religious holidays, and 21% of the believers had not attended a divine service for more than a year (Podmazov, "Sovremennoe staroobriadchestvo," p. 199). In a rural study, Ul'ianov discovered that only 12% of the believers attended services several times a month; while 30% attended only 3 or 4 times a year; 39.3%, only 1 or 2 times a year; and 14.3% of the believers had not attended church in the preceding five years ("Opyt," p. 224). According to Ugrinovich's study, 36% of the believers attended church only once or twice a year (*Vvedenie*, pp. 109–10).

Many Soviet researchers feel that church attendance is not a very widespread attribute of contemporary religious belief in the USSR. "The normative believer does not attend church very zealously. Concrete social research testifies that he goes to church a nominal once a month. True, when he is in church, he conscientiously places his coin on the collection plate and buys a candle, and he hears the church service in its entirety" (Duluman, *Sovremennyi veruiushchii*, p. 46). Safronov reports that "according to the data of the questionnaire, only 6 respondents [3.4%] regularly attend divine service in the local church (the church serves fifteen villages)"; he does not, however, indicate the distance to this church, but if it serves fifteen villages, transportation, which can often be very primitive in rural Russia, may be a significant factor in influencing the patterns of church attendance "Chto," p. 71). "In the town of Gnilets there is no church. And to attend the nearest church, which is located 25 km. away, takes no small amount of time. True, 53% of the believers questioned had not gone there once during the course of a year. But the remainder attended it (33% were there once a year, and the remainder— 14%—2 to 3 times and more)" (Gaidurova, "Zavisimost'," p. 31). It should be noted that Gaidurova failed to consider whether the believers were responding candidly. There are many disadvantages of a distant church, but one positive advantage is anonymity for those who attend, and it would not seem likely that all the believers who were questioned would surrender this valuable anonymity for the purposes of ensuring that the atheist's study would achieve technical accuracy.

In one fairly large-scale study, Klibanov discovered that among the Orthodox, only 10.7% attended church regularly, while 63.0% attended irregularly, and 26.3% did not attend at all (the figures for Baptists were 88%, 9%, and 3%, respectively; "Veruiushchii," p. 73). "Here is the distribution of answers, of people who count themselves among the believers, to the question 'Have you attended church often during the past year?': several times a week—0.6%; once a week—2.8%; 1 or 2 times a month— 8.3%; only on 'great' religious festivals (Easter, Christmas, 'Patron Saint')— 16.2%; 1 or 2 times a year—36.1%; have not attended—22.1%" (Ul'ianov, "Opyt," pp. 223–24). A study of patterns of church attendance yielded the percentages shown in table 11.1 for family members. It should be noted that these families embraced three generations (mother, father) or even four generations (other relatives). A study of two rural towns, neither of which possessed a church, showed that of 538 believers, only 24 (4.5%) managed to attend church more than twice a year, 250 (46.5%) attended once or twice a year, and 261 (48.5%) did not attend at all (Pashkov, "K voprosu," p. 153);[3] 43% of the believers had not attended a divine service in five years (ibid.; cf. Alekseev, "Metodika," p. 149).[4] Among a group of higher-education students who were wavering believers, however, only 4% were able to state that they did not visit church meetings and never had done so (Lebedev, "Studencheskaia molodezh'," p. 203). In a Belorussian village, 137 of 177 believers (77%) considered that church attendance was unnecessary (Safronov, "Chto," p. 70). As has been noted, only 8.4% of 235 working women living in a suburban Moscow dormitory attend church, and only 1 or 2 times a year as a rule (Ugrinovich, *Filosofskie problemy*, pp. 118–19).

In a study in Leningrad, Kobetskii found that only 10% of the

Religious Life

TABLE 11.1
A Study of Church Attendance

Attend church	Wife	Husband	Children	Mother	Father	Other relatives
On religious holidays	5.1%	0.2%	0.5%	13.5%	4.0%	33.3%
On Sundays	1.4	0.4	0.2	2.8	......	4.8
From time to time	7.9	3.2	3.3	17.9	......	38.0
Do not attend	85.6	96.2	96.0	65.8	96.0	23.9

SOURCE: Vasilevskaia, "Opyt," p. 395.
NOTE: The anomaly of more husbands attending church on Sundays than on religious holidays, when all other family members follow an opposite pattern, may be explained by the failure of the researcher to specify "*major* religious holidays." Many Russian Orthodox churches hold relatively brief morning or afternoon services on the minor holidays and saints' days, which occur as often as several times a week. With the exception of the breadwinner, who would normally be at work, these services might be more attractive to the members of the family than Sunday services, because the weekday services are usually less crowded and less likely to attract the attention of hostile authorities.

Baptists attended church regularly; the rest attended very infrequently indeed (*Sotsiologichesko izuchenie,* p. 41). This may well reflect the fact that early during the antireligious campaign, the Baptist church in Leningrad was forced to move, and at least until rather recently, Leningrad Baptists had to make a very inconvenient, time-consuming trip to the farther reaches of the metropolitan area in order to attend church.

Even where researchers find that patterns of church attendance are very low, disturbing data may appear. Tepliakov discovered that some members of the Communist Party attended church and prayer meetings (*Problemy,* p. 59). The consensus of Soviet sociological research, however, would seem to indicate that regular church attendance is by no means uniform among contemporary Soviet religious believers, and large proportions of them attend church rarely or not at all.

One of the chief reasons for the low levels of church attendance is, quite simply, the inadequate number of churches that are presently operating in the USSR. This factor is seldom mentioned in Soviet sociological writings. Pashkov, for example, goes to some lengths to make the point that for a number of reasons, observations of church attendance will not give an adequate index of the extent of religiousness in the population, but at no point does he mention that chief among the reasons is that there simply are not enough churches to serve the needs of more than a very small part of the religious population ("K voprosu," p. 149).

On the rare occasions when the number of churches are referred to, some fairly startling claims are made: in one case it was claimed that

177

currently there are fewer churches operating in the USSR than there were in 1940 (Duluman, *Sovremennyi veruiushchii*, p. 31). If true, this would be an astonishing revelation, for in 1941, after the church had recovered somewhat from the worst excesses of the thirties, by official figures there were only 4,225 Russian Orthodox churches still operating in the USSR, and informed estimates suggested that the true figure might be a great deal smaller.[5] Less extreme estimates suggest that perhaps one-tenth as many churches are now operating as existed before the Revolution (Il'inykh, "Osobennosti," p. 153); this estimate compares fairly well with at least one published figure that 7,500 Orthodox churches are currently operating in the USSR.[6] Compounding the problem is the uneven geographical distribution of the churches: one-third of the Baptist congregations and more than half of the Seventh Day Adventist and Pentecostal congregations, for example, are to be found in the Ukraine (Klibanov, *Religioznoe sektantstvo*, p. 76).

It is obvious that the number of churches that are presently allowed to operate legally is vastly below the number that would be needed in order to provide for the believing sector of the population. During the worst of the antireligious campaign, massive numbers of churches were being closed against the wishes of believers, and one still finds indications that such indifference to the needs of the religious people is not a thing of the past. For example, "At the present time nobody among the inhabitants of the village, where in former years a high level of religiousness was observed, attends church, and their participation in religious rites has been significantly reduced" (Selivanov, *Partiinoe rukovodstvo*, p. 76). It may well be that, as this report claims, this change is the result of vigorous antireligious work; but an abrupt closure of the church would just as easily account for it.

Baltanov warns against placing too much reliance on reports concerning the number of churches and attendance at them as indices of a decline in religion, for "the fact of the matter is that besides the official religious congregations in the country, there exists a multitude of unregistered religious congregations and clergymen who perform various rites" (*Sotsiologicheskie problemy*, p. 222). He is careful to remind his colleagues that "by means of concrete sociological research it has been established that the real number of religious congregations in our country is significantly higher than the number of officially registered religious associations" (ibid., p. 179).

The result of the diminished number of churches that are legally allowed to operate, of course, is a radical extension in the geographical territory that is served by individual churches.

During recent decades, substantial changes have taken place in the composition of parishioners. These are expressed first by a diminution in the number of parishioners in those population points that formerly constituted parishes, and in the second place in the increase in the number of points whose inhabitants participate in the activities of the parish. These are two interrelated processes, at the basis of which is the departure of the local population from religion and the decline in the number of churches. Thus, in the Ardatovsk district, Gorky region, in 1916 there were 18 parish churches, which served parishioners of 50 population points, while in 1966 two parishes were functioning. There was a corresponding diminution in the composition of the parishioners. [Ugrinovich, *Vvedenie,* p. 133]

"Now not a single pastor, not a single church elder can say how many parishioners there are in his church-parish congregation, for the borders of this congregation have dissipated, have become completely indeterminate" (Pashkov, "K voprosu," p. 153). In one church, more than 78% of the members inhabited neighboring villages and farms (Gaidurova, "Zavisimost'," p. 23).

There is a tendency towards a concentration of the remaining churches in the cities, at the expense of rural churches (Klibanov, *Religioznoe sektantstvo,* p. 89). This is only to be expected, for the larger population that the urban church is able to serve, due to higher densities of population and better networks of transportation, indicates that these will be stronger churches than those in the countryside and hence better able to withstand official hostility.

Infrequently, rural believers have been known to take matters into their own hands; one group of villagers built their own church:

Naturally, now the believers are very proud of the work of their hands; moreover, the church, in their opinion, is the village's distinguishing adornment (it does indeed give the impression of being the best building in the village, especially in comparison with the ugly clubhouse that stands next to it—a mud hut). (Footnote: Not only are the believers proud of the church building, a young collective farm woman, S. N. [32 years old] said, not without praise, "We have a fine church. Inside it is still better. They recognize us by our church. Wherever you may go they ask: 'And this is in Verkaniaia Plasovka, where there is the church?' ") [Gaidurova, "Zavisimost'," p. 23]

Naturally, with such a paucity of legally registered churches, unregistered (and illegal) churches abound. "At the beginning of 1971, in the territory of the [Voronezh] region, 48 registered congregations and 484 unregistered groups of the Orthodox Church were active; 8 registered congregations and 97 unregistered groups of the church of Evangelical Christians-Baptists; one registered congregation and 14 unregistered groups of Old Believers; 2 congregations of Molokans; 2 congregations of Sabbatarians; 10 groups of Pentecostals; 4 groups of Adventists; 1 Jewish congregation, and 23 groups of [underground] 'True Orthodox Christians'" (Tepliakov, *Problemy*, p. 169).

Nor can religious people afford to be selective concerning which churches they attend, given the scarcity of functioning churches. Crossing denominational boundaries is common. "Several Orthodox, in connection with the fact that the church in Ol'shany is not working, sometimes look in on the Baptist church and relate sympathetically to the Baptists themselves" (Fedorenko, *Sekty*, p. 235); Orthodox people commonly attend Old Believers churches, and vice versa.[7] Indeed, according to one researcher, adherents of different religions worship together: 21 of 148 Christians and 8 of 49 Muslims who were surveyed in Ossetia participated in both Christian and Muslim worship (*Gertsenovskie chteniia* 3 (1972): 14).

The churches that remain tend to be fairly active. "Of 56 [Orthodox] churches which were active in 1964, only in 10 are services held daily, in 11 they are held 2 or 3 times a week, and in the remaining 35, on religious holidays (70 days during the year)" (Tepliakov, *Problemy*, p. 147). Regular attendance at such churches provides the believer with substantial resources. "One of the directions of the activity of the Orthodox church is increasing the divine services of the church. In the churches of the region, each year from 8 to 9 thousand services are conducted. Convinced believers who attend church systematically listen to no fewer than 50 sermons per year" (ibid., p. 171). A typical rural church may attract 10 to 15 people to weekday services, 100 to 150 people on Sundays, and as many as 400 on major religious holidays (ibid., p. 147); some churches, of course, attract fewer (ibid., pp. 144–45).

According to Pivovarov, among those who attend church, usually 30% are 50 to 60 years old, and only 1% are 18 to 25 years old; 23.6% in rural churches and 13.2% in urban churches are between the ages of 20 and 40; and in urban churches, 10% more are over the age of 50 than in rural churches (*Struktura*, pp. 17–18). Pismanik found that those who were over 50 accounted for 70% and 55% of those who were attending two weekday services in the Moscow Baptist Church; among the Orthodox in Perm', they accounted for 80% on a weekday during working hours, 60% on a weekday during Holy Week, and 50% on Easter; among the Orthodox in a Moscow church, 87% on Saturday of Easter week were over 50, and "more than half" at a Moscow Catholic Sunday service were in this age group ("O sostoianii," p. 215). In a study of a Baptist congregation Stel'makov discovered that

> in it there is a significant percentage of comparatively young people with education from 7 to 10 years, and some believers have finished trade schools. In the congregation, prayer meetings are regularly conducted, and sermons are delivered that are distinguished not only by contents of interest to believers, but also by their powerful emotional coloring. Rank-and-file believers are actively encouraged to prepare and deliver short sermons and prayers. The setting of the prayer meetings that members of the expedition attended allows one to draw the conclusion that the feelings of believers are actively engaged in everything that happens.
>
> The majority of believers in this congregation are informed on the basic Baptist ideas and defend them tenaciously. ["O sootnoshenii," pp. 40–41]

By observing the Vladimir Cathedral in Moscow in 1965, Kobetskii discovered that 7% of the congregation at a weekday service and 4% of those attending the midnight service on Easter morning were children and adolescents; the researcher does not comment about the fact that this occurred when the campaign to prohibit church attendance by minors was at its height or about the possibility that some of the children, particularly during the Easter service (which typically lasts from 10:45 P.M. to 1:30 A.M. or later), may have been present due to problems with finding baby-sitters ("Obriad," pp. 167–68). "Analysis of the composition of participants in divine service shows that even on Sundays and also at evening services (i.e., at times when even workers in industry can attend church), women constitute more than 80% of the general number of worshipers. On weekdays, in the morning and afternoon, among the participants in divine services women constitute more than 90% of those present. According to the same data, it follows that approximately the same relative number of women and men are observed fulfilling the rites of confession and the Eucharist" (Pismanik, "O sostoianii," pp. 213–14). Average attendance figures for three Moscow churches suggested that 91%, 83%, and 72% of those present were women (Iablokov, "Obshchenie," p. 62). Pismanik acquired similar results in the Perm region ("O sostoianii," p. 213).

There have been some attempts to determine the reasons for attending church. Naturally, the satisfaction of religious needs occupies a significant place among these reasons, but there are other motivations as well

181

(Ul'ianov, "Opyt," pp. 224–25). Aesthetic reasons occupy a prominent place, "the splendor of the temple, the solemnity and beauty of the service, and first of all the church singing."[8] A considerable range of motivations operates among those who attend church. "For example, research on the motives of attendance at an Orthodox church by people who classify themselves as believers was conducted in the Penza region by L. N. Ul'ianov. Among those surveyed, 18.7% stated that they received comfort in church, 14.7% identified the motive for attendance as the desire to hear the sermon, 35.6% as the desire to confess and receive the Eucharist, 9.3% as the wish to listen to the singing, 1.4% as the need to meet with acquaintances, 0.9% as curiosity, and 3.4% as following tradition" (Ugrinovich, *Vvedenie*, pp. 113–14).[9] Ul'ianov's data appear in table 11.2.

Soviet sociological researchers have also devoted some attention to the observance of religious holidays. Although there are some data to the contrary, it would seem that religious holidays are almost universally observed, even in areas that have very few believers in the population (Kolbanovskii, *Kollektiv*, p. 247). Of the students at institutions of higher education who were wavering believers, only 11% stated categorically that they did not participate in religious holidays (Lebedev, "Studencheskaia molodezh'," p. 203). In a study of three collective farms, Alekseev found that 80% of the families observed the major religious holidays, even though there were no churches at the farm ("Metodika," p. 146). Among the nonreligious majority of the 30,000 surveyed in the Penza region, half admitted that they observed religious holidays at home (Selivanov, *Par-*

TABLE 11.2

REASONS FOR ATTENDING CHURCH

Reasons for attending church (each person could give one or several)	Percentage
To confess and communicate	36.0
I experience feeling of satisfaction, receive comfort	18.8
I listen to the sermon	14.8
I love to hear the singing	9.4
I place candle (s) to revered icons	7.5
Because many people come	3.4
To adore icons or appreciate paintings as works of art	2.5
I meet with acquaintances	1.4
Rest from cares	1.1
From curiosity	0.9
Other opinions	0.6
Difficult to answer	4.0

SOURCE: Ul'ianov, "Opyt," p. 223.

tiinoe rukovodstvo, p. 83). According to one study, almost half of the high-school students who were questioned expressed indifference to religious holidays, which, in view of the circumstances, probably indicated that a great many of them observed these festivals in one way or another (*Gertsenovskie chteniia* 3 (1972): 24). It was reported that one collective farm lost 30,000 man-days per year because of religious holidays (*Molodoi kommunist*, no. 12 (1963), pp. 20–21), and another farm observed 39 saints' days as holidays each year.[10] Similarly, in a formerly Sabbatarian village, where only 20 to 25 of the 1,200 inhabitants were believers, nobody worked on Saturdays (Tul'tseva, "Evoliutsiia," p. 214).

With regard to the observance of religious regulations regarding fasting (e.g., during Lent), Ul'ianov found that "more than 60% of the people who attach themselves to the group of believers do not observe fasts, and of the number who do fast, only about 15% are motivated by deep religious convictions" ("Opyt," p. 226). The corollary may be that nearly 40% of these believers did observe fasts. Tepliakov's study found that some 70% of the believers did not observe fasts ("Pobeda," pp. 154–55); while Ashirov, in a study of more than 1,500 Tatars, found that among the 396 believers, 40% of the women and 60% of the men did not observe the month-long fast of Ramadan. Analogous results were derived from other Muslim areas ("Evoliutsiia," p. 15).

Some studies have contradicted this suggestion that the observance of religious holidays is fairly widespread. Saparmukhamedova found that among 300 believing women, only 19.8% observed the holidays and fulfilled religious rites ("Obshchestvennoe mnenie," p. 21). On the other hand, Tepliakov discovered that 56% of the members of the Communist Party and 66.4% of the Komsomol members compromised with believing relatives in observing religious holidays (*Problemy*, p. 59). Particularly during the Easter season, an impressive number take part in the religious celebrations.

In all [three] Orthodox churches in Voronezh in 1966, 43,710 kissed the shroud, in 1967—35,342, in 1968—35,203, in 1969— 31,478, in 1970—31,742, and in 1971—27,909. Despite the absolute decline over the years in the number of those who kissed the cross while the population of Voronezh was growing, this unsanitary and nonsensical rite is still observed by a great many.

In 1971, believing parents and relatives brought 975 nursing children and preschoolers to kiss the shroud. It was established that 614 school children kissed the shroud.

On Easter Sunday, 21 April 1968, at the Voronezh cemeteries there were about 150,000 people, while on Easter Sunday, 18 April

183

1971, up to 90,000 people. Of them, about 30% came for religious reasons. [Ibid., p. 167]

Naturally, the reasons for observing religious holidays are by no means confined to religious motivations. In one case, only 10% of the people at a church for a holiday celebration had any idea of what the holiday was (Kampars, "Nekotorye problemy," p. 20). In other cases, "analysis demonstrated that 58% of the contemporary believers and waverers observed church holidays for other than religious motives" (Tepliakov *Problemy*, p. 143). Ul'ianov found that 56% were so motivated ("Opyt," p. 226). In one study conducted in three regions, Iablokov concluded that these observances "are motivated by faith in god only among 30% of those questioned. At the same time, 38% of those questioned participate in religious holidays and rituals with the goal of broadening their life by meeting with relatives and friends; 18% are attracted by the splendor and theatricality of the church service; and 14% are under the influence of social opinion of believers or relatives" (*Metodologicheskie problemy*, p. 122).

In a study of Old Believers, Podmazov found that among 444 adherents of this ancient form of Orthodoxy,

> only 104 (23.4%) systematically observe fasts, for "Christ himself fasted 40 days and 40 nights, driving the tempter from him," and "he who does not fast, by living for his own pleasure works not for god but for his own stomach; therefore his death will also be sooner, medicine proves this, and after death—eternal torments." Argumentation defending fasts has also changed, and the reasons stated above are rarely met. Most often of all, they now do not say that fasting helps "save the soul and is pleasing to god," but they speak of the danger of too much food, of the necessity of periodic unloadings of the organism, etc., citing for this, not the lord god, but medicine. Among the believers, 90 (20.3%) fast often, usually during the final week, infrequently during the first and the final weeks of Lent. Those who are forced to observe a fast under the influence of one of the members of the family belong to this group. Among these Old Believers, 250 (56.3%) have already dropped this custom. Some of them, while continuing to be believers, try to find justification for renouncing fasting in the "holy scriptures." "In the gospels it says," states M. (72 years old, second grade), "that not that which goes into the mouth defiles a man, but that which comes out, i.e., bad words. One may eat anything." ["Sovremennoe staroobriadchestvo," p. 198]

Nevertheless, the religious dimension of these holidays is still significant, and the effectiveness of the holiday ceremonies in eliciting a deep, religiously oriented response is considerable.

"Once," related A. A. Osipov, "in front of the mourners on the day of the 'burial of Christ,' one priest gave the following sermon: 'A grave before us! Are there words? The deceased died for us. A time to converse? For us! He died. And we live. Weep!' and silent, electrified by the situation, hypnotized by the power of the word, they began to weep." This sermon, which embraces 21 words, has all the qualities needed for expressing the inner effect: the connection between thoughts and feeling, concepts and the listeners nearby, beauty and conciseness, contrast in the composition of the phrases, intonational variety, composition of the question and statement, etc. [Iablokov, "Obshchenie," p. 61]

It is not entirely surprising, then, that the massive effort to replace religious holidays and rituals with secular substitutes has not enjoyed universal success.[11]

Soviet authorities are deeply concerned about the persistence of religious sacraments in the atheistic society. Baptism, religious weddings, and religious funerals have shown a surprising tenacity. In the Trans-Carpathian area, baptisms of children declined by only 15%; weddings, by 13.5%; and church funerals, by 11% over a decade.[12] In Latvia, for example, after nearly a decade of intensive effort, participation in these rites was reduced by a mere 6.8%;[13] eight years later this slow rate of decline was confirmed by a report that "from 1966 to 1975 the number of baptisms of newborn declined by 4.2% in the Republic; weddings, by 4.6%; and the number of funerals according to the church rite diminished by 10%" (Freiberg, "Rol'," p. 169). Changes this small may be completely insignificant and may reflect primarily the increased circumspection on the part of the participants.

Among college-aged students, only 55% of the wavering believers were able to state that they did not participate in religious rites and never had done so (Lebedev, "Studencheskaia molodezh'," p. 203). Indeed, even convinced atheists have not always renounced these rituals. "In practice, one meets from time to time with the performance of religious rites by members of atheistic families, and this relates, in the main, to representatives of the older generation. According to data of the research, such phenomena take place in not more than 2% of the atheistic families, and have an episodic character" (Vasilevskaia, "Opyt," p. 402). Not all Soviet commentators are quite so unconcerned. "A person of atheistic convictions, when he is among believing people and does not wish to complicate his relations with them, may fulfill religious rites and show his positive

185

relationship to religion outwardly. Our press brings out examples of such conduct on the part of individual Communists and members of the Komsomol" (Baltanov, *Sotsiologicheskie problemy*, p. 135). There is no room for complacency, for Soviet researchers have a healthy respect for the potential influence of religious rituals. Even when the motives are not religious, participation in such rituals indicates a friendliness toward religion or, at best, an indifferent, passive, or indiscriminate attitude— certainly such people are far from the Party-mindedness that is supposed to be the mark of the Soviet citizen (ibid., pp. 105–6).[14] "Sometimes participation in such rites serves as that 'hook' which enables an individual to be attracted into the sphere of the influence of the church" (Ugrinovich, *Vvedenie*, p. 136). Consequently, Soviet sociological researchers devote considerable attention to baptism, marriage, and funeral ceremonies in contemporary society.

With regard to baptism, there are not enough data to allow one to have any confidence in estimates of the percentage of the newly born in the USSR who are baptized. Exceedingly low figures are sometimes reported: "From conversations with Old Believers from [five villages] it is known that of the general number of newborn, not more than 10 percent are baptized by the preceptors."[15] Such a low estimate should not be accepted too credulously, for other evidence indicates that the rite is extremely tenacious among Old Believers (see below, p. 193). Even such an assertion as Aptekman's that "in previous years, as many as 25% of the total number of children born were baptized" ("Vitality," pp. 367–68) may be far too low. Studies in the Baltic states might serve to support such low readings, however. In one district in Latvia, 25.7% of the newborn were baptized.[16] In Estonia, only 11.8% of those born in 1969 were baptized.[17] In Lithuania, however, which is predominantly Catholic, as many as 51% of the newborn were baptized (Barkauskas, "Osushchestvlenie," p. 162), or perhaps even more.[18]

Conflicting reports have resulted from attempts to determine the practices of believers with regard to baptism. In the Voronezh study, "of 13,310 religious citizens surveyed, 11,846 (89%) answered that they had had their children and grandchildren baptized, and the remainder stated that they would have children and grandchildren baptized if they had them (Tepliakov, *Problemy*, p. 168). This surprising result, that virtually all believers practice baptism, has not always been supported by other researchers. "According to our data, in the group of people who number themselves among the believers, those who participate in the rite of baptism constitute 80%, and among waverers—66%. Not infrequently, nonbelievers also participate in this practice" (Ul'ianov, "Opyt," p. 227).

Tepliakov found that 38% of the believers did not baptize their children ("Pobeda," p. 154); but inasmuch as his research project mixed 2,075 convinced Orthodox and sectarian believers indiscriminantly, without distinguishing between the Orthodox, who practice pedobaptism, and Christian sectarians (such as the Baptists), who do not, this datum is meaningless.

According to Safronov's study, "To the question 'In order to be a moral and good person, is it essential to have one's children baptized?' 109 of those interviewed answered, 'no'; 12 said, 'I don't know'; and 56 said 'yes' " ("Chto," p. 70). It should be noted, however, that in this case the peculiar phrasing of the question almost guaranteed that a large number of the answers would be negative; a great many religious believers, regardless of how strongly they might adhere to baptism, would be unwilling to imply that moral goodness can be achieved only if one baptizes his children. In another study, it was found that there was a very low level of participation in baptism among Christians (13 out of 148 baptized their children or grandchildren) (*Gertsenovskie chteniia* 3 [1972]: 13). In this case, however, the study was conducted among the Ossetians, and no data were given concerning the number of churches. Many of the minor nationalities were only brought into the Orthodox fold rather recently, and under Soviet conditions, churches are exceedingly scarce in some of these areas.

Whether or not the levels of participation in the rite are as low as some of these studies would suggest, Soviet researchers recognize the potential danger of baptism.

> Participation in the rite even for unbelieving parents often does not pass them by without results. This, for example, is what N., a [female] worker at a box factory in Volkhov district, Leningrad region, said: "The rite was performed on both children. The first child was baptized at the age of 5 months; before the baptism the child was sickly, didn't sleep, misbehaved. After baptism he improved right away. Therefore, the second child was also baptized." N., who earlier was not religious, under the influence both of her mother and of the allegedly beneficial results of the baptism of the first child, became a believer. When she had the second child baptized, at the same time she was baptized herself. [Kobetskii, "Obriad," p. 164]

Understandably enough, Soviet researchers are vitally concerned with the motivations that lead people to have their children baptized. Purely religious considerations play only a rather small part in baptisms, according to many researchers. Galitskaia discovered that only 17% of the young parents who had their children baptized did so "because they consider that religion in a special, mysterious way exercises an influence on the life of the infant" ("K voprosu," p. 401). Two studies independently discovered that only 8% of those who have the rite performed are believers who act according to their convictions (Ugrinovich, *Vvedenie*, p. 136; Ul'ianov, "Opyt," p. 230). Similarly, according to a study among workers in Moscow, only 8.6% of those who had their children baptized did so for religious reasons (Iablokov, *Metodologicheskie problemy*, p. 123). Tepliakov asserts, "Research has shown that only 9.8% of the parents baptized children for religious motives, while the remainder had this rite performed for motives that speak of their indifference in regard to questions of world view" (*Problemy*, p. 143). Table 11.3 indicates the motivations according to Ul'ianov's study.

Many researchers agree that indifference plays a large role in baptism. Ul'ianov states that "more than 36% of the parents who baptized their children were guided by reasoning of the sort that 'we are all baptized, everyone does it,' 'this is a basic custom in which there is nothing bad'" ("Opyt," p. 230). More than 36% of the parents who were questioned gave such responses (Aptekman, "Vitality," p. 372).

Other motives play a part in baptism. According to Kapustin, the strength of tradition accounted for 60% of the contemporary baptisms.[19] Ul'ianov found that only a small portion of the parents were attracted by the beauty and splendor of the ritual ("Opyt," p. 230).

One of the most widespread motivations, however, is the influence that believing relatives have exerted on the infant's parents.

TABLE 11.3
REASONS FOR PARTICIPATION IN BAPTISM

Population group	Role in the rite	In past year	In past 5 yrs.	In past 10 yrs.	Over 10 yrs. ago
Considers self a believer	Baptized own child	5.1%	15.6%	15.9%	54.3%
	Was godparent	2.9	5.7	8.1	38.8
Considers self a waverer	Baptized own child	8.5	21.3	21.7	47.3
	Was godparent	4.0	8.5	6.3	39.3

SOURCE: Ul'ianov, "Opyt," p. 228.

188

Research on the motives for baptizing of children was conducted in Leningrad and the Leningrad region in 1965. More than 400 cases of baptism were analyzed according to objective data, supplemented by 73 cases of conversations conducted with parents with the aim of clarifying the motives for performing the rite. In all, 95 parents were questioned, with conversations being conducted with both parents in 22 cases and in 51 cases only with one parent.

Analysis of the results of these conversations showed: (1) in 4 cases, the rite was conducted on the strength of the personal religiousness of the parents (in 2 families only the mother was a believer, and in 2 others both parents, the mother and the father); (2) in 62 cases, the rite was conducted at the insistence of believing members of the family (basically, the grandmother) and also under the influence of relatives, acquaintances, etc.; (3) in 7 cases no religious influence for conduct of the rite was established. [Kobetskii, "Obriad," pp. 162–63]

Tepliakov, who found that only 9.8% of the parents baptized their children for religious reasons, asserted that all of the rest (90.2% of the total number) "came to the degrading rite under pressure from believing relatives, and by no means for religious motives" (*Problemy,* p. 170). Relatives exert a profound influence: "Thus, in explaining the reasons for baptizing children, it appeared that of 435 cases, 55% of the baptisms were performed under the influence of believing elderly relatives and acquaintances, and about 30% of the baptisms were performed by relatives and acquaintances without the knowledge of the parents" (Tepliakov, "So-

(TABLE 11.3—*continued*)

Reasons for participation					
Accept effectiveness of sacraments	Convinced rite determines child's fate	Rite gives peace	Attracted by emotion, beauty of rite	Tradition, no wish to be different from those who baptize	Other
10.3%	21.8%	11.9%	5.4%	37.9%	2.0%
1.8	5.9	4.8	11.6	56.5	2.6

stoianii," p. 37). Aptekman found that about one-third of the parents whose children were baptized had yielded to the demands of relatives; they described the blackmail that is commonly practiced by the baby sitter: grandmothers refuse to care for the child while both parents are working unless the child has been baptized ("Vitality," p. 371; cf. *Komsomol'skaia pravda,* 13 October 1971).

In view of the profound influence of believing relatives, the conclusion that religion provides the motivation for baptism only in a small percentage of the cases cannot be accepted without some modification. Kobetskii very astutely points out: "Nevertheless, research allows the assertion that religiousness is present almost always as one of the reasons for baptism. In the case where the parents of the infant are personally religious, there is no doubt. In the overwhelming majority of other cases, religiousness (a believing grandmother, for example) is evident as the means of getting past unbelievers" ("Obriad," p. 163).

Some attempts have been made to describe the profile of parents who have their children baptized: "It appeared that most often parents aged 28 to 33 baptize children. They constitute 41.7% of all parents who perform the rite of baptism. It strikes the attention that these are people who, by their age, are already beyond the influence of Komsomol organizations."[20] Aptekman disagrees, finding that the majority of the people who have their children baptized for religious reasons are over 35. Among them, unmarried mothers are common: "I don't usually go to church, but I arranged the baptism myself because my baby has no father, and people whom I know said that it is a sin not to baptize ("Vitality," p. 370). Pismanik found that fewer than 4% of the urban parents who had their children baptized had comparatively high industrial skills (a travel expert, a practical nurse, a laboratory assistant, two primary school teachers), and of 197 rural women, only 3 were skilled ("O sostoianii," p. 218). "The total number of parents who baptized their children were divided as follows in terms of education: higher, 0.6%; incomplete higher, 1.7%; specialized secondary, 9%; general secondary, 14%; 7-year school, 51.4%; and 4-year school, 23.3%" (Aptekman, "Vitality," p. 369). A great many of the children came from broken homes: "From this analysis it is apparent that, for example, for the period 1 May to 1 October 1962, of 141 women who baptized their children in the Dobrianskaia church, 71 were the sole parent; in the Chernushinskaia church, of 266 women, 138 were sole parents. For the first half of 1963, of 86 women who baptized their children in the Mytvenskaia church, 27 were sole parents; in the Egvinskaia church, of 152 women, 33 were sole parents; etc." (Pismanik, "O sostoianii," pp. 220–21).

Of considerable concern to the Soviet researchers is the uncomfortable fact that not even the atheists are entirely free from the influence of baptism. "A significant number of members and candidate members of the CPSU do not act against the religious rite of baptism of their children and grandchildren, and some even personally took part in it" (Tepliakov, *Problemy*, p. 59). In general, as many as 2.5% of the families that baptized their children were those of Party members, and 12.0% are families of Komsomol members (Aptekman, "Vitality," p. 375). "A survey of 403 Komsomol upperclassmen conducted in the summer of 1966 in the all-Russian camp 'Orlenok' showed that 52.7% of them had been baptized, 43.8% had not been baptized, 1.6% were unable to answer because they did not know, and 1.9% did not answer at all. (Footnote: The stated percentages relate only to those of the surveyed, 370 of 403, who belonged to nationalities that are historically considered to be Christian by tradition [Russian, Ukrainian, Belorussian, Armenian, etc.])" (Kobetskii, "Obriad," p. 170). These data included the percentages (shown in table 11.4) of these Komsomol upperclassmen, according to their home locales, who had or had not been baptized.

It should be noted, however, that there is no indication that any efforts whatsoever were expended to determine how candid the respondents had been in this study. These Komsomol upperclassmen would typically be in their early twenties, and their selection for this all-Russian camp experience would indicate that their career potentials were stellar; therefore, it would seem very probable that a great many of them would conceal the fact that they had been baptized if they thought that this could be kept a secret. Incidentally, concerning such phenomena as atheists having their children baptized, Kolbanovski notes wryly that because the incidence of Christian weddings is far lower than that of baptisms, "this amounts to a fairly absurd position from the church's point of view: unmarried parents baptize their children" (*Kollektiv*, p. 245).

It should not be assumed that only infants are presented for Baptism in Russian Orthodoxy. Indeed, this is far from the case.

TABLE 11.4
PLACES OF RESIDENCE

Komsomol upperclassmen	Village locale	Small city, workers' settlement	Large city
Baptized	61.2%	42.2%	44.9%
Not baptized	34.1	48.9	51.4

SOURCE: Kobetskii, "Obriad," p. 170.

The age at which those who were questioned had been baptized breaks down in the following manner: baptized at age:
Under 1 year—71.2%
1 to 3 years—17.3%
3 to 7 years—8.4%
Over 7—1.5%
Did not indicate age of baptism—1.6%

It is remarkable that the majority of those who had been baptized (79%) knew their "godfather and mother" (or one of them). The number of those who knew their "sponsors," with relation to the general number of those surveyed, constituted 40.5%. [Kobetskii, "Obriad," p. 170]

Among more than 300 who were baptized in the Vladimir Cathedral in Moscow on Easter, 1965, only 9% were under 1 year old; 49% were aged 1 to 3 years, 34% were aged 3 to 7 years, 6% were young school-age children, and 2% were adolescents (ibid., p. 167). Other research corroborates that at this time there was a resurgence of baptism: "In the process of the research this interesting fact also appeared: 45 families (out of 462) did not baptize the older children, and first returned to the rite of baptism in 1965–1966" (Pivovarov, *Struktura,* p. 61). One of the reasons for this return to baptism can be found in the state's policy toward religion. During the final years of Khrushchev's leadership, great pressure was brought to bear to discourage baptism. After he was removed from office in October 1964, for several months there was somewhat of a hiatus in the antireligious campaign, as local and regional administrators waited to find out what the policies of the collective leadership would be. Therefore, during the early months of 1965, it may have seemed that the risks involved in presenting children for baptizm had subsided, and parents might have been more inclined to ask that the rite be performed on older children who had not been baptized earlier for fear of reprisal.

Whatever the reason, it would appear that the pattern of baptizing older children continued and even, in some respects, increased after 1965 (see table 11.5). These figures demonstrate a steady increase in the percentage of older children who were being baptized; this might be an indication of a modest reduction in the antireligious campaign, at least locally. The notable increase during 1968 of children aged 1 to 3 (i.e., born in 1965 to 1967), again, may be explained by local fluctuations in official policy. It should be noted, however, that the researcher himself, Smirnov, suggests another reason for these delayed baptisms: "It turns out that until age three, grandmothers willingly baby-sit their unbaptized grandchildren, and then they refuse. But such a conclusion would not sound very convincing.

TABLE 11.5
AGES OF BAPTIZED CHILDREN

Age	Percentage of all baptized during		
	1967	1968	1969
Up to 1 year old	45.0	27.7	40.5
1 to 3 years old	33.0	45.6	27.0
3 to 7 years old	18.5	21.0	24.0
Over 7 years old	3.5	5.7	8.5

SOURCE: Smirnov, "Voprosy," p. 126.

Another is more likely. The fact, evidently, is that for the first three years, religious relatives manage to "work over" individual nonbelieving parents, convincing them of the necessity to baptize the child" ("Voprosy," p. 126). Such a hypothesis may be plausible, if not especially convincing, with regard to the first child only; it would be interesting to determine how many of those who were baptized later were the eldest child.

There is little doubt, however, about the most uncomfortable category of all for the atheistic observers: "To this time, albeit rarely, one still meets with cases in which grown people themselves receive the rite of baptism in Orthodox temples" (Selivanov, *Partiinoe rukovodstvo*, p. 51). Such instances are not completely inexplicable, however, in view of the statistical data mentioned in a previous chapter, which indicated a widespread return to Orthodoxy among middle-aged Soviet citizens.

According to ideological considerations, the popularity of baptism should be declining. Some Soviet researchers find that there has been a downward trend in the incidence of baptism, but there is no general agreement among them. One researcher found that in Estonia, for example, the percentage of the population that were baptized (presumably according to the Lutheran practice) decreased by almost 5 times in the decade prior to 1968.[21] In Latvia, Kampars claimed that baptisms declined by 50% in the 1960s ("Nekotorye problemy," p. 19). Podmazov is not quite so sanguine: "For example, from 1962 to 1966 among Catholics, the number who were baptized declined by 6.5%; among Old Believers, by 16.1%; among Orthodox, by 17.4%; and among Lutherans, by 39.2%. The data surveyed indicate that among the most widespread religious denominations in Latvia, only among Catholics did the number who were baptized decline more slowly than among Old Believers" ("Sovremennoe staroobriadchestvo," p. 201). It should be noted that it was during these years that the most intense antireligious efforts against baptism took place.

Thus far, the data that have been presented have been confined to pedobaptism and the religious denominations that practice it. Relatively little has been done concerning the rite of baptism (or cognate rituals) in other denominations. Klibanov, for example, finds that "from 1950 to 1964, in all the congregations of Baptists of the Voronezh region, 531 people were baptized, while 312 believers were excommunicated for 'un-Christian conduct,' and for this same period, another 202 people from the number of Evangelical Christian-Baptists broke entirely with religion" (*Religioznoe sektantstvo*, p. 77). This seems to be an incredibly small number of baptisms for the fourteen-year period in question, particularly in view of the large number of Baptist congregations in the region. Furthermore, inasmuch as Klibanov does not explain the apparent anomaly that the number of those who were excommunicated does not include those who embraced atheism, it seems difficult to draw conclusions from these data.

Similarly, very little has been done with regard to the Muslim practice of circumcision, which in some respects serves purposes that are similar to those of baptism among the Orthodox. One scholar reports that circumcision has disappeared entirely (*Gertsenovskie chteniia* 3 (1972): 14). This is certainly wishful thinking, for according to Baltanov, research in three districts of Uzbekistan "established that 81.9 percent of those who were questioned in essence support circumcision" (*Sotsiologicheskie problemy*, p. 209). To be sure, circumcision is not necessarily a sign of religious convictions; but in view of how closely religion and culture are intertwined among Muslim peoples, it is definitely a mark of national, and hence usually religious, consciousness under Soviet conditions (Filiminov, "Sotsiologicheskie issledovaniia," p. 81).

The rite of marriage has not displayed anything like the persistence of baptism, and of the three major rites, it would appear that the Christian wedding is the least popular. Even in Lithuania, where the traditions of Roman Catholicism remain a vigorous force in society, only some 38% of the marriages are solemnized with religious ceremonies (Pomerantsev, "Vchera," pp. 5–6). According to another study, 70% of the marriages in Lithuania are performed in civil ceremonies (Barkauskas, "Osushchestvlenie," pp. 161–62). In Latvia, not more than 10% of the newlyweds are married in church (Kampars, "Nekotorye problemy," p. 19), and in some districts the figure drops as low as 7% (Terent'eva, "Rasprostranenie," p. 65). In the Voronezh area, "from 1959 to 1970, only 3% of those getting married got married in church, which indirectly indicates the level of religiousness among people aged 18 to 30" (Tepliakov, *Problemy*, p. 143). Ranne claims that in Estonia, only 2.5% of the marriages are solemnized religiously ("Novye obriady," p. 183), and in another study, it was found that between 1959 and 1970 the number of religious weddings decreased by 12 times ("Razrabotka problem," p. 78). In Leningrad, less than 0.12% of the weddings were religious.[22] "In the Iaroslav region, for example, during the past ten years the number has diminished more than 6 times and constituted, in 1969, 0.16% of the number of all marriages contracted" (Vasilevskaia, "Opyt," pp. 395–96).

While these more extreme figures may not be representative, it would seem unquestionable that the prevalence of religious weddings is relatively low in the USSR. It is doubtful, however, that Soviet researchers have been successful in discovering all instances of church weddings, particularly when such weddings are conducted along with civil ·ceremonies. Means have been developed to solemnize weddings by correspondence[23] or in a quasi-religious manner by having the couple kiss an icon even when a priest is not available.[24] The religious ceremonies have also been simplified. In Islam, for example, "substantial changes have taken place in rites and ceremonies, in particular regarding the marriage. The external, ritual aspect of it is still preserved to a significant degree, but gradually there is an observable tendency toward simplification of the ceremony, dropping a number of details and only externally and formally fulfilling some customs. Performance of a number of customs and rituals at weddings, and also getting married according to the *Shariat,* is explained by the desire not to offend believing, elderly relatives."[25]

Perhaps more than in any other rite, participants in religious weddings tend to be motivated by nonreligious considerations. Ugrinovich discovered that "only 10% of the participants in religious weddings answered that they saw a religious meaning in it" (*Vvedenie,* p. 136). According to another report, "it is interesting to note that the increase in the positive attitude toward religious rites in many questionnaires of tenth graders, mainly girls, is explained in terms of motivation by the following: 'The rite of marriage pleases me (or is beautiful)'" (*Gertsenovskie chteniia* 3 [1972]: 24). Presumably (but not necessarily), such motivations were dominant when "on a single day in Kuibyshev 15 Komsomol members and shockworkers were married in church weddings."[26] Table 11.6 shows the range of motivations found in one study.

Religious funerals are the most persistent of all the rites. The percentage of religious funerals remains high, and attempts to replace them with secular rituals have certainly enjoyed very little success.

Some Soviet researchers report low levels of religious funerals, but not all of these reports are credible. For example, "of 148 Christians we surveyed, basically middle-aged, . . . 11 took part in funerals of deceased relatives" (Ul'ianov, "Opyt," p. 13). This figure, which at first glance

TABLE 11.6

REASONS FOR PARTICIPATING IN RELIGIOUS WEDDING

Population group	Role in the rite	Time of participation			
		In past year	In past 5 yrs.	In past 10 yrs.	Over 10 yrs. ago
Considers self a believer	Was bride/groom	0.7%	3.0%	4.2%	81.0%
	Married son/daughter	0.3	1.0	1.0	5.3
	Was sponsor	0.2	0.5	0.8	4.2
	Was a guest	0.5	2.3	2.8	8.9
Considers self a waverer	Was bride/groom	1.0	2.6	7.7	73.9
	Married son/daughter	0.5	......	1.0	4.1
	Was sponsor	0.2	0.2	0.8	2.6
	Was a guest	1.3	1.2	3.9	7.5

SOURCE: Ul'ianov, "Opyt," p. 232.

might seem to imply a level of religious funerals of 7.4%, may be misleading, for it apparently reports only those who acknowledge that they have actually taken part in funerals of deceased relatives, without raising the question of how many would be willing to do so should the occasion arise. Similarly, in a study in one Latvian district, Terent'eva found that only 19.4% of the funerals were church funerals ("Rasprostranenie," p. 65). In Estonia, "although the organization of civil funerals receives great attention, 40% of all who die in the republic to the present time are buried according to the church rite" (Ranne, "Novye obriady," p. 187). Another study in Estonia indicated that 46% of the funerals were religious ("Razrabotka problem," p. 78).

Much higher figures have commonly been reported, however. In Lithuania, 61% of the funerals were religious (Pomerantsev, "Vchera," pp. 5–6). The Jewish community in Riga, 75% of the deceased had received a religious funeral.[27] Among Catholics in Lithuania, 79% of the funerals were religious (Barkauskas, "Osushchestvlenie," pp. 161–62). Nor are these figures atypical. "Religious funeral and memorial rites are extraordinarily widespread traditions. Thus in a number of places, 80 to 90% of the people of the older generation who die are buried according to the church rite" (Kapustin, "O spetsifike," p. 95). During the most intense years of the antireligious campaign, the number of religious funerals among Old Believers and Catholics declined by only 1.5% (Pod-

(TABLE 11.6—*continued*)

Reasons for participation					
Accept effectiveness of rite	Convinced rite determines fate of marriage	Rite gives peace	Attracted by emotions, beauty	Tradition, no wish to be different from those who marry in church	Other
12.0%	26.6%	12.4%	8.0%	40.8%	1.4%
2.6	3.9	4.1	15.8	55.0	3.1

mazov, "Sovremennoe staroobriadchestvo," pp. 197, 201). According to Tepliakov's study of 13,310 religious citizens of the Voronezh area, "it was also clear that 3,826 (28.7%) buried their deceased relatives according to the religious rite, and the remainder were disposed to do likewise" (*Problemy*, p. 168). Thus, 100% of the religious people supported religious funerals, according to this study.

Tepliakov, in reporting this high level of support for Christian funerals, also notes that funerals by correspondence complicate the data on religious funerals (ibid., p. 171). Priests now apparently consider it to be acceptable for a bit of the earth from the grave to be blessed and returned to the grave where a person has been buried without a religious funeral (Demin, " 'Khristianskii kommunizm,' " pp. 185–86). One scholarly study reported that in 1966 in one district, 63 of 100 religious funerals were conducted by correspondence, as were 89% in another district.[28]

The motivations of people who participated in religious funerals revealed a very high level of direct religious sentiment. The range of motivations delineated in table 11.7 represents the low end of the spectrum; other studies find a much higher level of religious motivation. "Of 468 people who were representatively selected from the number of participants in religious funerals, 80 people (about 17%) participated through nonreligious motives (the solemnity of the ritual attracts them, they follow the example and the insistence of relatives), while 254 people (about 54%)—for religious motives."[29] More exactly, of these 468 participants

TABLE 11.7
REASONS FOR PARTICIPATING IN A RELIGIOUS FUNERAL

Population group	Role in the rite	In past year	In past 5 yrs.	In past 10 yrs.	Over 10 yrs. ago
			Time of participation		
Considers self a believer	Buried relative/friend; ordered funeral himself	12.0%	19.5%	14.9%	33.3%
	Buried relative; agreed to religious rite	2.0	5.3	4.0	8.0
	Civil funeral; correspondence religious rite	2.0	2.0	1.1	2.6
	Took part in religious funeral & memorial service	10.5	14.2	8.7	16.4
Considers self a waverer	Buried relative/friend; ordered funeral himself	14.4	20.6	12.7	22.6
	Buried relative; agreed to religious rite	3.2	7.0	4.5	5.4
	Civil funeral; correspondence religious rite	1.1	2.8	1.3	3.5
	Took part in religious funeral & memorial service	10.5	15.3	10.9	16.3

SOURCE: Ul'ianov, "Opyt," p. 234.

in funerals, 145 were motivated by religious convictions, 143 were following the dead relative's wish, for 131 it was a "Russian rite," 80 felt that the funeral made it easier to accept the loss of the loved one, 29 felt that a religious funeral was necessary for the afterlife, 55 were merely following the example of others, 12 liked the funeral, and 12 had other answers or were unclear. Obviously, some of the respondents named more than one motivation (Pivovarov, *Struktura*, p. 44). These figures may be misleading, however. Despite the fact that even Communist Party members on occasion arrange for and take part in religious funerals (Tepliakov, *Problemy*, p. 59), one highly respected scholar, Pivovarov, has asserted that *all* people are believers at funerals: 56% are convinced believers, and the remaining 44% are wavering believers (*Struktura*, p. 41).

On the whole, Soviet sociological scholarship has achieved an impressive level of credibility when attempting to delineate the religious practices

(TABLE 11.7—*continued*)

Reasons for participation					
Accept effective- ness of rite	Convinced rite deter- mines fate of deceased	Rite gives peace	Attracted by emotions, beauty	Tradition, no wish to be different	Other
12.0%	15.6%	13.6%	6.1%	38.6%	1.4%
2.2	3.5	5.6	12.3	56.5	2.8

of believers. There are still imbalances and contradictions in the data, but when these parameters are compared with excursions by atheistic researchers into more subtle areas of theology and the world view, the data on such concrete subjects as the possession of icons, patterns of church attendance and observance of religious holidays, and participation in religious rites seem to be relatively reliable. Much remains to be done, of course, and there is vast room for improvement. But the research is, by and large, good, and in this area, Soviet sociological research gives at least a preliminary indication of the achievements that are possible in matters that are definitely accessible to inspection by using the tools of sociological research.

12

CONCLUSIONS

The picture that emerges from a survey of Soviet sociology of religion provides useful insights into this important aspect of contemporary society in the USSR. The picture is not completely clear and sharply defined in all its aspects. Soviet sociological research is by no means free of problems; it is an imperfect tool. The problems and weaknesses described in the course of this study are not yet completely resolved and, from time to time, prevent the fullest achievement of the promise of that discipline. The conclusions to be drawn from this research are not always self-evident, and indeed, in many of the parameters, there is room for vigorous discussion concerning how the data should be evaluated.

It is lamentable that imperfect resources are no rarity in the study of the USSR. Particularly as regards religion, there are no sources of information that do not contain some limitations. No less than in other branches of Soviet studies, the student of religion must have recourse to a degree of inferential reconstruction in attempting to penetrate through to the actual situation; in weighing and evaluating the source materials, he must utilize all the methods and approaches that have been worked out over the years in the broader disciplines.[1] Not even when using concrete data drawn from sociological research can he construct an assessment of the actual situation which will be self-evident and which will elicit universal agreement. The data themselves, which seldom achieve absolute clarity, can be interpreted in a number of ways. To some degree, the matter becomes a question of taste; and if good taste is combined with discrimination based on some experience in working with other approaches to the subject of religion in the USSR, one may draw some tentative, credible estimates which may conform more or less to the actual situation.

On this basis, then, a composite picture may be drawn of the phenomenon described in the materials that were surveyed. The conclusions that follow are not absolute. Other conclusions are not in themselves excluded by the data, and depending on one's point of view, a broad range of interpretations is legitimate. Particularly where vested interests are involved (as in the case of some of the Soviet commentators), radically different conclusions can be supported with some eloquence. The conclusions that follow are not presented as demonstrated fact but rather as suggestions—indeed, interpretations—of what the shape of the reality might be as discerned through the insights presented by Soviet sociologists of religion.

It is a grave misfortune for Soviet sociology of religion that the central problem of the number of believers in Soviet society has still not been resolved. The problem of who is and who is not religious is fundamental to any assessment of other parameters concerning the believing citizens, and until this critical issue is resolved, the potential value of other findings of the research is gravely reduced. This problem will be discussed in some detail below, after a review of the other dimensions presented in the sociological research.

The evidence seems fairly strong that religious belief tends to concentrate among the older people in society. Certainly this would seem to be the case among those who outwardly participate in religious activities. Among these believers, at least half would be elderly, over the age of 50 or possibly even 60. It is important to note, however, that this tendency is not absolute. It is by no means unknown or unusual to discover religious belief in the younger strata of the population. Such data as have been presented concerning these age groups are not sufficient to allow one to draw any sweeping conclusion, particularly in view of the widespread tendency among the young to conceal any religious belief. That belief in God is present (or that active disbelief is absent) among some young people is indubitable; how many of the contemporary youth belong to this category cannot be estimated. The observable believers, once again, tend to be more elderly than the general population.

Soviet research also seems to be fairly persuasive in asserting that the majority of the religious believers are women. Certainly in the churches, and quite possibly absolutely, women believers are more numerous, outnumbering male believers by perhaps three or four to one.

The educational level of believers tends to be somewhat lower than that of the general population, but probably not by any great margin, particularly after adjustments are made for distribution according to age and gender. Discrimination against religious believers has effectively closed the possibilities of higher education for many of the believers, and this has certainly had some effect in lowering their aggregate educational level. It remains possible, although no very persuasive evidence has been presented, that believers, because of their interest in religion, are less interested in pursuing secular education and hence that the overall educational level among them may be somewhat lower than that which prevails in society at large.

Occupationally, a large proportion—30% or perhaps 40% or more—of the believers are not members of the labor force (retired, dependents, housekeepers, etc.). Those who are employed gravitate toward the lower levels of unskilled or semiskilled work. This last assessment, however, should be tempered by the consideration that job discrimination has been so widely practiced that those who are in more responsible positions would be well advised to conceal their religious beliefs, lest they be demoted to a lower work classification. Thus, the observable data concerning occupation have probably been shifted towards the lower end of the occupational spectrum by some unknown degree, because some of the workers in the higher occupational categories have concealed their religious beliefs.

Although the countryside continues to be the bastion of religiousness, with a higher proportion of the population remaining religious, urban believers tend to be stronger and more active in their faith. There seems to be less vacillation in their world view, and religion plays a more vigorous role in their lives than is the case with the average rural believer. In part, this may be due to the fact that churches are often available to the urban believer, whereas a very large percentage of the rural believers are virtually or absolutely denied any institutionalized expression of their faith. The greater anonymity possible to the urban dweller may also contribute to the increased vigor that is observable among urban believers—in the small village, religious observance is much more likely to attract attention than in the crowded city. Finally, urban believers tend to be somewhat better educated and considerably more sophisticated than their rural counterparts.

With regard to living conditions, despite the preponderance of unskilled (and hence poorly paid) workers in the religious population, the economic differences between believers and unbelievers are insignificant. The incidence of people who live alone (widows, divorcees, unmarried) is fairly high, and the remainder tend to live in an extended family that embraces three and sometimes four generations, which is a feature of Soviet society.

Religious people tend to make less use of newspapers, books, magazines, the cinema, and the like during their free time than is the average for nonbelievers. It should be noted, however, that the use of newspapers and attention to the radio are substantial among believers.

There are many indications that religious believers have a tendency to be alienated from society to one degree or another. Substantial minorities among the believers try to minimize their contacts with unbelievers, and a fairly large portion of the believers tend to distrust unbelievers, questioning whether in fact they can even be considered to be moral. Most believers relate favorably to social progress; however, participation in civic affairs is much lower among the believers than in the general population. The extent to which such indices of alienation are due to an undercurrent of hostility toward society or simply to the fact that believers tend to be interested in other matters is unclear.

The great majority of the religious believers were exposed to religious influences in childhood. Even those who had converted to one denomination or another generally were said to come from the religious sector, rather than the atheistic sector, of the population before their conversion. Such reports must be tempered somewhat: even though these people may have been believers in childhood, the considerable number who return to the church in middle age would be counted in the atheistic—or at least non-religious—sector prior to their reconversion. It would seem to be fairly well established, however, that the great majority of the believers became religious believers as children, whatever may have happened in the intervening years.

It seems fairly certain that most religious families engage in religious education of the children at home; data to the contrary do not seem very credible. Because of an almost universal practice of utilizing the services of grandparents to take care of children during the day (e.g., while both parents are at work), a great deal of this religious nurture in the home is transmitted from grandparents to grandchildren, by-passing the intervening generation.

Particularly where institutional religion has been liquidated, there are strong tendencies toward syncretism with indigenous folk beliefs. A relatively high incidence of various superstitions (fortunetelling, the evil eye, etc.) has been found among believers who did not have access to an open church. It should be noted, of course, that these superstitions are not confined to the religious population: they are quite common among unbelievers as well.

No clear picture of the world view of religious believers emerges from this research. The majority of the believers apparently find no inevitable contradiction between religion and science, although the sophistication and knowledge of science among some believers is very low. Soviet attempts to discriminate among the various concepts of God that prevail among believers have not been at all convincing. This is probably due both to an inadequate understanding of the complexity of the believer's concept of God and to the fact that such a discrimination may not be possible at all—believers may typically hold several different concepts of God simultaneously. There is some indication that belief in immortality is not universal among believers, although the data are fraught with difficulties. The congeniality of religion with morality seems to be all but universally maintained by the believers. The great majority of the believers, however, do not respond with religious concepts when they are asked about the meaning of life: very often their answers are couched in material, ethical, or family terms. Similarly, not all believers define happiness in religious terms.

A clearer picture emerges with regard to religious practices. Icons would seem to be exceedingly popular in traditionally Orthodox areas; the great majority of the homes contain icons whether or not the people who live there consider themselves to be believers. When churches are available, religious believers apparently attend them fairly regularly, although a significant percentage attend only occasionally. The inadequate number of functioning churches complicates the picture, however. The crossing of denominational boundaries is fairly common because of the small number of churches. When asked what their reasons for attending church are, a large fraction of the believers respond in nonreligious terms (aesthetic appreciation, tradition, etc.).

Religious holidays are widely observed in Soviet society, even among nonbelievers. Strict observance of the various fasting requirements, however, is relatively infrequent. Among the sacraments, baptism is still widely practiced; even nominal unbelievers have the rite performed on their children. Marriage, by contrast, is rather less popular; civil ceremonies suffice in the great majority of the cases. Religious funerals, however, are the most tenacious of the religious rites: a very high percentage of the funerals in the USSR are still religious, whether the ceremony is conducted directly or by correspondence.

This, briefly, is an impression that emerges from a survey of Soviet sociological research on religion. It should be emphasized that the picture is impressionistic, nothing more. Assertions that disagree with the above can be supported from some of the research data as readily as can this assessment, and no student of religion can afford a facile dogmatism in making such assertions. The above picture, however, would seem to be consistent with the overall impression given by the research.

One surprising aspect of the picture is the general impression of strength that is communicated by the data on religious believers. The Soviet believer would seem to be relatively vigorous in his faith. Despite the many pressures and discriminatory sanctions levied against religious belief, the typical Soviet believer would not appear to be in any sense demoralized or discouraged. The picture that emerges from Soviet sociological research is one of confidence and relative assurance on the part of Soviet believers.

There are other surprising dimensions to Soviet religion which can be found in Soviet sociological research. Particularly with regard to details, the research data very often deny widespread assumptions with regard to religious life in the USSR. The research tends to paint a picture that is different in a great many details from that which has been widely accepted.

One must conclude, then, that Soviet sociological research on religion is immensely valuable. It provides unique and indispensable insights into the subject of religion in the USSR. Indeed, the sociological research presented by Soviet scholars has already altered our impressions of religion in the USSR in many important respects.[2] It is a source of immense value for the serious student of religion in the USSR; indeed, it cannot be ignored. A study of religion in the USSR that neglects this important source of knowledge runs grave risks of being incomplete and possibly distorted.

Even more valuable is a dimension of Soviet sociology of religion that has not been touched upon in this survey except in passing. Many of the sociological reports include materials that illustrate the various statistical data. These illustrative materials regularly take the form of presenting the actual quoted responses of representative believers, and as such, they present an insight that can be found only rarely in other sources. These quoted responses from believers, while they are scarcely quantifiable as currently presented, provide a degree of intimacy that would otherwise be available only at first hand. These insights, as much as the statistical evidence, are what generate the indisputable value of Soviet sociological writings.

In large measure, in fact, these studies achieve their immense value precisely because of their firsthand, individualized, often person-to-person quality. In no other field of Soviet scholarship of atheism do researchers come into so much direct contact with the religious believers themselves, and sociological scholarship inevitably reflects this firsthand knowledge to a greater or lesser extent. Such immediate, concrete exposure to the real world of the believer is immensely enlightening. Despite the fact that every effort is made to quantify and generalize, Soviet sociologists very often achieve a direct portrait of the individual Soviet believer much more credibly and in much more detail than can be found in other research materials. This personalized dimension in Soviet sociology is what renders it so highly valuable, making Soviet sociological studies of religion indispensable for an understanding of contemporary religious life in the USSR.

Returning now to the central problem of the size of the religious sector of the population, it is apparent that Soviet researchers have not yet achieved general agreement among themselves in defining who is and who is not religious. Attempts to achieve some sort of behavioral criteria have not been persuasive nor widely accepted. The majority of the researchers have had recourse to some form of the cognitive approach, which is more or less reducible to the question of whether a person accepts or denies the concept of God. Obviously, this approach to the definition of religiousness is fairly crude, and Soviet researchers themselves are quick to recognize that it may include a great many people as believers who, to all intents and purposes, are not religious at all; conversely, it may exclude some persons who, however deeply religious they may be, do not emphasize the traditional concepts of God.

The problem is only made worse by attempts to refine the instrument. Classification schemes introduce a great deal of confusion into the picture, primarily because there is no general agreement concerning them. Two subgroups, in particular, are very difficult to handle.

"Waverers" is a category that embraces a multitude of variations, depending on the individual research project. Much of the time it is defined as "waverers between belief and unbelief," in which case an indeterminate portion of those who are included therein might be classifiable as believers rather than unbelievers. Other researchers define "waverers" as "wavering *believers*," in which case all of the members of this category must be included among the believers. Unfortunately, some of these researchers exclude this category from their aggregate figures, reporting only on the percentage of "believers"—and sometimes only "convinced believers"—in the population under study. Such figures, obviously, must be revised upward if a total figure for the religious sector is desired. The problem becomes immensely difficult when the report of the sociological research project does not present specific details concerning how the category of "waverers" was handled.

Similarly, the concept of "indifferent" is difficult to assess. The majority of the researchers do not use this category; when it is introduced, and particularly when it is used along with "wavering believers" and even "wavering unbelievers," it becomes uncertain how it should be treated. It may be that those who are indifferent should be completely excluded from the aggregate figures for believers; but perhaps an indeterminate number of people have been included in the "indifferent" category who should be counted among the believers when some overall assessment of the ratio of religious versus nonreligious members of the society is sought.

Thus the introduction of these two subcategories—"waverers" and "indifferent"—introduces great complexity into the search for an aggregate estimate. Perhaps the percentages of believers should be used as presented, without correction. But it would seem more reasonable that when a dichotomous, religious versus nonreligious, assessment is being sought, they should be revised upward by some amount if they are to conform to the actual situation.

Obviously, then, the data presented in chapter 4 could be utilized selectively to support a variety of estimates, from a very small figure to a substantial percentage of the population. The most general conclusion of Soviet sociologists is that 15 to 20% of the population is religious;[3] as will become apparent below, this figure is unrealistic. While it may be comforting to those who are seeking to confirm the predictions of Marxism, it can only be maintained by a completely uncritical acceptance of some—but by no means all—of the data presented by Soviet sociology of religion, without examination or analysis.

When the great mass of the data is brought together and reviewed, figures below 10% for the number of believers in the USSR would not seem to be realistic, for there are too many studies that indicate a higher incidence of religiousness. Conversely, in the Russian areas, figures as high as 50% may seem improbable. Perhaps the best estimate might suggest that in these parts of the country, 25% to 35% of the population continues to be religious.

At first glance, this estimate may seem high. However, close inspection of the data presented in chapter 4 will indicate that the lower percentages that are given there very often are confined to believers, excluding the large group classified as waverers or wavering believers, who must be included if the figures are to approach a realistic assessment. Furthermore, geographic imbalances must be considered, with low figures for urban areas being weighed against higher rural figures. The several large-scale studies consistently yield figures higher than 25%, sometimes higher than 30%. In the Penza study, in which more than 30,000 Soviet citizens were surveyed, it was found that 28.4% were religious.[4] The largest project reported to date, in the Voronezh region, despite its many inadequacies in design and execution, nevertheless indicated that no fewer than 22.4% were classifiable as believers and that an additional 27.8% could be classified as nonreligious but not unbelievers (whatever that may mean; obviously, the possibility must remain that some citizens who believe in God were included in this category). Thus, an aggregate estimate of 30% does not seem to be unreasonably high; indeed, lower estimates become increasingly difficult to justify on the basis of the data presented by Soviet sociological research.

But this figure applies only to the predominantly Russian areas. For the entire population, demographic factors complicate the picture. "Religiousness is not evenly distributed on the territories of the country. It is notably higher in the western regions of the Ukraine and Belorussia, which were united with the Soviet people later, and also in the Baltic Soviet republics, and also in Tadzhikistan, Uzbekistan and elsewhere, where the inhabitants formerly were under the influence of the Muslims. In the territories of the Russian Federation, religiousness is higher in the Moscow, Vladimir, Iaroslav, and other regions that used to be strongholds of the Russian Orthodox Church; less in the Urals and Western Siberia; and still less in the Altai and the Far East" (Kalashnikov, "Religiia," p. 23).

At present the Russians constitute slightly less than 50% of the population of the USSR. As noted above, in non-Russian areas the level of religiousness is much higher than in the Russian areas. An estimate that 60% or more of these people remain religious would seem to be fairly credible. Admittedly, several difficulties are inherent in any estimate such as this.

First, the estimate may seem high for the Ukrainians and Belorussians, who together constitute somewhat over 20% of the population of the USSR. The natural affinities due to common Slavic nationality and culture might suggest that patterns of religious adherence would approximate the Russian norm rather than that of non-Slavic cultures. However, the choice of a higher figure is indicated both by the consideration that portions of these areas were acquired during World War II—and thus a higher incidence of religiousness prevails in them than is the case in areas that have been a part of the Soviet Union for more than a half century—and by the consideration that a large proportion of the remaining churches are concentrated in the Ukraine. While the larger number of churches may indicate no more than vagaries of policy, it may also suggest and, indeed, contribute to a higher level of religiousness than is found in Russia proper. Hence, the actual figure for these areas is probably higher than the 30% estimated for the Russian nationality, although it might be debated vigorously whether it in fact is so high as 60%.

However, in other areas, 60% may be an unrealistically low figure. Among the Muslim nationalities, who constitute nearly 15% of the population, religion and culture are so intimately identified that it may be quite unrealistic to suggest that more than a fraction are nonreligious in any meaningful way—religion thus would have an impact in the lives of far more than 60% of these people. Soviet sociological research has done too little in these areas to provide any meaningful estimates concerning the viability of religion among the Muslim peoples. There are some data, however, concerning the use of their national languages, rather than Russian, as the mother tongue: 98.6% of the Uzbeks, 89.2% of the Tatars, 98% of the Kazakhs, 98.2% of the Azerbaijani, 98.5% of the Tadzhiks, 98.9% of the Turkmen, and 98.8% of the Kirgiz consider their national language to be their mother tongue. Fluency in Russian among these peoples ranges from a high of 62.5% among the Tatars to a low of 14.5% among the Uzbeks (Baltanov, *Sotsiologicheskie problemy*, p. 211). Not only does religiousness tend to accompany nationalism in Muslim areas (Filimonov, "Sotsiologicheskie issledovaniia," pp. 79–80); the lack of the Russian language virtually excludes these people from contact with atheism (Baltanov, *Sotsiologicheskie problemy*, pp. 211–12). These considerations, then, suggest that a figure of 60% for religious citizens among the Muslim nationalities is, if anything, a conservative estimate, and the actual situation may indicate a much higher figure.

Similarly, among the Armenians and Georgians (together constituting perhaps 3% of the population), religion and national culture are so intimately intertwined that 60% may be a very conservative estimate. The Jews represent an especially difficult case. Even though only 15% or fewer of them claim Hebrew or Yiddish as their mother tongue, it would be parlous to suggest that only this portion is religiously Jewish, for the Jewish religion and culture, again, are very closely identified. Very little is known concerning the pervasiveness of religion among the tribal peoples of Siberia and elsewhere. This may be in part because the Soviet researchers may not understand much about the strange congeries of shamanistic practices that often prevail. Such studies as have been conducted—for example, those among the Mari and Chechen-Ingush peoples—have suggested that they have a level of religiousness that is well above the Russian norm. And virtually nothing is known about the degree to which Lama Buddhism has survived among the small minority peoples of Central Asia since the institutional manifestations of that religion were virtually liquidated in the thirties.

In the Baltic republics, 60% may be a fairly good compromise estimate. It may be somewhat high for Latvia and Estonia, where some studies have suggested levels of religiousness of perhaps three-fourths this estimate. But it is certainly low for Lithuania. One might suppose that immigrants to this area will more or less reflect the degree of religiousness that prevails in their home regions; but for the vast majority who are Lithuanian, Catholicism is exceedingly strong and is virtually synonymous with nationality. To suggest that only 60% of the Lithuanians are still religious is probably completely unrealistic.

Thus, an overall estimate of 60% for the non-Russian half of the population does not, on closer inspection, seem to be unreasonably high.

Combining these two estimates—30% for the Russian half of the population, 60% for the rest—yields a composite figure of 45% for the religious sector of the Soviet population. This may seem unexpectedly high; but not all Soviet sociologists would necessarily be surprised by it. V. D. Kobetskii, for example, although he also acknowledges the received estimate of 15 to 20%, remarks that "during the years of Soviet rule, the level of religiousness has declined by approximately 50%" (*Sotsiologicheskoe izuchenie*, p. 90). He does not elaborate further. However, if the conventional wisdom is accepted that 90% or more of the population of the Russian Empire used to be religious (and he does cite Lunacharskii's statement that in the 1920s, a decade after atheism had been proclaimed as the official ideology, 80% of the Soviet people were religious [ibid., p. 21]), Kobetskii's remark would coincide very well with the 45% estimated here.

When this percentage is rendered into the number of people who are still religious in the USSR, the results are even more surprising. Soviet scholars have long ridiculed some of the more sanguine Western estimates that there may be as many as 100 million believers in the Soviet Union. "This figure exceeds by several times the real number of believers in the USSR, which has been made clear by means of concrete sociological research on religiousness" (Baltanov, *Sotsiologicheskie problemy,* p. 6). However, if the present review of this same concrete research is valid, this statement is not only quite wrong, the truth lies in the opposite direction.

For if 45% of the population is indeed religious, there must be some 115 million believers in the USSR.

This is a surprisingly high estimate, well above estimates that have been derived from sources other than Soviet sociological studies. Paul B. Anderson, for example, approaching the subject denominationally, derives a total estimate of only 64 million believers in the USSR.[5] These sociological studies that we have considered would suggest that the higher figure is the more persuasive. And the corollary must be that despite official hostility and intense antireligious pressure since the late 1950s, religion seems to be surviving rather handily. Indeed, it has grown.

After the aborted census of 1937, which included a question on belief

in God, E. Iaroslavskii, the head of the League of Militant Godless, estimated that one-third of the urban and two-thirds of the rural population
remained religious. The sociologist N. S. Timasheff, basing his estimates
on the degree of urbanization at the time, concluded—perhaps overpre-
cisely—that 56% of the population thus were religious, revising his figure
upwards from an earlier and lower estimate for 1937.[6] Using a population
base of 170 million, even though the USSR did not reach this figure until
1939, this would yield a total of some 95 million believers. However,
Iaroslavskii also claimed that only 80 million were believers, and the figure
of 90 million was much bruited about by his lieutenants (Fletcher, *Study
in Survival*, pp. 75–76). This last estimate, in the absence of any hard
or reliable data, seems to be a reasonable compromise.

It might be noted, incidentally, that the criterion for defining a person
as religious that was implied in the 1937 census is fully compatible with
the criteria that are being used by the majority of today's sociologists of
religion in the USSR. The census asked the question "Are you a believer
or not?" Inasmuch as most contemporary studies also utilize the cognitive
criterion of belief in God, the results derived in 1937 and during recent
surveys should be comparable.

Apparently, then, the religious sector of the population has declined
only from some 56% in 1937 to 45% today, and the absolute number of
religious citizens in Soviet society has actually increased from an estimated
90 or 95 million to an estimated 115 million people. These astonishing
results are extraordinarily difficult to reconcile with the ideological prediction that religion must disappear with the demise of capitalism. So
surprising are these results that one wonders again whether, in fact, the
estimate is too high. Yet reviewing the data, it is difficult to remain
comfortable with an overall figure much below 30% for the Russian half
of the population or with figures as low as 60% for the non-Russian half
of the population.

It must be reiterated, however, that this is an impressionistic estimate,
not one that is demanded, to the exclusion of all other estimates, by the
data. Particularly where vested interests would be served, it would be
eminently feasible to claim a much lower figure by selective use of the
data.

There is one factor that should be considered, however. As became
apparent in chapters 3 and 4, Soviet sociology of religion is an imperfect
tool, with many flaws and weaknesses. While some of the mistakes that
are inevitably made might conceivably result in an overestimate of the
numbers of religious respondents to the surveys, the contrary would seem
to be much more likely. Few if any of the researchers are motivated by a

desire to discover great strength and large numbers in the religious sector of the population. To the contrary, the ideology demands that religion must be weak, declining, and all but moribund in the socialist society. Consciously or unconsciously, then, when data are ambiguous, the Soviet researcher should be inclined to give the benefit of doubt to the unbelieving, rather than to the believing, dimension.

Much more important is the unresolved question of whether all of the respondents are being candid about whether or not, in their most interior privacy, they are believers. Given the tension of the times and given the fact that society and the antireligious campaign impose so many penalties upon believing citizens, there is every reason to suspect that some fraction of those who have been surveyed have found it advantageous to conceal their belief from the inquisitive and usually atheistic field workers who are pursuing officially sanctioned studies. Soviet sociologists, while they are often aware of this problem, have, to date, done little to rectify it; but there is ample evidence to suggest that some, at least, of those who have been classified as nonreligious may not ultimately belong in this classification, but in the other instead.

Thus, there is some reason to suspect that these Soviet field studies, which do not claim to be absolutely accurate, may err on the conservative side in reporting on how many Soviet citizens are religious. It seems fairly clear that these studies suggest that around 45%, and hence 115 million, of the population belong to the religious sector to some degree or another. And there is at least a chance that the true figures are even higher due to weaknesses in the sociological methods that have been employed.

Once again, these are tentative findings, and certainly the evidence is not so overwhelming that incautious conclusions may be drawn. There is more than enough evidence to support the conclusion that religion continues to be an important factor in Soviet society, perhaps a great deal more important than most observers suspect. To suggest that its importance will increase radically, however, and that it will become a dominant factor in the life of that society would be an excursion far beyond the bounds permitted by the present state of knowledge.

There may be a curious parallel, however, in Western experience regarding religion. In the United States, for example, many observers were surprised—indeed, they were amazed—by the resurgence of evangelical Protestantism during the 1970s. Prior to its reappearance, many commentators considered that the evangelical approach was a phenomenon of the receding past, which at least since the days of the *McGuffy Reader* and the "Tennessee Monkey Trial" was weak and declining, moribund at best. In retrospect, however, it is clear that this form of Christianity was not dead at all. For two generations it somehow maintained a corps of adherents in the American population, despite the many challenges of the rapidly changing industrial and then technological urbanized society. Then, when conditions somehow became favorable, during the 1970s it expanded rapidly, to such an extent that today great masses of Americans claim to be "born again," and this conservative approach to Christianity is exerting an ever greater influence on the social and political life of the country.

Similarly, in the USSR, most Soviet observers consider and the Marxist ideology demands that religion is a phenomenon of the receding past, that since the Great October Socialist Revolution it has been weak, declining, and moribund. And yet, there is much evidence that religion is not dead at all in the USSR. For four generations it has somehow maintained a corps of adherents in the Soviet population despite the many challenges of a rapidly changing society that is consciously structured against religion. And when conditions have been favorable, as in the wartime crisis or during the "Thaw" in the fifties, it has expanded rapidly. Current sociological research indicates that religion has by no means disappeared, and it may well be that what Soviet observers have considered a dying phenomenon is only dormant.

For all the many superficial similarities, however, the USSR is not the US, and there is no indication—none—that religion is now exercising or is destined to exercise anything like the influence it exerts in American life. One factor, however, is clear. On the basis of evidence presented by the Soviet sociology of religion, religious citizens are, and in any foreseeable future will remain, an important sector of the Soviet population.

NOTES

CHAPTER 1

1. For more detailed examination of the patterns of relations between the church and the state in the USSR see William C. Fletcher, *A Study in Survival: The Church in Russia, 1927–1943* (New York: Macmillan, and London: SPCK, 1965), and *Religion and Soviet Foreign Policy, 1945–1970* (London: Oxford University Press, for the Royal Institute of International Affairs, 1973).

2. William C. Fletcher, "USSR," in *Western Religion: A Country by Country Sociological Inquiry*, ed. Hans [J. J.] Mol (The Hague and Paris: Mouton, 1972), pp. 565–86.

3. *Pravda*, 11 November 1954.

4. William C. Fletcher, *The Russian Orthodox Church Underground, 1917–1970* (London: Oxford University Press, 1971), pp. 126, 226, 235; Nikita Struve, *Christians in Contemporary Russia*, tr. Lancelot Sheppard and A. Mason (London: Harvill Press, 1966), pp. 291–92.

5. For a summary treatment of the antireligious campaign see Donald A. Lowrie and William C. Fletcher, "Khrushchev's Religious Policy, 1959–1964," in *Aspects of Religion in the Soviet Union, 1917–1967*, ed. Richard H. Marshall, Jr. (Chicago: University of Chicago Press, 1971), pp. 131–55.

6. Fletcher, *Russian Orthodox Church*, pp. 219–29.

7. William C. Fletcher, *Nikolai: Portrait of a Dilemma* (New York: Macmillan, 1968), pp. 193–200.

8. *Ugolovnyi kodeks RSFSR* [Criminal Code of the RSFSR] (Moscow: "Juridical Literature" Press, 1964), p. 91.

9. E.g., *Literaturnaia gazeta*, 10 April 1962; *Sovetskaia Rossiia*, 21 June 1960; *Nauka i religiia*, no. 6 (1964), p. 78; *Pravda*, 7 October 1963; S. Ivanov, "Kak my organizuem nauchno-ateisticheskuiu propagandu" [How we organize scientific atheistic propaganda], *Kommunist Moldavii*, no. 7 (1961), pp. 52–57.

215

10. See below, pp. 177–79.
11. E.g., *Pravda*, 3 October 1964; M. G. Mikhailov, "Stavropolskie vstrechi" [Meetings in Stavropol], *Nauka i religiia*, no. 4 (1965), p. 20; *Sovetskaia Rossiia*, 26 May 1965.
12. E.g., *Leninskaia smena*, 20 September 1959; *Uchitel'skaia gazeta*, 20 November 1963.
13. For the Baptist protest movement see Michael A. Bourdeaux, *Religious Ferment in Russia* (London: Macmillan, 1968), and *Faith on Trial in Russia* (New York: Harper & Row, 1971).
14. For the Orthodox protest see Michael A. Bourdeaux, *Patriarch and Prophets* (London: Macmillan, 1969).
15. *New York Times*, 9 April 1972; cf. William C. Fletcher, "Solzhenitsyn and the Merger of Dissent," *Worldview*, vol. 16, no. 8 (1972), pp. 5–8.
16. A. I. Rogov, "Nash golos v efire" [Our voice in the ether], *Nauka i religiia*, no. 3 (1962), pp. 10–11; V. Uryvskii and M. Tepliakov, "Radiozhurnal 'Nauka i religiia'" [The radio magazine "Science and religion"], *Agitator*, no. 13 (1965), p. 33; V. Buslinskii, "Tonkoe delo" [A delicate matter], *Agitator*, no. 7 (1961), p. 49; "Ob uluchshenii sovetskogo radioveshchaniia i dal'neishem razvitii televedenii" [Improving Soviet radio broadcasting and the farthest development of television], *Partiinaia zhizn'*, no. 4 (1960).
17. Rogov, "Nash golos," pp. 10–11; A. Shamaro, "Svet golubnogo ekrana" [The light of the blue screen], *Nauka i religiia*, no. 3 (1962), p. 11; B. Zaikin, "Pered samoi bol'shoi auditoriei" [Before the largest audience], *Agitator*, no. 20 (1966), pp. 44–45; V. Rudnev, "Nasha sistema anti-religioznoi propagandy" [Our system of antireligious propaganda], *Agitator*, no. 11 (1965), pp. 42–44; V. Komarov, "Tvorcheskaia dolzhnost'" [A creative duty], *Nauka i religiia*, no. 4 (1967), p. 35.
18. *Komsomol'skaia pravda*, 31 August 1962; D. M. Ugrinovich, "Neobkhodima produmannaia sistema nauchno-ateisticheskogo vospitaniia" [A thought-out system of scientific atheistic education is essential], *Kommunist*, no. 9 (1962), p. 100; L. N. Mitrokhin, "Izucheniia sektantstva v Tambovskoi oblasti" [The study of sectarianism in the Tambov region], *Voprosy filsofii*, no. 1 (1960), pp. 143–48; G. Koleda and Ia. Seidov, "On ochen khotel zhit'" [He very much wanted to live], *Nauka i religiia*, no. 1 (1969), pp. 52–62.
19. A. Voss, "Vazhnyi uchastok ideologicheskoi raboty" [An important sector of ideological work], *Partiinaia zhizn'*, no. 15 (1962), p. 24.
20. *Komsomol'skaia pravda*, 26 January 1968; A. Olshauskas, "'Reshitel'nye mery' tsely ne dostigaiut" ["Decisive measures" do not achieve the goal], *Nauka i religiia*, no. 6 (1963), pp. 72–73.
21. E. Bondar, "Desiat' tysach 'pochemu'" [Ten thousand "why's"], *Agitator*, no. 23 (1964), p. 40; S. Kurshakov, "V gorode na Volge" [In a city on the Volga], *Nauka i religiia*, no. 4 (1968), p. 43; E. Riumin, "Zhivoe slovo i glubina soderzhaniia" [The living word and depth of contents], *Agitator*, no. 6 (1967), p. 45.

22. *Uchitel'skaia gazeta*, 23 August 1966; *Komsomol'skaia pravda*, 13 October 1971; V. Iakub, "Muzei v shkole" [A museum in the school], *Nauka i religiia*, no. 9 (1964), pp. 46–49.
23. *Pravda*, 6 March 1964; *Sovetskaia Rossia*, 6 January 1972; *Uchitel'skaia gazeta*, 29 January 1972; A. Gorelov, "Dokhodit' do kazhdogo" [Go to each one], *Partiinaia zhizn'*, no. 12 (1971), p. 48.
24. Cf. L. Il'ichev, "Formirovanie nauchnogo mirovozzreniia i ateisticheskoe vospitanie" [The formation of a scientific world view and atheistic education], *Kommunist*, no. 1 (1964), pp. 23–46; "O meropriiatiiakh po usileniiu ateisticheskogo vospitaniia naseleniia" [Measures for strengthening the atheistic education of the population], *Partiinaia zhizn'*, no. 2 (1964), p. 23.
25. *Pravda*, 11 November 1954.
26. *Pravda*, 2 March 1964; "V dobry chas!" [High time!], *Nauka i religiia*, no. 9 (1964), p. 53.

CHAPTER 2

1. A. P. Sheptulin, "Zadachi povysheniia urovnia prepodovaniia osnov nauchnogo ateizma" [Tasks of raising the level of teaching of the fundamentals of scientific atheism], in *Voprosy nauchnogo ateizma* [Problems of scientific atheism; hereafter cited as *VNA*], ed. A. F. Okulov (Moscow: "Mysl'," semi-annually), vol. 15 (1973), pp. 19–20.
2. S. P. Trapeznikov, "Razvitie obshchestvennykh nauk i povyshenie ikh roli v kommunisticheskom stroitel'stve" [The development of social sciences and the increase of their role in building communism], *Voprosy filosofii*, no. 11 (1967), p. 9.
3. Karl Marx and F. Engels, *On Religion* (Moscow: State Publishing House for Political Literature, 1955), pp. 41–42.
4. V. I. Lenin, *Sochineniia* [Works], 4th ed. (Moscow: State Publishing House for Political Literature, 1942–66), vol. 10, pp. 65–66.
5. See the discussion in M. F. Kalashnikov, "Religiia kak obshchestvennyi fenomen" [Religion as a social phenomenon], in *Nauchnyi ateizm: Voprosy metodologii i sotsiologii* [Scientific atheism: problems of methodology and sociology], ed. M. F. Kalashnikov, 3d ed. (Perm': Perm State Pedagogical Institute, 1974), pp. 29–33. V. N. Nikitin, "Dialektika prichinnoi sviazi i problema religioznosti v usloviiakh sotsializma" [The dialectic of causal links and the problem of religiousness in conditions of socialism], in ibid., p. 35, presents an instructive survey of the explanations for the survival of religion by fifty Soviet antireligious authors.
6. A. D. Sukhov, *Religiia kak obshchestvennyi fenomen* [Religion as a social phenomenon] (Moscow: "Mysl'," 1972), p. 40.
7. I. N. Iablokov, *Metodologicheskie problemy sotsiologii religii* [Methodological problems of the sociology of religion] (Moscow: Moscow University Press, 1972), p. 128.

8. I. D. Pantskhava, ed., *O nekotorykh osobennostiakh sovremennoi religioznoi ideologii* [Certain peculiarities of contemporary religious ideology] (Moscow: Moscow University Press, 1964), p. 7.

9. P. D. Selivanov, *Partiinoi rukovodstvo ateisticheskim vospitaniem* [Party leadership in atheistic education] (Moscow: Publishing House for Political Literature, 1973), p. 52.

10. N. Mizov, "Protsess preodoleniia religii i upravlenie im" [The process of overcoming religion and its guidance], *Voprosy filosofii*, no. 7 (1973), p. 78.

11. Iablokov, *Metodologicheskie Problemy*, p. 7.

12. V. S. Nemchinov, "Sotsiologii i statistika" [Sociology and statistics], *Voprosy filosofii*, 1955, quoted in R. G. Baltanov, *Sotsiologicheskie problemy v sisteme naucho-ateisticheskogo vospitaniia* [Sociological problems in the system of scientific atheistic education] (Kazan': Kazan University Press, 1973), p. 15.

13. Sukhov, *Religiia*, p. 6.

14. Vusia Aronovna Cherniak, *Formirovanie nauchno-materialisticheskogo ateisticheskogo mirovozzreniia* [The formation of a scientific, materialistic, atheistic world view] (Alma-Ata: "Nauka," 1969), p. 19 n.4.

15. Cf. D. M. Ugrinovich, "O predmete marksistskoi sotsiologii" [The subject matter of Marxist sociology], in *Ocherki metodologii poznaniia sotsial'nykh iavlenii* [Essays on the methodology of understanding social phenomena], ed. L. N. Dorogova (Moscow: "Mysl'," 1970), pp. 11–46.

16. V. P. Fedotov and V. I. Klushin, reviewing B. A. Chagin, *Ocherki istorii sotsiologicheskoi mysli v SSSR (1917–1969 gg)* [Essays on the history of sociological thought in the USSR (1917–1969)] (Leningrad: "Nauka," 1971), in *Voprosy filosofii*, no. 11 (1973), pp. 167–68.

17. I. A. Galitskaia, "K voprosu ob izuchenii religioznosti molodezhi" [The question of the study of the religiousness of youth], in *VNA* 7 (1969): 390.

18. A. I. Klibanov, *Religioznoe sektantstvo i sovremennost'* [Religious sectarianism and contemporaneity] (Moscow: "Nauka," 1969), p. 24.

19. *Gertsenovskie chteniia: Nauchnyi ateizm, etika, estetika* [Herzen readings: scientific atheism, ethics, aesthetics] (Leningrad: State Teacher Training Institute, annually), vol. 1 (1970), p. 15; V. D. Kobetskii, *Sotsiologicheskoe izuchenie religioznosti i ateizma* [Sociological study of religiousness and atheism] (Leningrad: Leningrad University Press, 1978), pp. 8–11, 14–21, and passim.

20. E. Duluman, B. Lobovik, and V. Tancher, *Sovremennyi veruiushchii* [The contemporary believer] (Moscow: Publishing House for Political Literature, 1970), p. 4.

21. Klibanov, *Religioznoe sektantstvo*, p. 24.

22. Fletcher, *Study in Survival*, pp. 75–76; John Shelton Curtiss, *The Russian Church and the Soviet State, 1917–1950* (Boston: Little, Brown, 1953), p. 283; N. S. Timasheff, *Religion in Soviet Russia, 1917–1942* (New York: Sheed & Ward, 1942), p. 92; Leopold L. Braun, *Religion in Russia, from Lenin to*

Khrushchev: An Uncensored Account (Paterson, N.J.: Saint Anthony Guild Press, 1959), pp. 38–41.

23. For a convenient and impressive example see Akademiia Nauk SSSR (hereafter cited as AN SSSR), *Voprosy istorii religii i ateizma* [Problems of the history of religion and atheism] (Moscow: AN SSSR, annually), vol. 9 (1961) passim.

24. Sukhov, *Religiia*, p. 6.

25. I. D. Pantskhava, "Vvedenie" [Introduction], in *Konkretno-sotsiologicheskoe izuchenie sostoianiia religioznosti i opyta ateisticheskogo vospitaniia* [Concrete sociological study of the condition of religiousness and the experience of atheistic education], ed. I. D. Pantskhava (Moscow: Moscow University Press, 1969), p. 4.

26. *Gertsenovskie chteniia* 1 (1970): 16.

27. "V institute nauchnogo ateizma" [In the institute of scientific atheism], *Nauka i religiia*, no. 7 (1972), p. 6.

28. A. F. Okulov, *Sovetskaia filosofskaia nauka i ee problemy* [Soviet philosophical science and its problems] (Moscow: "Mysl'," 1970), p. 29.

29. See the bibliographies in Kobetskii, *Sotsiologicheskoe izuchenie*, pp. 108–17, and Baltanov, *Sotsiologicheskie problemy*, pp. 234–49.

30. Duluman, *Sovremennyi veruiushchii*, p. 5.

31. A. Kozhenikov, "Ateisticheskoe vospitanie na sele" [Atheistic education in the village], *Nauka i religiia*, no. 12 (1971), p. 2.

32. Klibanov, *Religioznoe sektantstvo*, p. 42.

33. Pantskhava, "Vvedenie," p. 5.

34. N. P. Krasnikov, "O nekotorykh voprosakh raboty s veruiushchimi" [Certain problems of work with believers], in *Voprosy preodoleniia religioznykh perezhitkov v SSSR* [Problems of overcoming religious survivals in the USSR], ed. N. P. Krasnikov (Moscow: "Nauka," 1966), p. 7.

35. Duluman, *Sovremennyi veruiushchii*, p. 5.

36. L. T. Sytenko, "O nravstvennom oblike sovremennogo veruiushchego" [The moral aspect of the contemporary believer], in *VNA* 3 (1967): 126.

37. M. K. Tepliakov, "Pobeda ateizma v razlichnykh sotsial'nykh sloiakh sovetskogo obshchestva" [The victory of atheism in various social strata of Soviet society], in *VNA* 4 (1967): 32.

38. T. Mering, "Konkretno o samom vazhnom" [Concretely on the most important], *Nauka i religiia*, no. 3 (1969), p. 40.

39. M. K. Tepliakov, *Problemy ateisticheskogo vospitaniia v praktike partiinoi raboty* [Problems of atheistic education in the practice of Party work] (Voronezh: Voronezh University Press, 1972), p. 32.

40. Iu. Safronov, "Chto pokazali otvety" [What the answers showed], *Kommunist Belorussii*, no. 3 (1967), p. 69.

41. A. Eryshev and P. Kosukha, "Instilling Irreconcilability," *Lyudina i svit*, no. 2 (January 1969), in *Religion in Communist Dominated Areas*, vol. 8 (1969), p. 136 (translation from *Digest of the Soviet Ukrainian Press*).

42. B. V. Kniazev, "Sistema ateisticheskogo vospitaniia—vazhneishee uslovie preodoleniia religioznykh perezhitkov" [The system of atheistic education—the most important condition for overcoming religious survivals], in Pantskhava, *Konkretno-sotsiologicheskoe izuchenie*, p. 248; Sytenko, "O nravstvennom oblike," p. 126.

43. V. N. Kolbanovskii, *Kollektiv kolkhoznikov: Sotsial'no-psikhologicheskoe issledovanie* [The collective of the collective farmers: social-psychological research] (Moscow: "Mysl'," 1967), p. 232.

44. I. S. Gusev, "Konkretnost', nauchnost', deistvennost'" [Concreteness, science, effectiveness], in *VNA* 19 (1976): 23–24.

45. M. K. Tepliakov, "Sotsial'nye issledovaniia v sisteme ateisticheskogo vospitaniia" [Social reseach in the system of atheistic education], in *VNA* 9 (1970): 108.

46. N. S. Vasilevskaia, "Opyt konkretno-sotsiologicheskogo issledovaniia otnosheniia k religii v sovremennoi gorodskoi sem'e" [Experience of concrete sociological research on the relationship to religion in the contemporary urban family], in *VNA* 13 (1972): 384–85 and passim.

47. V. Cherniak, "Nuzhen nauchnyi podkhod" [A scientific approach is necessary], *Nauka i religiia*, no. 5 (1971), p. 25.

48. V. S. Solov'ev, "O vliianii ateizma na dukhovnoe razvitie lichnosti" [The influence of atheism on the intellectual development of the personality], in *VNA* 14 (1973): 187.

49. Klibanov, *Religioznoe sektantstvo*, pp. 59–68 and passim.

50. V. G. Pivovarov, "Sotsiologicheskoe issledovanie problem byta, kul'tury, natsional'nykh traditsii i verovanii v Checheno-Ingushskoi ASSR" [Sociological research on the problems of the manner of life, culture, national traditions, and beliefs in the Chechen-Ingush ASSR], in *VNA* 17 (1975): 310–19.

51. E.g., I. A. Galitskaia, "Izuchenie kanalov vosproizvodstva religioznosti v novykh pokoleniiakh—odno iz trebovanii sistemy ateisticheskogo vospitaniia" [Study of the channels of the reproduction of religiousness in new generations—one of the requirements for a system of atheistic education], in *VNA* 9 (1970): 56.

52. G. Osipov and M. Yovchuk, "Some Principles of Theory, Problems and Methods of Research in Sociology in the USSR: A Soviet View," in *Soviet Sociology: Historical Antecedents and Current Appraisals*, ed. Alex Simirenko (Chicago: Quadrangle Books, 1966), p. 302.

53. A. I. Klibanov, "Nauchno-organizatsionnyi i metodicheskii opyt konkretnykh issledovanii religioznosti" [Scientific organizational and methodological experience of concrete research on religiousness], in *Konkretnye issledovaniia sovremennykh religioznykh verovanii (metodika, organizatsiia, rezul'taty)* [Concrete research on contemporary religious faiths (methodolgy, organization, results)], ed. A. I. Klibanov (Moscow: "Mysl'," 1967), p. 19.

54. E.g., K. I. Nikonov, "O nekotorykh tendentsiiakh v propovednicheskoi deiatel'nosti sovremennogo baptizma" [Certain tendencies in the preaching

activity of contemporary Baptists], in Pantskhava, *Konkretno-sotsiologicheskoe izuchenie*, pp. 174–76.

55. The Council for Religious Affairs was formed in 1966 by a merger of the Council for the Affairs of Religious Cults and the Council for the Affairs of the Russian Orthodox Church (*Izvestiia*, 30 August 1966). The latter was formed in 1943 under the Council of Ministers of the USSR. The Council for Religious Affairs has branch offices throughout the country.

56. Iu. V. Gagarin, "Otkhod ot sektantstva v Komi ASSR" [The departure from sectarianism in the Komi ASSR], in *Po etapam razvitiia ateizma v SSSR* [Stages of the development of atheism in the USSR], ed. N. P. Krasnikov (Leningrad: "Nauka," 1967), p. 169 n.1; Klibanov, "Nauchno-organizatsionnyi i metodicheskii opyt," pp. 7, 24.

57. A. Iarygin, "Baptistskaia propoved': Chemu ona uchit?" [Baptist preaching: what does it teach?], *Nauka i religiia*, no. 5 (1972), p. 55.

58. L. M. Ignatenko and E. S. Prokoshina, "Opyt konkretnykh issledovanii psikhologii baptistov v BSSR [Experience of concrete research on the psychology of Baptists in the B(elorussian)SSR], in *VNA* 11 (1971): 251.

59. Cf. V. Nestorov, "Pravoslavnaia tserkov' v Latvii" [The Orthodox Church in Latvia], in *Ateizm i religiia* [Atheism and religion], ed. Z. B. Balevits (Riga: "Zinatne," 1969), pp. 146–50.

60. N. P. Alekseev, "Metodika i rezul'taty izucheniia religioznosti sel'skogo naseleniia" [Methods and results of the study of religiousness of the rural population], in *VNA* 3 (1967): 141–42.

61. K. A. Vimmsaare, "Ob ispol'zovanii rezul'tatov konkretno-sotsiologicheskikh issledovanii v uchebno-vospitatel'nom protsesse" [The use of results of concrete sociological research in the educational upbringing process], in *VNA* 15 (1973): 226–27. The text of two such questionnaires, one for university students and the other for the general public, is given in Kobetskii, *Sotsiologischeskoe izuchenie*, pp. 95–107.

62. D. M. Ugrinovich and I. N. Iablokov, "Izuchenie religioznogo soznaniia veruiushchikh v sotsialisticheskom obshchestve i zadachi ateisticheskogo vospitaniia" [The study of the religious consciousness of believers in socialist society and the tasks of atheistic education], in *Obshchestvennaia psikhologiia i kommunisticheskoe vospitanie* [Social Psychology and Communist education], ed. D. M. Ugrinovich (Moscow: Moscow University Press, 1967), pp. 142–43.

63. Cf. G. E. Kudriashov, "Metod kartiinogo interv'iu izuchenii religioznogo vliianiia na doshkol'nikov" [The method of the picture interview in studying religious influence on preschoolers], in *VNA* 11 (1971): 276–86 passim.

64. V. A. Saprykin, "Ateisticheskaia rabota partiinoi organizatsii v usloviiakh goroda" [Atheistic work of the Party organization in urban conditions], in *VNA* 9 (1970): 223–24. Incidentally, the following typical findings are given (p. 224): "Here are results from research in school No. 23 in a neighborhood that is distinguished by relatively high religiousness. 205 students took part in the survey. 194 school children answered the question of what is a cos-

monaut, what is god—27, what is hell—45, what is heaven—34 (many approximately), 57 knew what the Bible is, 2 had read it. The holidays they like: May First and the Anniversary of the October Revolution—177, New Years'—82, Easter—5 ("because they decorate eggs and bake buns," "because mama decorates eggs and buys candy"). Everyone in the family prays—2, only father and mother—3, grandmother and grandfather—15. Believe in god—2. The Bible tells about god—1, parents—1, teachers and books—5, grandmother and grandfather—12."

65. A. I. Dem'ianov, "K voprosu o sovremennom sostoianii religioznogo techeniia 'Istinno Pravoslavnykh Khristian' " [On the question of the contemporary condition of the religious movement "True Orthodox Christians"], in *VNA* 16 (1974): 103–22.

66. M. A. Popova, "Kritika priemov i metodov konkretnykh issledovanii v amerikanskoi psikhologii religii" [A critique of modes and methods of concrete research in American psychology of religion], in Pantskhava, *Konkretnosotsiologicheskoe izuchenie*, pp. 261–81.

CHAPTER 3

1. T. G. Gaidurova, "Zavisimost' obydennogo religioznogo soznaniia veruiushchikh ot uslovii ikh zhizni" [The dependence of the ordinary religious consciousness of believers on the conditions of their lives], in Pantskhava, *Konkretno-sotsiologicheskoe izuchenie*, p. 31.

2. Kolbanovskii, *Kollektiv*, p. 236. The third collective farm is highly atypical; it may be a site that was uninhabited during tsarist times.

3. This is reminiscent of a case cited by Kobetskii, *Sotsiologicheskoe veruiushchii*, p. 30: in the thirties, "a teacher asked the pupils of one group which of them believes in god, and who doesn't. There seemed to be twenty believers, three unbelievers. But afterwards, when the pupils learned that the teacher herself does not believe, all of them, except for five people, also said they were unbelievers." Kobetskii concludes that their beliefs were not very firm; it seems just as reasonable to conclude that children are quick to learn how to take on protective coloration.

4. V. Evdokimov, "Konkretnye sotsial'nye issledovaniia i ateizm" [Concrete social research and atheism], *Nauka i religiia*, no. 1 (1968), p. 24.

5. Constantin de Grunwald, *The Churches and the Soviet Union*, tr. G. J. Robinson-Paskevsky (New York: Macmillan, 1962), p. 222.

6. Paul Hollander, "The Dilemmas of Soviet Sociology," in Simirenko, *Soviet Sociology*, p. 308.

7. I. N. Iablokov, "Obshchenie veruiushchikh kak faktor formirovaniia psikhologii religioznoi gruppy" [The congregation of believers as a factor in the formation of the psychology of the religious group], in Pantskhava, *Konkretnosotsiologicheskoe izuchenie*, p. 55.

8. Iu. I. Stel'makov, "O sootnoshenii ratsional'nogo i emotsional'nogo v soznanii

veruiushchikh" [The relationship of the rational and the emotional in the consciousness of believers], in Pantskhava, *Konkretno-sotsiologicheskoe izuchenie*, pp. 32–46 passim.

9. M. G. Pismanik, "Metodika sotsial'no-psikhologicheskikh issledovanii religioznosti" [Methods of social-psychological research on religiousness], in *VNA* 11 (1971): 214.

10. Cf. I. N. Iablokov, "Transformatsiia religioznoi morali v soznanii veruiushchikh v usloviiakh sotsializma" [The transformation of religious morality in the consciousness of believers in the conditions of socialism], in Pantskhava, *Konkretno-sotsiologicheskoe izuchenie*, p. 144.

11. L. P. Kharakhorkin and A. P. Andreev, "Kritika baptistskoi interpretatsii nauki i nauchno-tekhnicheskogo progressa" [A critique of the Baptist interpretation of science and scientific-technological progress], in *Gertsenovskie chteniia* 30 (1977): 45.

12. N. N. Kozachishin, "Konkretno-sotsiologicheskie issledovanii i ikh rol' v sovershenstvovanii ateisticheskogo vospitaniia v vuzakh" [Concrete sociological research and its role in improving atheistic education in institutions of higher education], in *VNA* 15 (1973): 218.

13. L. N. Mitrokhin, "O metodologii konkretnykh issledovanii v oblasti religii" [The methodology of concrete research in the field of religion], in *Sotsiologiia v SSSR* [Sociology in the USSR] (Moscow: "Mysl'," 1966), vol. 1, p. 319.

14. V. Arsenkin et al., "Molodezhi—ateisticheskuiu zakalku!" [Youth—atheistic toughness!], *Nauka i religiia*, no. 11 (1971), p. 15.

15. D. M. Ugrinovich, "Religiia kak predmet sotsiologicheskogo issledovaniia" [Religion as a subject of sociological research], in Dorogova, *Ocherki*, p. 156.

16. Cf. the great difficulties experienced and the instructive results achieved by Bulgarian sociologists in attempting to overcome the problem of conscious or unconscious deception by believers: Jivko Ochavkov, "Bulgaria," in Mol, *Western Religion*, pp. 83–99.

17. A. A. Lebedev, "Studencheskaia molodezh' i ateizm" [Student youth and atheism], in *VNA* 15 (1973): 201.

18. K. Mamaeva, "O nekotorykh ob"ektivnykh i sub"ektivnykh faktorakh v ateisticheskom vospitanii sel'skogo naseleniia" [Some objective and subjective factors in atheistic education of the rural population], in Balevits, *Ateizm*, p. 85.

19. D. M. Ugrinovich, *Vvedenie v teoreticheskoe religiovedenie* [Introduction to theoretical religious studies] (Moscow: "Mysl'," 1973), p. 85.

20. L. A. Tul'tseva, "Evoliutsiia starogo russkogo sektantstva" [The evolution of old Russian sectarianism], in *VNA* 7 (1969): 210–11.

21. M. G. Pismanik, "O sostoianii religioznosti i nekotorykh osobennostiakh nauchno-ateisticheskogo vospitaniia sredi zhenshchin" [The situation of religiousness and certain peculiarities of scientific atheistic education among women], in Pantskhava, *Konkretno-sotsiologicheskoe izuchenie*, p. 222 and passim.

22. V. V. Korolev, "Rol' sotsial'noi aktivnosti v formirovanii ateisticheskogo mirovozzreniia" [The role of social activism in the formation of an atheistic world view], in *VNA* 13 (1972): 153.

23. *Financial Times,* 28 June 1974; cf. *Electronics,* 1 September 1969, p. 105.

24. Cherniak, *Formirovanie,* pp. 267–68; V. P. Bichany and T. A. Sypacheva, "Rol' obshchestvennoi aktivnosti v formirovanii ateisticheskoi ubezhdennosti molodezhi" [The role of social activism in the formation of atheistic convictions of youth], in Kalashnikov, *Nauchnyi ateizm,* pp. 106–7.

25. For a detailed examination of this problem see Fletcher, "USSR," passim.

26. Cf. *Sobranie uzakonenii i rasporiazhenii rabochekrest'ianskogo pravitel'stva RSFSR* [Collection of legislation and orders of the workers and peasants government of the RSFSR], no. 35 (1929), text no. 353; and amendments in ibid., no. 8 (1932), text no. 41, vol. 2, p. 6; N. Orleanskii, *Zakon o religioznykh ob"edineniiakh RSFSR* [The law concerning religious associations of the RSFSR] (Moscow: State Publishing House for Political Literature, 1930), pp. 26–39; Fletcher, *Study in Survival,* p. 114.

27. D. M. Aptekman, "The Vitality of the Baptismal Ceremony under Modern Soviet Conditions: An Empirical Study," in Simirenko, *Soviet Sociology,* p. 376.

28. V. G. Pivovarov, *Struktura religioznoi obshchiny* [The structure of the religious congregation] (Groznyi: Chechen-Ingush Book Press, 1970), p. 56.

29. E.g., see above, note to table 3.1.

30. Klibanov, *Konkretnye issledovaniie,* pp. 150–51; M. K. Tepliakov, "Sostoianie religioznosti naseleniia i otkhod veruiushchikh ot religii v Voronezhskoi oblasti (1961–1964 gg)" [The situation of the religiousness of the population and the departure of believers from religion in the Voronezh region (1961–1964)], in Krasnikov, *Voprosy,* p. 36.

31. S. V. Koltuniuk, "K probleme effektivnosti nauchno-ateisticheskogo vospitaniia" [The problem of the effectiveness of scientific atheistic education], in *VNA* 12 (1971): 143.

32. N. A. Pashkov, "K voprosu o kharaktere obydennogo religioznogo soznaniia pravoslavnykh khristian" [The problem of the character of the ordinary religious consciousness of Orthodox Christians], in Pantskhava, *Konkretno-sotsiologicheskoe izuchenie,* p. 150.

33. A. I. Klibanov, "Veruiushchii v sovremennom mire" [The believer in the contemporary world], *Nauka i religiia,* no. 11 (1970), p. 73.

34. B. G. Furov, "Sovetskoe gosudarstvo i tserkov'" [The Soviet government and the church], in *Ateizm, religiia, sovremennost'* [Atheism, religion, contemporaneity], ed. G. A. Razumova (Leningrad: State Museum of the History of Religion and Atheism, 1977), p. 55.

35. *Voprosy filosofii i sotsiologii,* nos. 1–5 (1969–73), reverse title page.

36. E.g., M. T. Iovchuk et al., "Aktual'nye teoreticheskie problemy Marksistsko-Leninskoi sotsiologii v SSSR" [Pressing theoretical problems of Marxist-Leninist sociology in the USSR], *Filosofskie nauki,* no. 5 (1970), pp. 3–13.

CHAPTER 4

1. Review of *Prichiny sushchestvovaniia i puti preodoleniia religioznykh pere-zhitkov* [Causes of the existence of and ways of overcoming religious survivals] (Minsk: "Nauka i Tekhnika," 1965), in *VNA* 3 (1967): 365.
2. A. S. Onishchenko, "Tendentsii izmeneniia sovremennogo religioznogo soz-naniia" [Tendencies of change of contemporary religious consciousness], in *VNA* 2 (1966): 92.
3. Ugrinovich, *Obshchestvennaia psikhologiia*, p. 145; cf. N. Krasnikov, "Blizhe k zhizni—blizhe k uspekhu" [Nearer to life—nearer to success], *Nauka i religiia*, no. 12 (1965), p. 5.
4. R. A. Lopatkin, "Nekotorye sotsial'no-psikhologicheskie problemy ateistiche-skogo vospitaniia" [Certain social-psychological problems of atheistic educa-tion], in *VNA* 11 (1971): 296–97.
5. "O chem govorit statistika?" [What do the statistics say?], *Nauki i religiia*, no. 1 (1967), p. 35.
6. Ibid., citing *Antireligioznik*, no. 6 (1935), p. 2.
7. N. I. Puchkov, "Vliianie vnutriklassovykh izmenenii v sotsialisticheskom ob-shchestve na razvitie massogo ateizma" [The influence of intraclass changes in Socialist society on the development of mass atheism], in *VNA* 13 (1972): 119.
8. Duluman, *Sovremennyi veruiushchii*, p. 33; Ugrinovich, *Vvedenie*, p. 179; A. Gur'ianov, "Bogi ne umiraiut sami" [The gods do not die by themselves], *Nauka i religiia*, no. 9 (1969), p. 16.
9. A. Vinokur, "Ugasenie drevnei very" [Extinction of an ancient faith], *Nauka i religiia*, no. 1 (1967), p. 41.
10. N. P. Andrianov, "Evoliutsiia nravstvennogo oblika sovremennogo veruiu-shchego" [The evolution of the moral make-up of the contemporary believer], in *Ateizm, religiia, nravstvennost'* [Atheism, religion, morality], ed. A. I. Garadzha (Moscow: "Mysl'," 1972), p. 171.
11. These percentages should be 74.9 and 13.0.
12. A. Okulov, "Nauchno-ateisticheskoe vospitanie segodnia" [Scientific atheistic education today], *Nauka i religiia*, no. 8 (1967), p. 16.
13. D. M. Ugrinovich, *Filosofskie problemy kritiki religii* [Philosophical problems of the critique of religion] (Moscow: Moscow University Press, 1965), pp. 118–19.
14. E. G. Filimonov, "Sotsiologicheskie issledovaniia protsessa preodoleniia religii v sel'skoi mestnosti: Itogi, problemy, perspektivy" [Sociological research on the process of overcoming religion in the rural locale: results, problems, perspectives], in *VNA* 16 (1974): 73.
15. V. Pivovarov, "Pod rukovodstvom partiinykh organov" [Under the leadership of party organs], *Nauka i religiia*, no. 9 (1972), p. 90.
16. A. F. Okulov and D. M. Ugrinovich, "VII mezhdunarodnyi sotsiologicheskii kongress: Problemy sotsiologii religii" [The VII international sociological congress: problems of the sociology of religion], in *VNA* 12 (1971): 238.
17. R. Baltanov, "Iz nashego opyta issledovaniia religioznosti naseleniia" [Our

experience studying the religiousness of the population], *Nauka i religiia*, no. 8 (1967), p. 18.

18. Filimonov, "Sotsiologicheskie issledovaniia," p. 73, citing *K obshchestvu, svobodnomu ot religii* [Toward a society free from religion] (Moscow: "Mysl'," 1970), p. 267.

19. Iu. B. Pishchik, "Sovremennyi protestantizm: Problemy teorii i praktiki" [Contemporary protestantism: problems of theory and practice], in *VNA* 13 (1972): 410.

20. N. Ashirov, "Evoliutsiia Islama v SSSR: Izmeneniia v kul'te" [The evolution of Islam in the USSR: changes in the cultus], *Nauka i religiia*, no. 9 (1971), p. 15.

21. M. V. Vagabov, "Bol'she vnimaniia sovetskomu islamovedeniiu" [More attention to Soviet Islamic studies], *Voprosy filosofii*, no. 12 (1966), p. 173; cf. I. A. Makatov, "Kul't sviatykh v islame" [The cult of saints in Islam], in *VNA* 3 (1967): 164; Geoffrey Wheeler, "The Muslims of Central Asia," *Problems of Communism*, September/October 1967, p. 78; and William C. Fletcher, "Religious Dissent in the USSR in the 1960s," *Slavic Review*, vol. 30, no. 2 (June 1971), pp. 306–8.

22. The official figure of 328,000 Baptists would yield a figure of less than 0.15% of the total population of the USSR.

23. Serge Bolshakoff, *Russian Nonconformity* (Philadelphia: Westminster, 1950), pp. 122–28; Charles Foltz, Jr., "Religion in Russia Today: A First-hand Report," *US News and World Report*, 10 February 1964, p. 57.

24. It is more likely that their churches were forcibly closed. The futility of using such methods is evident from the fact that the number of unregistered Baptist communities remained exactly the same (123).

25. A. Podmazov, "Sovremennoe staroobriadchestvo v Latvii" [Contemporary Old Believers in Latvia], in Balevits, *Ateizm*, p. 201. There is a possibility that these figures may reflect a degree of preferential treatment due to a state policy of favoring the smaller denominations as competitors to the major religion.

26. Tepliakov, "Pobeda," p. 156. F. Fedorenko, in *Sekty, ikh vera i dela* [The sects, their faith and works] (Moscow: Publishing House for Political Literature, 1965), provides a useful but by no means exhaustive description of more than 400 religious denominations in the USSR. Very little of his information is derived from sociological research, however.

27. Cf. A. N. Kochetov, "Izuchenie buddizma v SSSR" [The study of Buddhism in the USSR], in *VNA* 4 (1967): 427–44; AN SSSR, *Kritika ideologii lamaizma i shamanizma* [A critique of the ideology of Lamaism and shamanism] (Ulan-Ude: Buriat Book Press, 1965), passim.

CHAPTER 5

1. A Mennik, "Nasushchnye zadachi ateisticheskogo vospitaniia" [Urgent tasks

of atheistic education], in Balevits, *Ateizm*, p. 10.

2. Interestingly enough, in the city of Penza, 100% of those over 80 years old were religious, while in the region, only 80.1% were. Surely, such incongruous figures might deserve some elaboration.

3. A. M. Orlov, "Opyt issledovaniia protsessa sekuliarizatsii v tatarskikh selakh" [Experience of research on the process of secularization in Tatar villages], in *VNA* 16 (1974): 93.

4. G. Lialina, "Sud'ba odnoi utopii" [The fate of one utopia], *Nauka i religiia*, no. 11 (1970), p. 90.

5. I. A. Ulybin, "Iz opyta prepodovaniia nauchnogo ateizma v sel'skokhoziaistvennom vuze" [Experience in teaching scientific atheism in agricultural institutions of higher education], in *VNA* 15 (1973): 109.

6. V. Ershov, "Zachem neveruiushchemu ateizm?" [Why atheism for the nonbeliever?], *Nauka i religiia*, no. 7 (1971), p. 76.

7. L. Freiberg, "Rol' intelligentsii v formirovanii materialisticheskogo mirovozzreniia" [The role of the intelligentsia in the formation of a materialistic world view], in *VNA* 21 (1977): 164.

8. The sources for these data are academic dissertations for advanced degrees.

9. A. S. Barkauskas, "Osushchestvlenie leninskikh idei ob ateisticheskom vospitanii v prakticheskoi deiatel'nosti partiinykh organizatsii" [The implementation of Leninist ideas on atheistic education in the practical activity of Party organizations], in *VNA* 10 (1970): 162.

10. A. I. Klibanov, "Sovremennoe sektantstvo v Lipetskoi oblasti" [Contemporary sectarianism in the Lipetsk region], in AN SSSR, *Voprosy* 10 (1962): 165–66.

11. N. I. Il'inykh, "Osobennosti organizatsii i deiatel'nosti mennonitskikh obshchin" [Peculiarities of the organization and activity of Mennonite congregations], in Pantskhava, *Konkretno-sotsiologicheskoe izuchenie*, p. 202.

12. A. D. Sukhov, "O konservativnosti religioznykh traditsii" [The conservatism of religious traditions], *Voprosy filosofii*, no. 8 (1961), p. 150.

13. O. Osipov, "Priglashenie v klub" [An invitation to the club], *Nauka i religiia*, no. 11 (1971), p. 31.

14. N. S. Sofronov, "Ateisticheskoe vospitanie v sel'skoi mestnosti" [Atheistic education in the rural locale], in *VNA* 9 (1970): 239. It may be noted that retired people, because they are no longer vulnerable to job discrimination, are often more willing than others to serve on the official church board (*dvadsatka*).

15. Klibanov, *Religioznoe sektantstvo*, p. 74; A. I. Klibanov and L. N. Mitrokhin, "Raskol v sovremennom baptizme" [Schism among contemporary Baptists], in *VNA* 3 (1967): 92; Tepliakov, *Problemy*, pp. 156–57.

16. E. Ia. Bograd, "Opyt izuchenii sovremennogo sektantstva v Michurinskom raione" [Experience of studying contemporary sectarianism in the Michurin district], in AN SSSR, *Voprosy* 9 (1961): 127.

17. E. F. Murav'ev and Iu. V. Dmitrev, "O konkretnosti v izuchenii i preodolenii religioznykh perezhitkov" [Concreteness in studying and overcoming religious survivals], *Voprosy filosofii*, no. 3 (1961), p. 64.

18. I. A. Malakhova, "Istoriki izuchaiut sovremennye religioznye techeniia" [Historians are studying contemporary religious trends], *Istoriia SSSR*, no. 2 (1961), p. 234.

19. More accurately, the last two percentages should read 22.4 and 37.0.

20. It should be noted, with regard to the last figure, that the minimum age at which a citizen may legally belong to a religious organization is 18.

21. This datum is suspect; see above, p. 53.

22. E. Duluman, "Vosproizvodstvo religii" [The origin of religion], *Nauka i religiia*, no. 7 (1968), p. 10.

23. Cf. *Kazakhstanskaia pravda*, 8 December 1963; Fletcher, *Russian Orthodox Church*, pp. 223–25.

24. Cf. William C. Fletcher, "Protestant Influences on the Outlook of the Soviet Citizen Today," in *Religion and the Search for New Ideals in the USSR*, ed. William C. Fletcher and Anthony J. Strover (New York: Praeger, for the Institute for the Study of the USSR, 1967), pp. 75–76.

25. Harvey Fireside, *Icon and Swastika: The Russian Orthodox Church under Nazi and Soviet Control* (Cambridge, Mass.: Harvard University Press, 1971), pp. 7–9.

26. G. G. Ershov, "Kritika v ateisticheskoe literature religioznogo ucheniia o bessmertii" [Criticism in atheistic literature of the religious doctrine of immortality], in Krasnikov, *Po etapam*, pp. 247–48.

27. Cf. Nathaniel Davis, "Religion and Communist Government in the Soviet Union and Eastern Europe" (Ph.D. dissertation, Fletcher School of Law and Diplomacy, Tufts University, 1960), p. 88.

28. Klibanov, *Religioznoe sektantstvo*, pp. 74, 82, 100–101; Ugrinovich, *Filosofskie problemy*, p. 120; Tepliakov, "Sostoianie," p. 34; Tepliakov, "Sotsial'nye issledovaniia," p. 110; Gaidurova, "Zavisimost'," p. 28; E. I. Lisavtsev and S. I. Nikoshov, "Rukovodiashchaia rol' partiinykh organizatsii v sisteme ateisticheskogo vospitaniia" [The guiding role of Party organizations in the system of atheistic education], in *VNA* 9 (1970): 103; Alekseev, "Metodika," p. 149; Tepliakov, *Problemy*, p. 157.

29. Nikonov, "O nekotorykh tendentsiiakh," pp. 174–75; Lisavtsev, "Rukovodiashchaia rol'," pp. 102–3; Klibanov, "Raskol," p. 93; Klibanov, *Religioznoe sektantstvo*, pp. 74, 80, 96; Pismanik, "O sostoianii," pp. 213–14; Mering, "Konkretno o samom vazhnom," p. 40; Malakhova, "Istoriki," p. 233; Tepliakov, *Problemy*, p. 157; Iablokov, "Obshchenie," p. 62; Ugrinovich, *Filosofskie problemy*, p. 119; Saprykin, "Ateisticheskaia rabota," p. 223.

30. Klibanov, *Religioznoe sektantstvo*, pp. 82, 88, 95, 97; Malakhova, "Istoriki," p. 233; Tepliakov, *Problemy*, p. 144; Duluman, *Sovremennyi veruiushchii*, p. 37; Pashkov, "K voprosu," p. 150; Kozhevnikov, "Ateisticheskoe vospitanie," p. 2; Gagarin, "Otkhod," p. 186; Ugrinovich, *Filosofskie problemy*, p. 120; Murav'ev, "O konkretnosti," pp. 67–68; Nesterov, "Pravoslavnaia tserkov'," p. 145; B. Saparmukhamedova, "Obshchestvennoe mnenie protiv religii"

[Social opinion against religion], *Nauka i religiia*, no. 11 (1971), p. 21; Lisavtsev, "Rukovodiashchaia rol'," p. 102.

31. Malakhova, "Istoriki," p. 233; Klibanov, *Religioznoe sektantstvo*, pp. 74, 81–82, 90, 101, 114; Klibanov, "Raskol," p. 93; Saprykin, "Ateisticheskaia rabota," p. 225; Gagarin, "Otkhod," p. 186; Tul'tseva, "Evoliutsiia," p. 209; Iablokov, "Obshchenie," p. 62.

32. Cf. Davis, *Religion*, pp. 403–4. It would be interesting to compare the greater longevity of women with the higher incidence of religion among them. If Soviet data indicating a radical increase in the percentage of religiousness with advancing age are correct, then naturally the total number of religious women would be greater than the number of religious men, as would the percentage of religious people among the women versus men.

CHAPTER 6

1. Kozhevnikov, "Ateisticheskoe vospitanie," p. 2; I. A. Malakhova, "Religioznoe sektantstvo v Tambovskoi oblasti v posleoktiabr'skii period i v nashi dni" [Religious sectarianism in the Tambov region in the post-October period and in our days], in AN SSSR, *Voprosy* 9 (1961): 95.

2. William C. Fletcher, "Khrushchev on Religion in the USSR," *Communist Affairs*, vol. 1, no. 4 (1962), p. 5. He did attend a school for Party workers later, as an adult.

3. M. Ia. Lensu, V. A. Cherniak, and A. I. Artem'ev, "Differentsirovannyi podkhod v ateisticheskom vospitanii" [A differentiated approach to atheistic education], in *VNA* 9 (1970): 136.

4. V. P. Bukin, "XXV C"ezd KPSS i formirovanie nauchnogo mirovozzreniia" [The Twenty-fifth Congress of the CPSU and the formation of a scientific world view], in Razumova, *Ateizm*, pp. 10–11.

5. Klibanov, *Religioznoe sektantstvo*, pp. 82, 100–101; Osipov, "Priglashenie," p. 31; Gaidurova, "Zavisimost'," p. 17; Tepliakov, "Sostoianie," pp. 34–35; Alekseev, "Metodika," p. 149; Pivovarov, *Struktura*, p. 21; Malakhova, "Istoriki," p. 234; Saprykin, "Ateisticheskaia rabota," p. 225; V. Dobrotvor and M. Pastukh, "Naucho-ateisticheskoe vospitanie i preodolenie religioznykh perezhitkov" [Scientific atheistic education and overcoming religious survivals], *Kommunist Ukrainy*, no. 9 (1967), p. 67.

6. Klibanov, *Religioznoe sektantstvo*, pp. 79, 82; Gaidurova, "Zavisimost'," pp. 17–18; Gagarin, "Otkhod," p. 186; Iablokov, "Obshchenie," p. 52; Lensu, "Differentsirovannyi podkhod," p. 148.

7. Baltanov, *Sotsiologicheskie problemy*, p. 149, quoting G. N. Plechov, "Ob"ektivnye usloviia izzhivaniia religioznosti" [Objective conditions for getting rid of religiousness], in *K Obshchestvu*, p. 77.

8. Baltanov, *Sotsiologicheskie problemy*, p. 150, citing N. A. Nosenko, "Nekotorye rezul'taty izucheniia religioznosti naseleniia v Novosibirskoi oblasti" [Some results of the study of the religiousness of the population in the

Novosibirsk region], *Informatsionnyi biulleten' Instituta nauchnogo ateizma AON pri TsK KPSS,* no. 3 (1968), p. 70.

9. By implication, 75% are nonworkers and 9.6% are collective farmers.

10. I have supplied the percentages independently; those given by the authors are incorrect (31.6%, 8.1%, 0.6%, 24.2%, and 35.5% respectively).

11. What became of the other 7.8% is not specified.

12. A. I. Klibanov, "Sektantstvo v proshlom i nastoiashchem" [Sectarianism in the past and present], in AN SSSR, *Voprosy* 9 (1961): 23; Malakhova, "Religioznoe sektantstvo," p. 95; Bograd, "Opyt," p. 142.

13. Tepliakov, *Problemy,* p. 37; Lensu, "Differentsirovannyi," p. 134; S. Shimkus, "Mesto ateizma v sisteme kommunisticheskogo vospitaniia" [The place of atheism in the system of Communist education], *Nauka i religiia,* no. 8 (1967), p. 19; Evdokimov, "Konkretnye sotsial'nye issledovaniia," pp. 24–25.

14. D. A. Kapparov and V. A. Cherniak, "O prichinakh i usloviiakh zhivuchesti religioznykh perezhitkov" [Reasons and conditions for the vitality of religious survivals], *Voprosy filosofii,* no. 6 (1967), p. 67.

CHAPTER 7

1. E.g., Matthew Spinka, *The Church in Soviet Russia* (New York: Oxford University Press, 1956), p. 80.

2. I have changed the last percentage from the author's 8.4, which is incorrect.

3. Christel Lane, *Christian Religion in the Soviet Union* (Albany: State University of New York Press, 1978), pp. 149, 235–39.

4. William C. Fletcher, "American Influence on Russian Religion: The Case of the Pentecostals," *Journal of Church and State,* vol. 20, no. 2 (Spring 1978), p. 232.

5. These figures seem surprisingly high; they may refer only to annual money income.

CHAPTER 8

1. E. Bairamov, "Propaganda ateizma v klube" [The propaganda of atheism in the club], in *VNA* 9 (1970): 250.

2. I have revised his percentage figure from 18.4, which is incorrect.

3. I have revised the first percentage figure from 89.9, which is incorrect.

4. A. I. Rogov, "Ateisticheskie radioperedachi" [Atheistic radio broadcasts], in *VNA* 9 (1970): 312.

5. "Vazhnaia tema" [An important theme], *Nauka i religiia,* no. 5 (1972), p. 27.

6. I have changed his figure of 37.9%, which is incorrect, to 37.7%.

7. D. A. Meikshane, "Metody izucheniia otnosheniia uchashchikhsia k religii" [Methods of studying the relationship of pupils to religion], in *VNA* 11 (1971): 267.

8. Reading aloud in the family may be included.

9. M. G. Pismanik, "Religioznaia kontseptsiia 'grekhovnosti' i nravstvennyi progress" [The religious conception of "sinfulness" and moral progress], in Garadzha, *Ateizm*, p. 149.

10. L. Prokoshchenkov, "Sotsial'nyi kollektiv—osnova vospitaniie" [The social collective—the basis of education], *Nauka i religiia*, no. 7 (1972), pp. 11–12.

CHAPTER 9

1. I have changed the second percentage figure from ˙10.7, which is inaccurate.

2. E.g., *Pravda*, 3 October 1964; *Izvestiia*, 20 June 1962; cf. *Posev*, no. 11 (1969), p. 12. For ideological background, see *Izvestiia*, 17 April 1962; *Sovetskaia iustitsiia*, no. 21 (1961) (translation in *Soviet Law and Government* [spring 1963], pp. 46–47); *Kazakhstanskaia pravda*, 24 June 1964.

3. V. D. Kobetskii, "Obriad kreshcheniia kak proiavlenie religioznosti" [The rite of baptism as a manifestation of religiousness], in Pantskhava, *Konkretno-sotsiologicheskoe izuchenie*, p. 167.

4. M. A. Abdurakhimov, "Rol' nravstvennogo dolga v semeinobytovoi morali" [The role of moral duty in family life morals], in *Sotsiologicheskii sbornik* [A sociological anthology], ed. Z. A. Kolmakova (Makhachkala, Dagestan: AN SSSR, Dagestan Branch, 1970), p. 125.

5. Z. A. Tazhurina, "Mistifikatsiia obydennykh otnoshenii v sueveriiakh" [The mystification of ordinary relationships in superstitions], in Pantskhava, *Konkretno-sotsiologicheskoe izuchenie*, pp. 84–85.

6. No indication is given concerning the attitude of the two remaining village believers.

CHAPTER 10

1. AN SSSR, *Uspekhi sovremennoi nauki i religiia* [Contemporary science's successes and religion] (Moscow: AN SSSR, 1961), p. 8; V. Chertikhin, "Chto propoveduet pravoslavie?" [What is Orthodoxy preaching?], *Nauka i religiia*, no. 11 (1961), pp. 28–29.

2. A. S. Iukhimenko, "Izuchenie religioznogo sektantstva na Ukraine" [The study of religious sectarianism in the Ukraine], in *VNA* 21 (1977): 256.

3. A. F. Iarygin, "Kharakter sovremennoi baptistskoi propovedi" [The character of contemporary Baptist preaching], in *VNA* 12 (1971): 152.

4. This question doubtless was ill conceived; see above, pp. 33–34.

5. Iu. Iu. Iunosov, "K voprosy o kharaktere prestupnosti v Dagestanskoi ASSR v sovremennyi period" [The problem of the character of criminality in the Dagestan ASSR in the contemporary period], in Kolmakova, *Sotsiologicheskii sbornik*, p. 153.

6. P. Kampars, "Nekotorye problemy grazhdanskoi obriadnosti" [Some problems of civil rites], in Balevits, *Ateizm*, p. 20.

7. P. S. Sedykh, "Esteticheskaia otsenka iavlenii deistvitel'nosti kak kriterii

formirovanii nauchno-ateisticheskogo mirovozzreniia" [The aesthetic evaluation of phenomena of reality as a criterion of the formation of a scientific-atheistic world view], in *Gertsenovskie chteniia* 30 (1977): 13.

CHAPTER 11

1. L. N. Ul'ianov, "Opyt issledovaniia motivatsii religioznogo povedeniia" [Experience of study of the motivation of religious conduct], in *VNA* 11 (1971): 222.
2. Iu. V. Arutiunian, "Sotsial'naia struktura sel'skogo naseleniia" [The social structure of the rural population], *Voprosy filosofii*, no. 5 (1966), p. 60.
3. What happened to the other 3 believers is not specified.
4. It should be noted that the caveat mentioned above, that believers may not have surrendered the anonymity of their church attendance in a distant town by answering frankly, applies here also.
5. The figure of 4,225 was given by *Religious Communities in the Soviet Union* (London: Press Department of the Soviet Embassy, 1941), p. 2. A. Veschikov, "Etapy bol'shogo puti" [Stages of a great way], *Nauka i religiia*, no. 11 (1962), p. 60, states that "in 1941 there were *nearly* 4,000 Orthodox churches" (italics mine); Dmitrii Konstantinov, *Religious Persecution in USSR* (London, Ont., Canada: SBONR, 1965), p. 17, estimates that there were 3,200; Kurt Hutten, *Iron Curtain Christians*, tr. Walter G. Tillmanns (Minneapolis, Minn.: Augsburg Publishing House, 1967), p. 13, estimates 1,500; and Michael Bourdeaux, *Opium of the People* (London: Faber & Faber, 1965), p. 58, without specifying the basis for the estimate, places the number of operating churches on the eve of World War II at 100.
6. *Spravochnik propagandista i agitatora* [Reference book of the propagandist and agitator] (Moscow, 1965), pp. 149–50, translated in *Research Materials,* October 1969, p. 1. According to *Ezhegodnik Rossii za 1914* [Annual of Russia for 1914] (St. Petersburg, 1914), p. 99, there were 77,766 churches and chapels in Russia in 1914. The figure of 78,767 on the eve of the Revolution is given by N. I. Iudin, *Pravda o Petersburgskikh "sviatyniakh"* [The truth about the Petersburg "shrines"] (Leningrad: Leningrad Publishing House, 1962).
7. V. F. Milovidov, "Staroobriadchestvo i sotsial'nyi progress" [Old Believers and social progress], in *VNA* 2 (1964): 221.
8. V. V. Pavliuk, "K voprosy o 'religioznykh' potrebnostiakh" [The problem of "religious" needs], in *VNA* 11 (1971): 157.
9. Reasons for the differences between his figures and those presented by Ul'ianov (below) remain obscure.
10. A Vestnikov, "Narod sozdaiet traditsii" [The people are establishing traditions], *Nauka i religiia*, no. 1 (1964), p. 61.
11. For a convenient, if somewhat credulous, summary of these efforts, see Jennifer McDowell, "Soviet Civil Ceremonies," *Journal for the Scientific Study of Religion*, vol. 13, no. 3 (September 1974), pp. 265–79.

12. I. P. Timchenko, "Sistemnost'—glavnoe uslovie deistvennosti ateisticheskogo vospitaniia" [Being systematic—the major condition for effectiveness of atheistic education], in *VNA* 19 (1976): 40.

13. B. Shneidere, "Sovetskie obriady—partiinoe delo" [Soviet rites—a Party matter], *Nauka i religiia,* no. 2 (1969), p. 36.

14. It is interesting that this stern condemnation, which in effect suggests that even the smallest lapses indicate some degree of failure to accept the Marxist ideals on the part of the participant, approaches—indeed, almost coincides with—that mistaken dogma of Western anticommunism that religious people in the USSR, actually or potentially, are politically hostile to the state; cf. Joseph Johnston, *God's Secret Armies within the Soviet Empire* (New York: Putnam, 1954), p. 18.

15. V. F. Vinogradov, "Staroobriadchestvo na territoriiakh pskovskoi i novgorodskoi oblastei" [Old Believers in the territories of the Pskov and Novgorod regions], in *Gertsenovskie chteniia* 30 (1977): 37–40.

16. L. N. Terent'eva, "Rasprostranenie ateisticheskogo mirovozzreniia i bezreligioznykh form byta sredi kolkhoznikov latyshei (po materialam Ekabpilsskogo raiona Latviiskoie SSR)" [The prevalence of the atheistic world view and irreligious forms of life among Lettish collective farmers (according to materials from the Ekabpils district, Latvian SSR)], in Krasnikov, *Voprosy,* p. 65.

17. V. Ia. Ranne, "Novye obriady i ikh mesto v dukhovnoi zhizni sovetskikh liudei" [New rites and their place in the spiritual life of Soviet people], in *VNA* 13 (1972): 183, 188.

18. V. Pomerantsev, "Vchera i segodnia" [Yesterday and today], *Nauka i religiia,* no. 4 (1966), pp. 5–6.

19. N. S. Kapustin, "O spetsifike nekotorykh religiozno-bytovykh perezhitkov" [Specifics of certain survivals of religious life], in Pantskhava, *Konkretno-sotsiologicheskoe izuchenie,* p. 96.

20. V. I. Smirnov, "Voprosy ateisticheskogo vospitaniia v ideologicheskoi rabote partiinykh organizatsii" [Problems of atheistic education in the ideological work of Party organizations], in *VNA* 12 (1971): 126–27.

21. "Razrabotka problem nauchnogo ateizma v soiuznykh respublikakh: Belorusskaia SSR, Gruzinskaia SSR, Moldavskaia SSR, Estonskaia SSR" [Elaboration of the problems of scientific atheism in the Union Republics: Belorussian SSR, Georgian SSR, Moldavian SSR, Estonian SSR], in *VNA* 14 (1973): 78.

22. V. A. Rudnev, "Kommunisticheskomu bytu—novye sovetskie traditsii" [To Communist living conditions—new Soviet traditions], in Krasnikov, *Voprosy,* p. 169.

23. M. V. Demin, " 'Khristianskii kommunizm' kak otrazhenie krizisa sovremennoi religioznoi ideologii" ["Christian communism" as a reflection of the deepening crisis of contemporary religious ideology], in Pantskhava, *O nekotorykh osobennostiakh,* pp. 185–86.

24. I. Kryvelev, "Vazhnaia storona byta" [An important aspect of living conditions], *Kommunist,* no. 8 (May 1961), p. 68.
25. M. M. Ikhilov, "Izmenenie kul'tury i byta kolkhoznogo krest'ianstva Dagestana" [Changes in the culture and living conditions of the collective-farm peasantry of Dagestan], in Kolmakova, *Sotsiologicheskii sbornik,* p. 31.
26. N. Sviridov and G. Marchik, "Za deistvennost' ideologicheskoi raboty" [For the effectiveness of ideological work], *Molodoi kommunist,* no. 8 (1962), p. 30.
27. G. Gerodnik, "Printsipial'nost' ateista" [An atheist's principles], *Nauka i religiia,* no. 11 (1966), p. 53.
28. N. P. Andrianov, R. A. Lopatkin, and V. V. Pavliuk, *Osobennosti sovremennogo religioznogo soznaniia* [Peculiarities of contemporary religious understanding] (Moscow: "Mysl'," 1966), p. 213.
29. I have changed his second percentage figure from 53, which is inaccurate.

CHAPTER 12

1. For a brief review of these techniques see Fletcher, *Study in Survival,* pp. 8–11.
2. For example, with regard to illegal Orthodoxy; see Fletcher, *Russian Orthodox Church,* passim, but especially pp. 8–15.
3. E.g., Kobetskii, *Sotsiologicheskoe izuchenii,* p. 24; Kalashnikov, "Religiia," pp. 22–23.
4. Selivanov, *Partiinoe rukovodstvo,* p. 40; Filimonov, "Sotsiologicheskie issledovaniia," p. 73. Tepliakov, *Problemy,* p. 121, places the figure at 30.3%.
5. United States, House of Representatives, Committee on Foreign Affairs, *Recent Developments in the Soviet Bloc* (Washington, D.C.: U.S. Government Printing Office, 1964), pt. 1, pp. 100–101.
6. Nicholas S. Timasheff, "Urbanization, Operation Antireligion and the Decline of Religion in the USSR," *American Slavic and East European Review* 14 (April 1955): 232.

REFERENCE BIBLIOGRAPHY
OF WORKS CITED

The acronym AN SSSR is used for Akademiia Nauk SSSR; *VNA* is used for *Voprosy nauchnogo ateizma* [Problems of scientific atheism], edited by A. F. Okulov (Moscow: "Mysl'").

BOOKS

Akademiia Nauk SSSR [AN SSSR]. *Voprosy istorii religii i ateizma* [Problems of the history of religion and atheism]. Moscow: AN SSSR, annually.

——. *Kritika ideologii lamaizma i shamanizma* [A critique of the ideology of Lamaism and shamanism]. Ulan-Ude: Buriat Book Press, 1965.

——. *Uspekhi sovremennoi nauki i religiia* [Contemporary science's successes and religion]. Moscow: AN SSSR, 1961.

Andrianov, N. P., Lopatkin, R. A., and Pavliuk, V. V. *Osobennosti sovremennogo religioznogo soznaniia* [Peculiarities of contemporary religious understanding]. Moscow: "Mysl'," 1966.

Balevits, Z. B., ed. *Ateizm i religiia* [Atheism and religion]. Riga: "Zinatne," 1969.

Baltanov, R. G. *Sotsiologicheskie problemy v sisteme nauchno-ateisticheskogo vospitaniia* [Sociological problems in the system of scientific atheistic education]. Kazan': Kazan' University Press, 1973.

Bolshakoff, Serge. *Russian Nonconformity*. Philadelphia: Westminster, 1950.

Bourdeaux, Michael A. *Faith on Trial in Russia*. New York: Harper & Row, 1971.

——. *Opium of the People*. London: Faber & Faber, 1965.

——. *Patriarch and Prophets*. London: Macmillan, 1969.

——. *Religious Ferment in Russia*. London: Macmillan, 1968.

Braun, Leopold L. *Religion in Russia, from Lenin to Khrushchev: An Uncensored Account*. Paterson, N.J.: Saint Anthony Guild Press, 1959.

Chagin, B. A. *Ocherki istorii sotsiologicheskoi mysli v SSSR (1917–1969 gg)* [Essays on the history of sociological thought in the USSR (1917–1969)]. Leningrad: "Nauka," 1969.

Cherniak, Vusia Aronovna. *Formirovanie nauchno-materialisticheskogo ateisticheskogo mirovozzreniia* [The formation of a scientific, materialistic, atheistic world view]. Alma-Ata: "Nauka," 1969.

Curtiss, John Shelton. *The Russian Church and the Soviet State, 1917–1950.* Boston: Little, Brown, 1953.

Davis, Nathaniel. "Religion and Communist Government in the Soviet Union and Eastern Europe." Ph.D. dissertation, Fletcher School of Law and Diplomacy, Tufts University, 1960.

Dorogova, L. N., ed. *Ocherki metodologii poznaniia sotsial'nykh iavlenii* [Essays on the methodology of understanding social phenomena]. Moscow: "Mysl'," 1970.

Duluman, E., Lobovik, B., and Tancher, V. *Sovremennyi veruiushchii* [The contemporary believer]. Moscow: Publishing House for Political Literature, 1970.

Ezhegodnik Rossii za 1914 [Annual of Russia for 1914]. St. Petersburg, 1914.

Fedorenko, F. *Sekty, ikh vera i dela* [The sects, their faith and works]. Moscow: Publishing House for Political Literature, 1965.

Fireside, Harvey. *Icon and Swastika: The Russian Orthodox Church under Nazi and Soviet Control.* Cambridge, Mass.: Harvard University Press, 1971.

Fletcher, William C. *Nikolai: Portrait of a Dilemma.* New York: Macmillan, 1968.

———. *Religion and Soviet Foreign Policy, 1945–1970.* London: Oxford University Press, for the Royal Institute of International Affairs, 1973.

———. *The Russian Orthodox Church Underground, 1917–1970.* London: Oxford University Press, 1971.

———. *A Study in Survival: The Church in Russia, 1927–1943.* New York: Macmillan, and London: SPCK, 1965.

———, and Strover, Anthony J., eds. *Religion and the Search for New Ideals in the USSR.* New York: Praeger, for the Institute for the Study of the USSR, 1967.

Garadzha, A. I. *Ateizm, religiia, nravstvennost'* [Atheism, religion, morality]. Moscow: "Mysl'," 1972.

Gertsenovskie chteniia: Nauchnyi ateizm, etika, estetika [Herzen readings: scientific atheism, ethics, aesthetics]. Leningrad: State Teacher Training Institute, annually.

Grunwald, Constantin de. *The Churches and the Soviet Union.* Translated by G. J. Robinson-Paskevsky. Macmillan, 1962.

Hutten, Kurt. *Iron Curtain Christians.* Translated by Walter G. Tillmanns. Minneapolis, Minn.: Augsburg Publishing House, 1967.

Iablokov, I. N. *Metodologicheskie problemy sotsiologii religii* [Methodological problems of the sociology of religion]. Moscow: Moscow University Press, 1972.

Iudin, N. I. *Pravda o Petersburgskikh "sviatyniakh"* [The truth about the Petersburg "shrines"]. Leningrad: Leningrad Publishing House, 1962.

Johnston, Joseph. *God's Secret Armies within the Soviet Empire*. New York: Putnam, 1954.

Kalashnikov, M. F., ed. *Nauchnyi ateizm: Voprosy metodologii i sotsiologii* [Scientific atheism: problems of methodology and sociology]. 3d edition. Perm': Perm State Pedagogical Institute, 1974.

Klibanov, A. I., ed. *Konkretnye issledovaniia sovremennykh religioznykh verovanii (metodika, organizatsiia, rezul'taty)* [Concrete research on contemporary religious faiths (methodology, organization, results)]. Moscow: "Mysl'," 1967.

―――. *Religioznoe sektantstvo i sovremennost'* [Religious sectarianism and contemporaneity]. Moscow: "Nauka," 1969.

Kobetskii, V. D. *Sotsiologicheskoe izuchenie religioznosti i ateizma* [Sociological study of religiousness and atheism]. Leningrad: Leningrad University Press, 1978.

―――. *K obshchestvu, svobodnomu ot religii* [Toward a society free from religion]. Moscow: "Mysl'," 1970.

Kolbanovskii, V. N. *Kollektiv kolkhoznikov: Sotsial'no-psikhologicheskoe issledovanie* [The collective of the collective farmers: social-psychological research]. Moscow: "Mysl'," 1967.

Kolmakova, Z. A., ed. *Sotsiologicheskii sbornik* [A sociological anthology]. Makhachkala, Dagestan: AN SSSR, Dagestan Branch, 1970.

Konstantinov, Dmitrii. *Religious Persecution in USSR*. London, Ont., Canada: SBONR, 1965.

Krasnikov, N. P., ed. *Po etapam razvitiia ateizma v SSSR* [Stages of the development of atheism in the USSR]. Leningrad: "Nauka," 1967.

―――, ed. *Voprosy preodoleniia religioznykh perezhitkov v SSSR* [Problems of overcoming religious survivals in the USSR]. Moscow: "Nauka," 1966.

Lane, Christel. *Christian Religion in the Soviet Union*. Albany: State University of New York Press, 1978.

Lenin, V. I. *Sochineniia* [Works]. 4th edition. Moscow: State Publishing House for Political Literature, 1942–66.

Marshall, Richard H., Jr., ed. *Aspects of Religion in the Soviet Union, 1917–1967*. Chicago: University of Chicago Press, 1971.

Marx, Karl, and Engels, Friedrich. *On Religion*. Moscow: State Publishing House for Political Literature, 1955.

Mol, Hans [J. J.], ed. *Western Religion: A Country by Country Sociological Inquiry*. The Hague: Mouton, 1972.

Okulov, A. F. *Sovetskaia filosofskaia nauka i ee problemy* [Soviet philosophical science and its problems]. Moscow: "Mysl'," 1970.

―――, ed. *Voprosy nauchnogo ateizma* [*VNA*; Problems of scientific atheism]. Moscow: "Mysl'," semiannually.

Orleanskii, N. *Zakon o religioznykh ob"edineniiakh RSFSR* [The law concerning religious associations of the RSFSR]. Moscow: State Publishing House for Political Literature, 1930.

Pantskhava, I. D., ed. *Konkretno-sotsiologicheskoe izuchenie sostoianiia religioznosti i opyta ateisticheskogo vospitaniia* [Concrete sociological study of the condition of religiousness and the experience of atheistic education]. Moscow: Moscow University Press, 1969.

———, ed. *O nekotorykh osobennostiakh sovremennoi religioznoi ideologii* [Certain peculiarities of contemporary religious ideology]. Moscow: Moscow University Press, 1964.

Pivovarov, V. G. *Struktura religioznoi obshchiny* [The structure of the religious congregation]. Groznyi: Chechen-Ingush Book Press, 1970.

Prichiny sushchestvovaniia i puti preodoleniia religioznykh perezhitkov [Causes of the existence of and ways of overcoming religious survivals]. Minsk: "Nauka i Tekhnika," 1965. A review of this work appears in *VNA* 3 (1967): 365.

Razumova, G. A., ed. *Ateizm, religiia, sovremennost'* [Atheism, religion, contemporaneity]. Leningrad: State Museum of the History of Religion and Atheism, 1977.

Religious Communities in the Soviet Union. London: Press Department of the Soviet Embassy, 1941.

Selivanov, P. D. *Partiinoe rukovodstvo ateisticheskim vospitaniem* [Party leadership in atheistic education]. Moscow: Publishing House for Political Literature, 1973.

Simirenko, Alex, ed. *Soviet Sociology: Historical Antecedents and Current Appraisals*. Chicago: Quadrangle Books, 1966.

Sobranie uzakonenii i rasporiazhenii rabochekrest'ianskogo pravitel'stva RSFSR [Collection of legislation and orders of the workers and peasants government of the RSFSR]. Moscow: State Publishing House for Political Literature, 1930.

Sotsiologiia v SSSR [Sociology in the USSR]. Moscow: "Mysl'," 1966.

Spinka, Matthew. *The Church in Soviet Russia*. New York: Oxford University Press, 1956.

Spravochnik propagandista i agitatora [Reference book of the propagandist and agitator]. Moscow, 1965.

Struve, Nikita. *Christians in Contemporary Russia*. Translated by Lancelot Sheppard and A. Mason. London: Harvill Press, 1966.

Sukhov, A. D. *Religiia kak obshchestvennyi fenomen* [Religion as a social phenomenon]. Moscow: "Mysl'," 1972.

Tepliakov, M. K. *Problemy ateisticheskogo vospitaniia v praktike partiinoi raboty* [Problems of atheistic education in the practice of Party work]. Voronezh: Voronezh University Press, 1972.

Timasheff, N. S. *Religion in Soviet Russia, 1917–1942*. New York: Sheed & Ward, 1942.

Ugolovnyi kodeks RSFSR [Criminal Code of the RSFSR]. Moscow: "Juridical Literature" Press, 1964.

Reference Bibliography

Ugrinovich, D. M. *Filosofskie problemy kritiki religii* [Philosophical problems of the critique of religion]. Moscow: Moscow University Press, 1965.

——, ed. *Obshchestvennaia psikhologiia i kommunisticheskoe vospitanie* [Social psychology and Communist education]. Moscow: Moscow University Press, 1967.

——. *Vvedenie v teorteticheskoe religiovedenie* [Introduction to theoretical religious studies]. Moscow: "Mysl'," 1973.

United States, House of Representatives, Committee on Foreign Affairs. *Recent Developments in the Soviet Bloc.* Washington, D.C.: U.S. Government Printing Office, 1964.

ARTICLES

Abdurakhimov, M. A. "Rol' nravstvennogo dolga v semeinobytovoi morali" [The role of moral duty in family life morals]. In *Sotsiologicheskii sbornik* [A sociological anthology], edited by Z. A. Kolmakova. Makhachkala, Dagestan: AN SSSR, Dagestan Branch, 1970.

Alekseev, N. P. "Metodika i rezul'taty izucheniia religioznosti sel'skogo naseleniia" [Methods and results of the study of religiousness of the rural population]. In *VNA* 3 (1967): 131–50.

Andrianov, N. P. "Evoliutsiia nravstvennogo oblika sovremennogo veruiushchego" [The evolution of the moral make-up of the contemporary believer]. In *Ateizm, religiia, nravstvennost'* [Atheism, religion, morality], edited by V. I. Garadzha, pp. 170–81. Moscow: "Mysl'," 1972.

Aptekman, D. M. "The Vitality of the Baptismal Ceremony under Modern Soviet Conditions: An Empirical Study." In *Soviet Sociology,* edited by Alex Simirenko, pp. 367–76. Chicago: Quadrangle Books, 1966.

Arsenkin, V., et al. "Molodezhi—ateisticheskuiu zakalku!" [Youth—atheistic toughness!]. *Nauka i religiia,* no. 11 (1971), pp. 2–20.

Arutiunian, Iu. V. "Sotsial'naia struktura sel'skogo naseleniia" [The social structure of the rural population]. *Voprosy filosofii,* no. 5 (1966), pp. 51–61.

Ashirov, N. "Evoliutsiia Islama v SSSR: Izmeneniia v kul'te" [The evolution of Islam in the USSR: changes in the cultus]. *Nauka i religiia,* no. 9 (1971), pp. 14–19.

Bairamov, E. "Propaganda ateizma v klube" [The propaganda of atheism in the club]. In *VNA* 9 (1970): 249–63.

Baltanov, R. "Iz nashego opyta issledovaniia religioznosti naseleniia" [Our experience studying the religiousness of the population]. *Nauka i religiia,* no. 8 (1967), p. 18.

Barkauskas, A. S. "Osushchestvlenie leninskikh idei ob ateisticheskom vospitanii v prakticheskie deiatel'nosti partiinykh organizatsii" [The implementation of Leninist ideas on atheistic education in the practical activity of Party organizations]. In *VNA* 10 (1970): 151–65.

Bichany, V. P., and Sypacheva, T. A. "Rol' obshchestvennoi aktivnosti v formirovanii ateisticheskoi ubezhdennosti molodezhi" [The role of social activism in the formation of atheistic convictions of youth]. In *Nauchnyi atiezm* [Scientific atheism], edited by M. F. Kalashnikov, pp. 102–10. Perm': Perm' State Pedagogical Institute, 1974.

Bograd, E. Ia. "Opyt izuchenii sovremennogo sektantstva v Michurinskom raione" [Experience of studying contemporary sectarianism in the Michurin district]. In *Voprosy istorii religii i ateizma* [Problems of the history of religion and atheism], vol. 9, pp. 113–43. Moscow: AN SSSR, 1961.

Bondar, E. "Desiat' tysach 'pochemu' " [Ten thousand "why's"]. *Agitator*, no. 23 (1964), pp. 40–43.

Bukin, V. P. "XXV C"ezd KPSS i formirovanie nauchnogo mirovozzreniia" [The Twenty-fifth Congress of the CPSU and the formation of a scientific world view]. In *Ateizm, religiia, sovremennost'* [Atheism, religion, contemporaneity], edited by G. A. Razumova, pp. 3–18. Leningrad: State Museum of the History of Religion and Atheism, 1977.

Buslinskii, V. "Tonkoe delo" [A delicate matter]. *Agitator*, no. 7 (1961), pp. 49–51.

Cherniak, V. "Nuzhen nauchnyi podkhod" [A scientific approach is necessary]. *Nauka i religiia*, no. 5 (1971), pp. 24–27.

Chertikhin, V. "Chto propoveduet pravoslavie?" [What is Orthodoxy preaching?]. *Nauka i religiia*, no. 11 (1961), pp. 28–33.

Dem'ianov, A. I. "K voprosu o sovremennom sostoianii religioznogo techeniia 'Istinno Pravoslavnykh Khristian' " [On the question of the contemporary condition of the religious movement, "True Orthodox Christians"]. In *VNA* 16 (1974): 103-22.

Demin, M. V. " 'Khristianskii kommunizm' kak otrazhenie krizisa sovremennoi religioznoi ideologii" ["Christian communism" as a reflection of the deepening crisis of contemporary religious ideology]. In *O nekotorykh osobennostiakh sovremennoi religioznoi ideologii* [Certain peculiarities of contemporary religious ideology], edited by I. D. Pantskhava, pp. 178–215. Moscow: Moscow University Press, 1964.

Dobrotvor, V., and Pastukh, M. "Nauchno-ateisticheskoe vospitanie i preodolenie religioznykh perezhitkov" [Scientific atheistic education and overcoming religious survivals]. *Kommunist Ukrainy*, no. 9 (1967), p. 64–71.

Duluman, E. "Vosproizvodstvo religii" [The origin of religion]. *Nauka i religiia*, no. 7 (1968), pp. 9–13.

Ershov, G. G. "Kritika v ateisticheskoi literature religioznogo ucheniia o bessmertii" [Criticism in atheistic literature of the religious doctrine of immortality]. In *Po etapam razvitiia ateizma v SSSR* [Stages of the development of atheism in the USSR], edited by N. P. Krasinkov. Leningrad: "Nauka," 1967.

Ershov, V. "Zachem neveruiushchemu ateizm?" [Why atheism for the nonbeliever?]. *Nauka i religiia*, no. 7 (1971), pp. 75–76.

Eryshev, A., and Kosukha, P. "Instilling Irreconcilability." *Lyudina i svit*, no. 2

(January 1969). In *Religion in Communist Dominated Areas*, vol. 8 (1969), pp. 134–36, translation from *Digest of the Soviet Ukrainian Press*.

Evdokimov, V. "Konkretnye sotsial'nye issledovaniia i ateizm" [Concrete social research and atheism]. *Nauka i religiia*, no. 1 (1968), pp. 22–25.

Filimonov, E. G. "Sotsiologicheskie issledovaniia protsessa preodoleniia religii v sel'skoi mestnosti: Itogi, problemy, perspektivy" [Sociological research on the process of overcoming religion in the rural locale: results, problems, perspectives]. In *VNA* 16 (1974): 71–88.

Fletcher, William C. "American Influence on Russian Religion: The Case of the Pentecostals." *Journal of Church and State*, vol. 20, no. 2 (spring 1978), pp. 215–32.

———. "Khrushchev on Religion in the USSR." *Communist Affairs*, vol. 1, no. 4 (1962), pp. 5–6.

———. "Protestant Influences on the Outlook of the Soviet Citizen Today." In *Religion and the Search for New Ideals in the USSR*, edited by William C. Fletcher and Anthony J. Strover. New York: Praeger, for the Institute for the Study of the USSR, 1967.

———. "Religious Dissent in the USSR in the 1960s." *Slavic Review*, vol. 30, no. 2 (June 1971), pp. 298–316.

———. "Solzhenitsyn and the Merger of Dissent." *Worldview*, vol. 16, no. 8 (1972), pp. 5–8.

———. "USSR." In *Western Religion: A Country by Country Sociological Inquiry*, edited by Hans [J. J.] Mol, pp. 565–86. The Hague: Mouton, 1972.

Foltz, Charles, Jr. "Religion in Russia Today: A First-hand Report." *US News and World Report*, 10 February 1964, pp. 56–57.

Freiberg, L. "Rol' intelligentsii v formirovanii materialisticheskogo mirovozzreniia" [The role of the intelligentsia in the formation of a materialistic world view]. In *VNA* 21 (1977): 159–69.

Furov, B. G. "Sovetskoe gosudarstvo i tserkov' " [The Soviet government and the church]. In *Ateizm, religiia, sovremennost'* [Atheism, religion, contemporaneity], edited by G. A. Razumova, pp. 33–56. Leningrad: State Museum of the History of Religion and Atheism, 1977.

Gagarin, Iu. V. "Otkhod ot sektantstva v Komi ASSR" [The departure from sectarianism in the Komi ASSR]. In *Po etapam razvitiia ateizma v SSSR* [Stages of the development of atheism in the USSR], edited by N. P. Krasnikov, pp. 168–87. Leningrad: "Nauka," 1967.

Gaidurova, T. G. "Zavisimost' obydennogo religioznogo soznaniia veruiushchikh ot uslovii ikh zhizni" [The dependence of the ordinary religious consciousness of believers on the conditions of their lives]. In *Konkretno-sotsiologicheskoe izuchenie sostoianiia religioznosti i opyta ateisticheskogo vospitaniia* [Concrete sociological study of the condition of religiousness and the experience of atheistic education], edited by J. D. Pantskhava, pp. 12–31. Moscow: Moscow University Press, 1969.

Galitskaia, I. A. "Izuchenie kanalov vosproizvodstva religioznosti v novykh pokoleniiakh—odno iz trebovanii sistemy ateisticheskogo vospitaniia" [Study of the channels of the reproduction of religiousness in new generations—one of the requirements for a system of atheistic education]. In *VNA* 9 (1970): 55–78.

———. "K voprosu ob izuchenii religioznosti molodezhi" [The question of the study of the religiousness of youth]. In *VNA* 7 (1969): 389–405.

Gerodnik, G. "Printsipial'nost' ateista" [An atheist's principles]. *Nauka i religiia*, no. 11 (1969), pp. 52–54.

Gorelov, A. "Dokhodit' do kazhdogo" [Go to each one]. *Partiinaia zhizn'*, no. 12 (1971), pp. 46–48.

Gur'ianov, A. "Bogi ne umiraiut sami" [The gods do not die by themselves]. *Nauka i religiia*, no. 9 (1969), pp. 14–22.

Gusev, I. S. "Konkretnost', nauchnost', deistvennost'" [Concreteness, science, effectiveness]. In *VNA* 19 (1976): 19–31.

Hollander, Paul. "The Dilemmas of Soviet Sociology." In *Soviet Sociology: Historical Antecedents and Current Appraisals,* edited by Alex Simirenko, pp. 306–26. Chicago: Quadrangle Books, 1966.

Iablokov, I. N. "Obshchenie veruiushchikh kak faktor formirovaniia psikhologii religioznoi gruppy" [The congregation of believers as a factor in the formation of the psychology of the religious group]. In *Konkretno-sotsiologicheskoe izuchenie sostoianiia religioznosti i opyta ateisticheskogo vospitaniia* [Concrete sociological study of the condition of religiousness and the experience of atheistic education], edited by I. D. Pantskhava, pp. 47–67. Moscow: Moscow University Press, 1969.

———. "Transformatsiia religioznoi morali v soznanii veruiushchikh v usloviiakh sotsializma" [The transformation of religious morality in the consciousness of believers in the conditions of socialism]. In ibid., pp. 127–47.

Iakub, V. "Muzei v shkole" [A museum in the school]. *Nauka i religiia*, no. 9 (1964), pp. 46–49.

Iarygin, A. "Baptistskaia propoved': Chemu ona uchit?" [Baptist preaching: what does it teach?]. *Nauka i religiia*, no. 5 (1972), pp. 53–55.

———. "Kharakter sovremennoi baptistskoi propovedi" [The character of contemporary Baptist preaching]. In *VNA* 12 (1971): 149–63.

Ignatenko, L. M., and Prokoshina, E. S. "Opyt konkretnykh issledovanii psikhologii baptistov v BSSR" [Experience of concrete research on the psychology of Baptists in the B(elorussian)SSR]. In *VNA* 11 (1971): 250–63.

Ikhilov, M. M. "Izmenenie kul'tury i byta kolkhoznogo krest'ianstva Dagestana" [Changes in the culture and living conditions of the collective-farm peasantry of Dagestan]. In *Sotsiologicheskii sbornik* [A sociological anthology], edited by Z. A. Kolmakova, pp. 19–35. Makhachkala, Dagestan: AN SSSR, Dagestan Branch, 1970.

Il'ichev, L. "Formirovanie nauchnogo mirovozzreniia i ateisticheskoe vospitanie" [The formation of a scientific world view and atheistic education]. *Kommunist*, no. 1 (1964), pp. 23–46.

Reference Bibliography

Il'inykh, N. I. "Osobennosti organizatsii i deiatel'nosti mennonitskikh obshchin" [Peculiarities of the organization and activity of Mennonite congregations]. In *Konkretno-sotsiologicheskoe izuchenie sostoianiia religioznosti i opyta ateisticheskogo vospitaniia* [Concrete sociological study of the condition of religiousness and the experience of atheistic education], edited by I. D. Pantskhava, pp. 200–212. Moscow: Moscow University Press, 1969.

Iovchuk, M. T., et al. "Aktual'nye teoreticheskie problemy Marksistsko-Leninskoi sotsiologii v SSSR" [Pressing theoretical problems of Marxist-Leninist sociology in the USSR]. *Filosofskie nauki*, no. 5 (1970), pp. 3–13.

Iukhimenko, A. S. "Izuchenie religioznogo sektantstva na Ukraine" [The study of religious sectarianism in the Ukraine]. In *VNA* 21 (1977): 248–61.

Iunosov, Iu. Iu. "K voprosy o kharaktere prestupnosti v Dagestanskoi ASSR v sovremennyi period" [The problem of the character of criminality in the Dagestan ASSR in the contemporary period]. In *Sotsiologicheskii sbornik* [A sociological anthology], edited by Z. A. Kolmakova, pp. 136–55. Makhachkala, Dagestan: AN SSSR, Dagestan Branch, 1970.

Ivanov, S. "Kak my organizuem nauchno-ateisticheskuiu propagandu" [How we organize scientific atheistic propaganda]. *Kommunist Moldavii*, no. 7 (1961), pp. 52–57.

Kalashnikov, M. F. "Religiia kak obshchestvennyi fenomen" [Religion as a social phenomenon]. In *Nauchnyi ateizm: Voprosy metodologii i sotsiologii* [Scientific atheism: problems of methodology and sociology], edited by M. F. Kalashnikov, pp. 3–33. Perm': Perm' State Pedagogical Institute, 1974.

Kampars, P. "Nekotorye problemy grazhdanskoi obriadnosti" [Some problems of civil rites]. In *Ateizm i religiia* [Atheism and religion], edited by Z. B. Balevits. Riga: "Zinatne," 1969.

Kapparov, D. A., and Cherniak, V. A. "O prichinakh i usloviiakh zhivuchesti religioznykh perezhitkov" [Reasons and conditions for the vitality of religious survivals]. *Voprosy filosofii*, no. 6 (1967), pp. 65–72.

Kapustin, N. S. "O spetsifike nekotorykh religiozno-bytovtykh perezhitkov" [Specifics of certain survivals of religious life]. In *Konkretno-sotsiologicheskoe izuchenie sostoianiia religioznosti i opyta ateisticheskogo vospitaniia* [Concrete sociological study of the condition of religiousness and the experience of atheistic education], edited by I. D. Pantskhava, pp. 89–100. Moscow: Moscow University Press, 1969.

Kharakhorkin, L. P., and Andreev, A. P. "Kritika baptistskoi interpretatsii nauki i nauchno-tekhnicheskogo progressa" [A critique of the Baptist interpretation of science and scientific-technological progress]. *Gertsenovskie chteniia* 30 (1977): 43–46.

Klibanov, A. I. "Nauchno-organizatsionnyi i metodicheskii opyt konkretnykh issledovanii religioznosti" [Scientific organizational and methodological experience of concrete research on religiousness]. In *Konkretnye issledovaniia sovremennykh religioznykh verovanii (metodika, organizatsiia, rezul'taty)* [Concrete

research on contemporary religious faiths (methodology, organization, results)],
edited by A. I. Klibanov, pp. 5–34. Moscow: "Mysl'," 1967.

———. "Sektantstvo v proshlom i nastoiashchem" [Sectarianism in the past and
present]. In *Voprosy istorii religii i ateizma* [Problems of the history of
religion and atheism], vol. 9, pp. 9–34. Moscow: AN SSSR, 1961.

———. "Sovremennoe sektantstvo v Lipetskoi oblasti" [Contemporary sectarianism in the Lipetsk region]. In *Voprosy istorii religii i ateizma* [Problems of the
history of religion and atheism], vol. 10, pp. 157–85. Moscow: AN SSSR, 1962.

———. "Veruiushchii v sovremennom mire" [The believer in the contemporary
world]. *Nauka i religiia,* no. 11 (1970), pp. 70–74.

———, and Mitrokhin, L. N. "Raskol v sovremennom baptizme" [Schism among
contemporary Baptists]. In *VNA* 3 (1967): 84–110.

Kniazev, B. V. "Sistema ateisticheskogo vospitaniia—vazhneishee uslovie preodoleniia religioznykh perezhitkov" [The system of atheistic education—the most
important condition for overcoming religious survivals]. In *Konkretno-
sotsiologicheskoe izuchenie sostoianiia religioznosti i opyta ateisticheskogo
vospitaniia* [Concrete sociological study of the condition of religiousness and
the experience of atheistic education], edited by I. D. Pantskhava, pp. 231–60.
Moscow: Moscow University Press, 1969.

Kobetskii, V. D. "Obriad kreshcheniia kak proiavlenie religioznosti" [The rite of
baptism as a manifestation of religiousness]. In ibid., pp. 162–73.

Kochetov, A. N. "Izuchenie buddizma v SSSR" [The study of Buddhism in the
USSR]. In *VNA* 4 (1967): 427–44.

Koleda, G., and Seidov, Ia. "On ochen khotel zhit'" [He very much wanted to
live]. *Nauka i religiia,* no. 1 (1969), pp. 52–62.

Koltuniuk, S. V. "K probleme effecktivnosti nauchno-ateisticheskogo vospitaniia"
[The problem of the effectiveness of scientific atheistic education]. In *VNA*
12 (1971): 134–48.

Komarov, V. "Tvorcheskaia dolzhnost'" [A creative duty]. *Nauka i religiia,* no.
4 (1967), pp. 35–36.

Korolev, V. V. "Rol' sotsial'noi aktivnosti v formirovanii ateisticheskogo mirovozzreniia" [The role of social activism in the formation of an atheistic world
view]. In *VNA* 13 (1972): 127–54.

Kozachishin, N. N. "Konkretno-sotsiologicheskie issledovanii i ikh rol' v sovershenstvovanii ateisticheskogo vospitaniia v vuzakh" [Concrete sociological
research and its role in improving atheistic education in institutions of higher
education]. In *VNA* 15 (1973): 214–22.

Kozhevnikov, A. "Ateisticheskoe vospitanie na sele" [Atheistic education in the
village]. *Nauka i religiia,* no. 12 (1971), pp. 2–4.

Krasnikov, N. P. "Blizhe k zhizni—blizhe k uspekhu" [Nearer to life—nearer to
success]. *Nauka i religiia,* no. 12 (1965), pp. 4–6.

———. "O nekotorykh voprosakh roboty s veruiushchimi" [Certain problems of
work with believers]. In *Voprosy preodoleniia religioznykh perezhitkov v*

SSSR [Problems of overcoming religious survivals in the USSR], edited by N. P. Krasnikov, pp. 3–16. Moscow: "Nauka," 1966.

Kryvelev, I. "Vazhnaia storona byta" [An important aspect of living conditions]. *Kommunist*, no. 8 (May 1961), pp. 65–72.

Kudriashov, G. E. "Metod kartiinogo interv'iu pri izuchenii religioznogo vliianiia na doshkol'nikov" [The method of the picture interview in studying religious influence on preschoolers]. In *VNA* 11 (1971): 276–86.

Kurshakov, S. "V gorode na Volge" [In a city on the Volga]. *Nauka i religiia*, no. 4 (1968), p. 43.

Lebedev, A. A. "Studencheskaia molodezh' i ateizm" [Student youth and atheism]. In *VNA* 15 (1973): 199–213.

Lensu, M. Ia., Cherniak, V. A., and Artem'ev, A. I. "Differentsirovannyi podkhod v ateisticheskom vospitanii" [A differentiated approach to atheistic education]. In *VNA* 9 (1970): 81–105.

Lialina, G. "Sud'ba odnoi utopii" [The fate of one utopia]. *Nauka i religiia*, no. 11 (1970), pp. 89–90.

Lisavtsev, E. I., and Nikoshov, S. I. "Rukovodiashchaia rol' partiinykh organizatsii v sisteme ateisticheskogo vospitaniia" [The guiding role of Party organizations in the system of atheistic education]. In *VNA* 9 (1970): 81–105.

Lopatkin, R. A. "Nekotorye sotsial'no-psikhologicheskie problemy ateisticheskogo vospitaniia" [Certain social-psychological problems of atheistic education]. In *VNA* 9 (1971): 289–307.

———. "Vzaimodeistvie sredstv, form i metodov ateisticheskogo vospitaniia" [The interaction of means, forms, and methods of atheistic education]. In *VNA* 9 (1970): 177–94.

Lowrie, Donald A., and Fletcher, William C. "Khrushchev's Religious Policy, 1959–1964." In *Aspects of Religion in the Soviet Union, 1917–1967*, edited by Richard H. Marshall, Jr. Chicago: University of Chicago Press, 1971.

McDowell, Jennifer. "Soviet Civil Ceremonies." *Journal for the Scientific Study of Religion*, vol. 13, no. 3 (September 1974), pp. 265–79.

Makatov, I. A. "Kul't sviatykh v islame" [The cult of saints in Islam]. In *VNA* 3 (1967): 164–84.

Malakhova, I. A. "Istoriki izuchaiut sovremennye religioznye techeniia" [Historians are studying contemporary religious trends]. *Istoriia SSSR*, no. 2 (1961), pp. 233–35.

———. "Religioznoe sektantstvo v Tambovskoi oblasti v posleoktiabr'skii period i v nashi dni" [Religious sectarianism in the Tambov region in the post-October period and in our days]. In *Voprosy istorii religii i ateizma* [Problems of the history of religion and atheism], vol. 9, pp. 77–112. Moscow: AN SSSR, 1961.

Mamaeva, K. "O nekotorykh ob"ektivnykh i sub"ektivnykh faktorakh v ateisticheskom vospitanii sel'skogo naseleniia" [Some objective and subjective factors in atheistic education of the rural population]. In *Ateizm i religiia*

[Atheism and religion], edited by Z. B. Balevits, pp. 77–92. Riga: "Zinatne," 1969.

Meikshane, D. A. "Metody izucheniia otnosheniia uchashchikhsia k religii" [Methods of studying the relationship of pupils to religion]. In *VNA* 11 (1971): 264–75.

Mennik, A. "Nasushchnye zadachi ateisticheskogo vospitaniia" [Urgent tasks of atheistic education]. In *Ateizm i religiia* [Atheism and religion], edited by Z. B. Balevits, pp. 5–14. Riga: "Zinatne," 1969.

Mering, T. "Konkretno o samom vazhnom" [Concretely on the most important]. *Nauka i religiia,* no. 3 (1969), pp. 40–41.

Mikhailov, M. G. "Staroobriadchestvo i sotsial'nyi progress" [Old Believers and social progress]. In *VNA* 2 (1962): 198–224.

———. "Stavropolskie vstrechi" [Meetings in Stavropol]. *Nauka i religiia,* no. 4 (1965), p. 20.

Milovidov, V. F. "Staroobriadchestvo i sotsial'nyi progress" [Old Believers and social progress]. In *VNA* 2 (1964): 221.

Mitrokhin, L. N. "Izucheniia sektantstva v Tambovskoi oblasti" [The study of sectarianism in the Tambov region]. *Voprosy filosofii,* no. 1 (1960), pp. 143–48.

———. "O metodologii konkretnykh issledovanii v oblasti religii" [The methodology of concrete research in the field of religion]. In *Sotsiologiia v SSSR* [Sociology in the USSR], pp. 299–324. Moscow: "Mysl'," 1966.

Mizov, N. "Protsess preodoleniia religii i upravlenie im" [The process of overcoming religion and its guidance]. *Voprosy filosofii,* no. 7 (1973), pp. 77–82.

Murav'ev, E. F., and Dmitrev, Iu. V. "O konkretnosti v izuchenii i preodolenii religioznykh perezhitkov" [Concreteness in studying and overcoming religious survivals]. *Voprosy filosofii,* no. 3 (1961), pp. 63–73.

Nestorov, V. "Pravoslavnaia tserkov' v Latvii" [The Orthodox Church in Latvia]. In *Ateizm i religiia* [Atheism and religion], edited by Z. B. Balevits, pp. 137–52. Riga: "Zinatne," 1969.

Nikitin, V. N. "Dialektika prichinnoi sviazi i problema religioznosti v usloviiakh sotsializma" [The dialectic of causal links and the problem of religiousness in conditions of socialism]. In *Nauchnyi ateizma: Voprosy metodologii i sotsiologii* [Scientific atheism: problems of methodology and sociology], pp. 34–61. Perm': Perm' State Pedagogical Institute, 1974.

Nikonov, K. I. "O nekotorykh tendentsiiakh v propovednicheskoi deiatel'nosti sovremennogo baptizma" [Certain tendencies in the preaching activity of contemporary Baptists]. In *Konkretno-sotsiologicheskoe izuchenie sostoianiia religioznosti i opyta ateisticheskogo vospitaniia* [Concrete sociological study of the condition of the religiousness and the experience of atheistic education], edited by I. D. Pantskhava, pp. 179–99. Moscow: Moscow University Press, 1969.

"Ob uluchshenii sovetskogo radioveshchaniia i dal'neishem razvitii televedenii" [Improving Soviet radio broadcasting and the farthest development of television]. *Partiinaia zhizn',* no. 4 (1960), pp. 26–34.

Reference Bibliography

Ochavkov, Jivko. "Bulgaria." In *Western Religion,* edited by Hans Mol, pp. 83–99. The Hague: Mouton, 1972.

"O chem govorit statistika?" [What do the statistics say?]. *Nauka i religiia,* no. 1 (1967), p. 35.

Okulov, A. "Nauchno-ateisticheskoe vospitanie segodnia" [Scientific atheistic education today]. *Nauka i religiia,* no. 8 (1967), pp. 15–17.

————, and Ugrinovich, D. M. "VIII mezhdunarodnyi sotsiologicheskii kongress: Problemy sotsiologii religii" [The VII international sociological congress: problems of the sociology of religion]. In *VNA* 12 (1971): 325–42.

Olshauskas, A. " 'Reshitel'nye mery' tseli ne dostigaiut" ["Decisive measures" do not achieve the goal]. *Nauka i religiia,* no. 6 (1963), pp. 72–73.

"O meropriiatiiakh po usileniiu ateisticheskogo vospitaniia naseleniia" [Measures for strengthening the atheistic education of the population]. *Partiinaia zhizn',* no. 2 (1964), pp. 22–26.

Onishchenko, A. S. "Tendentsii izmeneniia sovremennogo religioznogo soznaniia" [Tendencies of change of contemporary religious consciousness]. In *VNA* 2 (1966): 91–109.

Orlov, A. M. "Opyt issledovaniia protsessa sekuliarizatsii v tatarskikh selakh" [Experience of research on the process of secularization in Tatar villages]. In *VNA* 16 (1974): 89–102.

Osipov, G., and Yovchuk, M. "Some Principles of Theory, Problems and Methods of Research in Sociology in the USSR: A Soviet View." In *Soviet Sociology: Historical Antecedents and Current Appraisals,* edited by Alex Simirenko, pp. 298–305. Chicago: Quadrangle Books, 1966.

Osipov, O. "Priglashenie v klub" [An invitation to the club]. *Nauka i religiia,* no. 11 (1971), pp. 29–31.

Pashkov, N. A. "K voprosu o kharaktere obydennogo religioznogo soznaniia pravoslavnykh khristian" [The problem of the character of the ordinary religious consciousness of Orthodox Christians]. In *Konkretno-sotsiologicheskoe izuchenie sostoianiia religioznosti i opyta ateisticheskogo vospitaniia* [Concrete sociological study of the condition of religiousness and the experience of atheistic education], edited by I. D. Pantskhava, pp. 148–61. Moscow: Moscow University Press, 1969.

Pavliuk, V. V. "K voprosu o 'religioznykh' potrebnostiakh" [The problem of "religious" needs]. In *VNA* 11 (1971): 151–61.

Pishchik, Iu. B. "Sovremennyi protestantizm: Problemy teorii i praktiki" [Contemporary protestantism: problems of theory and practice]. In *VNA* 13 (1972): 409–12.

Pismanik, M. G. "Metodika sotsial'no-psikhologicheskikh issledovanii religioznosti" [Methods of social-psychological research on religiousness]. In *VNA* 11 (1971): 205–18.

————. "O sostoianii religioznosti i nekotorykh osobennostiakh nauchno-ateisticheskogo vospitaniia sredi zhenshchin" [The situation of religiousness and certain peculiarities of scientific atheistic education among women]. In *Kon-*

kretno-sotsiologicheskoe izuchenie sostoianiia religioznosti i opyta ateisticheskogo vospitaniia [Concrete sociological study of the condition of religiousness and the experience of atheistic education], edited by I. D. Pantskhava, pp. 213–30. Moscow: Moscow University Press, 1969.

————. "Religiozniaia kontseptsiia 'grekhovnosti' i nravstvennyi progress" [The religious conception of "sinfulness" and moral progress]. In *Ateizm, religiia, nravstvennost'* [Atheism, religion, morality], edited by A. I. Garadzha, pp. 129–51. Moscow: "Mysl'," 1972.

Pivovarov, V. "Pod rukovodstvom partiinykh organov" [Under the leadership of Party organs]. *Nauka i religiia,* no. 9 (1972), pp. 88–90.

————. "Sotsiologicheskoe issledovanie problem byta, kul'tury, natsional'nykh traditsii i verovanii v Checheno-Ingushskoi ASSR" [Sociological research on the problems of the manner of life, culture, national traditions, and beliefs in the Chechen-Ingush ASSR]. In *VNA* 17 (1975): 310–19.

Podmazov, A. "Sovremennoe staroobriadchestvo v Latvii" [Contemporary Old Believers in Latvia]. In *Ateizm i religiia,* edited by Z. B. Balevits, pp. 173–207. Riga: "Zinatne," 1969.

Pomerantsev, V. "Vchera i segodnia" [Yesterday and today]. *Nauka i religiia,* no. 4 (1966), pp. 2–7.

Popova, M. A. "Kritika priemov i metodov konkretnykh issledovanii v amerikanskoi psikhologii religii" [A critique of modes and methods of concrete research in American psychology of religion]. In *Konkretno-sotsiologicheskoe izuchenie sostoianiia religioznosti i opyta ateisticheskogo vospitanii* [Concrete sociological study of the condition of religiousness and the experience of atheistic education], edited by I. D. Pantskhava, pp. 261–81. Moscow: Moscow University Press, 1969.

Prokoshchenkov, L. "Sotsial'nyi kollektiv—osnova vospitaniie" [The social collective—the basis of education]. *Nauka i religiia,* no. 7 (1972), pp. 11–12.

Puchkov, N. I. "Vliianie vnutriklassovykh izmenenii v sotsialisticheskom obshchestve na razvitie massogo ateizma" [The influence of intraclass changes in socialist society on the development of mass atheism]. In *VNA* 13 (1972): 101–26.

Ranne, V. Ia. "Novye obriady i ikh mesto v dukhovnoi zhizni sovetskikh liudei" [New rites and their place in the spiritual life of Soviet people]. In *VNA* 13 (1972): 181–97.

"Razrabotka problem nauchnogo ateizma v soiuznykh respublikakh: Belorusskaia SSR, Gruzinskaia SSR, Moldavskaia SSR, Estonskaia SSR" [Elaboration of the problems of scientific atheism in the Union Republics: Belorussian SSR, Georgian SSR, Moldavian SSR, Estonian SSR]. In *VNA* 14 (1973): 53–86.

Riumin, E. "Zhivoe slovo i glubina soderzhaniia" [The living word and depth of contents]. *Agitator,* no. 6 (1967), pp. 43–45.

Rogov, A. I. "Ateisticheskie radioperedachi" [Atheistic radio broadcasts]. In *VNA* 9 (1970): 305–16.

Reference Bibliography

———. "Nash golos v efire" [Our voice in the ether]. *Nauka i religiia*, no. 3 (1962), pp. 10–11.

Rudnev, V. A. "Kommunisticheskomu btyu—novye sovetskie traditsii" [To Communist living conditions—new Soviet traditions]. In *Voprosy preodoleniia religioznykh perezhitkov v SSSR* [Problems of overcoming religious survivals in the USSR], edited by N. P. Krashnikov, pp. 158–76. Moscow: "Nauka," 1966.

———. "Nasha sistema anti-religioznoi propagandy" [Our system of antireligious propaganda]. *Agitator*, no. 11 (1965), pp. 42–44.

Safronov, Iu. "Chto pokazali otvety" [What the answers showed]. *Kommunist Belorussii*, no. 3 (1967), pp. 66–71.

Saparmukhamedova, B. "Obshchestvennoe mnenie protiv religii" [Social opinion against religion]. *Nauka i religiia*, no. 11 (1971), pp. 21–22.

Saprykin, V. A. "Ateisticheskaia rabota partiinoi organizatsii v usloviiakh goroda" [Atheistic work of the Party organization in urban conditions]. In *VNA* 9 (1970): 216–34.

Schneidere, B. "Sovetskie obriady—partiinoe delo" [Soviet rites—a Party matter]. *Nauka i religiia*, no. 2 (1969), pp. 36–37.

Sedykh, P. S. "Esteticheskaia otsenka iavlenii deistvitel'nosti kak kriterii formirovanii nauchno-ateisticheskogo mirovozzreniia" [The aesthetic evaluation of phenomena of reality as a criterion of the formation of a scientific-atheistic world view]. *Gertsenovskie chteniia*, vol. 30 (1977), pp. 10–14.

Severchuk, I. P. "Sredstva massovoi informatsii i propagandy v sisteme ateisticheskogo vospitaniia" [Mass information media and propaganda in the system of atheistic education]. In *VNA* 13 (1972): 198–218.

Shamaro, A. "Svet golubnogo ekrana" [The light of the blue screen]. *Nauka i religiia*, no. 3 (1962), p. 11.

Sheptulin, A. P. "Zadachi povysheniia urovnia prepodavaniia osnov nauchnogo ateizma" [Tasks of raising the level of teaching of the fundamentals of scientific atheism]. In *VNA* 15 (1973): 4–22.

Shimkus, S. "Mesto ateizma v sisteme kommunisticheskogo vospitaniia" [The place of atheism in the system of Communist education]. *Nauka i religiia*, no. 8 (1967), p. 19.

Smirnov, V. I. "Voprosy ateisticheskogo vospitaniia v ideologicheskoi rabote partiinykh organizatsii" [Problems of atheistic education in the ideological work of Party organizations]. In *VNA* 12 (1971): 121–33.

Sofronov, N. S. "Ateisticheskoe vospitanie v sel'skoi mestnosti" [Atheistic education in the rural locale]. In *VNA* 9 (1970): 235–48.

Solov'ev, V. S. "O vliianii ateizma na dukhovnoe razvitie lichnosti" [The influence of atheism on the intellectual development of the personality]. In *VNA* 14 (1973): 186–95.

Stel'makov, Iu. I. "O sootnoshenii ratsional'nogo i emotsional'nogo v soznanii veruiushchikh" [The relationship of the rational and the emotional in the consciousness of believers]. In *Konkretno-sotsiologicheskoe izuchenie sostoia-*

niia religioznosti i opyta ateisticheskogo vospitaniia [Concrete sociological study of the condition of religiousness and the experience of atheistic education], edited by I. D. Pantskhava, pp. 32–46. Moscow: Moscow University Press, 1969.

Sukhov, A. D. "O konservativnosti religioznykh traditsii" [The conservatism of religious traditions]. *Voprosy filosofii*, no. 8 (1961), pp. 144–50.

Sviridov, N., and Marchik, G. "Za deistvennost' ideologicheskoi raboty" [For the effectiveness of ideological work]. *Molodoi kommunist*, no. 8 (1962), pp. 23–33.

Sytenko, L. T. "O nravstvennom oblike sovremennogo veruiushchego" [The moral aspect of the contemporary believer]. In *VNA* 3 (1967): 113–30.

Tazhurina, Z. A. "Mistifikatsiia obydennykh otnoshenii v sueveriiakh" [The mystification of ordinary relationships in superstitions]. In *Konkretnosotsiologicheskoe izuchenie sostoianiia religioznosti i opyta ateisticheskogo vospitaniia* [Concrete sociological study of the condition of religiousness and the experience of atheistic education], edited by I. D. Pantskhava, pp. 68–88. Moscow: Moscow University Press, 1969.

Tepliakov, M. K. "Pobeda ateizma v razlichnykh sotsial'nykh sloiakh sovetskogo obshchestva" [The victory of atheism in various social strata of Soviet society]. In *VNA* 4 (1967): 130–56.

——. "Sostoianie religioznosti naseleniia i otkhod veruiushchikh ot religii v Voronezhskoi oblasti (1961–1964 gg)" [The situation of the religiousness of the population and the departure of believers from religion in the Voronezh region (1961–1964)]. In *Voprosy preodoleniia religioznykh perezhitkov v SSSR* [Problems of overcoming religious survivals in the USSR], edited by N. P. Krasnikov, pp. 31–52. Moscow: "Nauka," 1966.

——. "Sotsial'nye issledovaniia v sisteme ateisticheskogo vospitaniia" [Social research in the system of atheistic education]. In *VNA* 9 (1970): 106–22.

Terent'eva, L. N. "Rasprostranenie ateisticheskogo mirovozzreniia i bezreligioznykh form byta sredi kolkhoznikov latyshei (po materialam Ekabpilsskogo raiona Latviiskoi SSR)" [The prevalence of the atheistic world view and irreligious forms of life among Lettish collective farmers (according to materials from the Ekabpils district, Latvian SSR)]. In *Voprosy preodoleniia religioznykh perezhitkov v SSSR* [Problems of overcoming religious survivals in the USSR], edited by N. P. Krasnikov, pp. 53–78. Moscow: "Nauka," 1966.

Timasheff, Nicholas S. "Urbanization, Operation Antireligion and the Decline of Religion in the USSR." *American Slavic and East European Review* 14 (April 1955): 224–38.

Timchenko, I. P. "Sistemnost'—glavnoe uslovie deistvennosti ateisticheskogo vospitaniia" [Being systematic—the major condition for effectiveness of atheistic education]. In *VNA* 19 (1976): 32–41.

Trapeznikov, S. P. "Razvitie obshchestvennykh nauk i povyshenie ikh roli v kommunisticheskom stroitel'stve" [The development of social sciences and the increase of their role in building communism]. *Voprosy filosofii*, no. 11 (1967), pp. 3–27.

Tul'tseva, L. A. "Evoliutsiia starogo russkogo sektantstva" [The evolution of old Russian sectarianism]. In *VNA* 7 (1969): 210–11.

Ugrinovich, D. M. "O predmete marksistskoi sotsiologii" [The subject matter of Marxist sociology]. In *Ocherki metodologii poznaniia sotsial'nykh iavlenii* [Essays on the methodology of understanding social phenomena], edited by L. N. Dorogova, pp. 11–46. Moscow: "Mysl'," 1970.

———. "Neobkhodima produmannaia sistema nauchno-ateisticheskogo vospitaniia" [A thought-out system of scientific atheistic education is essential]. *Kommunist*, no. 9 (1962), pp. 93–100.

———. "Religiia kak predmet sotsiologicheskogo issledovaniia" [Religion as a subject of sociological research]. In *Ocherki metodologii poznaniia sotsial'nykh iavlenii* [Essays on the methodology of understanding social phenomena], edited by L. N. Dorogova, pp. 121–59. Moscow: "Mysl'," 1970.

———, and Iablokov, I. N. "Izuchenie religioznogo soznaniia veruiushchikh v sotsialisticheskom obshchestve i zadachi ateisticheskogo vospitaniia" [The study of the religious consciousness of believers in socialist society and the tasks of atheistic education], in *Obshchestvennaia psikhologiia i kommunisticheskoe vospitanie* [Social psychology and Communist education], edited by D. M. Ugrinovich, pp. 140–64. Moscow: Moscow University Press, 1967.

Ul'ianov, L. N. "Opyt issledovaniia motivatsii religioznogo povedeniia" [Experience of study of the motivation of religious conduct]. In *VNA* 11 (1971): 219–35.

Ulybin, I. A. "Iz opyta prepodavaniia nauchnogo ateizma v sel'skokhoziaistvennom vuze" [Experience in teaching scientific atheism in agricultural institutions of higher education]. In *VNA* 15 (1973): 103–14.

Uryvskii, V., and Tepliakov, M. "Radiozhurnal 'Nauka i religiia'" [The radio magazine "Science and Religion"]. *Agitator*, no. 13 (1965), pp. 31–33.

Vagabov, M. V. "Bol'she vnimaniia sovetskomu islamovedeniiu" [More attention to Soviet Islamic studies]. *Voprosy filosofii*, no. 12 (1966), pp. 172–75.

Vasilevskaia, N. S. "Opyt konkretno-sotsiologicheskogo issledovaniia otnosheniia k religii v sovremennoi gorodskoi sem'e" [Experience of concrete sociological research on the relationship to religion in the contemporary urban family]. In *VNA* 13 (1972): 383–404.

"Vazhnaia tema" [An important theme]. *Nauka i religiia*, no. 5 (1972), pp. 26–28.

"V dobry chas!" [High time!]. *Nauka i religiia*, no. 9 (1964), p. 53.

Veschikov, A. "Etapy bol'shogo puti" [Stages of a great way]. *Nauka i religiia*, no. 11 (1962), pp. 56–60.

Vestnikov, A. "Narod sozdaiet traditsii" [The people are establishing traditions]. *Nauka i religiia*, no. 1 (1964), pp. 60–61.

Vimmsaare, K. A. "Ob ispol'zovanii rezul'tatov konkretno-sotsiologicheskikh issledovanii v uchebno-vospitatel'nom protsesse" [The use of results of concrete sociological research in the educational upbringing process]. In *VNA* 15 (1973): 223–29.

Vinogradov, V. F. "Staroobriadchestvo na territoriiakh pskovskoi i novgorodskoi oblastei" [Old Believers in the territories of the Pskov and Novgorod regions]. *Gertsenovski chteniia,* vol. 30 (1977), pp. 37–40.

Vinokur, A. "Ugasenie drevnei very" [Extinction of an ancient faith]. *Nauka i religiia,* no. 1 (1967), pp. 41–43.

"V institute nauchnogo ateizma" [In the institute of scientific atheism]. *Nauka i religiia,* no. 7 (1972), p. 6.

Voss, A. "Vazhnyi uchastok ideologicheskoi raboty" [An important sector of ideological work]. *Partiinaia zhizn',* no. 15 (1962), p. 24.

Wheeler, Geoffrey. "The Muslims of Central Asia." *Problems of Communism,* September/October 1967, pp. 72–81.

Zaikin, B. "Pered samoi bol'shoi auditoriei" [Before the largest audience]. *Agitator,* no. 20 (1966), pp. 44–45.

INDEX

76–79, 115; and college, 98–99; and Bibles, 131; and superstitions, 151; and religious rites, 191, 195. *See also* Children

DATE DUE

MAR 3 0 1985			
APR 1 2 1985			

GAYLORD   PRINTED IN U.S.A